Elizabeth Madox Roberts

AMERICAN NOVELIST

HARRY MODEAN CAMPBELL

AND RUEL E. FOSTER

~~☙*~☙*~*~☙*~☙*~☙*~*~☙*~*~☙*~☙*~*~☙*~*

Elizabeth
Madox
Roberts

AMERICAN NOVELIST

~~☙*~☙*~*~☙*~☙*~☙*~*~☙*~*~☙*~☙*~*~☙*~*

With a Foreword by J. Donald Adams

NORMAN: UNIVERSITY OF OKLAHOMA PRESS

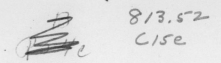

BY HARRY MODEAN CAMPBELL
AND RUEL E. FOSTER

William Faulkner: A Critical Appraisal (Norman, 1951)

Elizabeth Madox Roberts: American Novelist (Norman, 1956)

Library of Congress Catalog Card Number 56–11237

Copyright 1956 by the University of Oklahoma Press,
Publishing Division of the University.

Composed and printed at Norman, Oklahoma, U.S.A.,
by the University of Oklahoma Press.

First edition.

To Donald Davidson Again

Foreword

by J. Donald Adams

ᘯ When the late Stefan Zweig, a writer of great sensitivity, sailed for South America on his last voyage, I gave him a copy of *The Time of Man* for shipboard reading. He was unacquainted with the work of Miss Roberts, and I felt sure that she was a writer whose quality he would at once perceive. Before his arrival at Rio de Janeiro he wrote me to express his astonishment that a novelist of this stature should be so little known in Europe. He had, he said, been greatly impressed, not only by the beauty of her writing, but by her deeply perceptive understanding of the human heart.

If Stefan Zweig found it difficult to comprehend why Miss Roberts was not more widely appreciated abroad, there is much more reason for wonder over her neglect at home. In the earlier years of her career she was accorded much acclaim by American critics, and in one or two books achieved a considerable popular recognition. But as the authors of this welcome book point out, during the last few years of her life, and since her death in 1941, little has been written about her. Theirs is the first full-scale attempt to assess her work as a whole and to tell the story of her life in some detail. This is the more surprising in view of the fact that she was one of those few contemporary writers whose work is distinguished by a timeless quality. Nothing she wrote is dated, and what is excellent in her work will be excellent always.

It is my conviction, held over many years, that *The Time of Man* is one of the best American novels, one that stands as good a chance as any of being read and held in high esteem a hundred years hence. It is both indigenous and universal, and its insights are both original and profound. It is one of the rare examples in our fiction of the successful welding of realism and poetry. It has the ageless quality of folksong, and the sharp impact of life truly and unflinchingly observed. It is, as I have elsewhere remarked, "an epic in folk terms of the human journey, of mankind's never ending hope for some fairer land, some more desirable world. Human aspiration speaks in Ellen Chesser, child of a tenant farmer, whom we watch repeat the pattern of her parents' lives, and who sees her own hopes and yearnings reborn again in her own children, asking, as the book ends, the same questions of life which she herself had asked as a child." Also, it is one of those books, like *Moby Dick* and *The Scarlet Letter,* which stand alone. It resembles nothing else in American literature.

In the same way, Miss Roberts' one venture in the historical novel, *The Great Meadow,* resembles nothing else, so far as I am aware, in that genre. Its combination of narrative interest with philosophical suggestion is a rare one. Outwardly, its theme is the settlement of Kentucky by the pioneers who followed in the path of Daniel Boone; inwardly, it is the power of mind and will over the material world. Incidentally, I know of no comparably powerful handling of the Enoch Arden story. Miss Roberts' presentation of Diony's choice, by frontier custom, between the husband, returned from Indian captivity, whom she had believed dead, and the man to whom he found her married, is a remarkable piece of writing.

One aspect of Miss Roberts' work that I find of particular interest is her effort to fuse the techniques of literature and music. More than any other writer I can think of, she strove to give her longer works a symphonic structure. She had a passionate love of music, and frequently used it as a kind of preparation for the actual work of writing. She made repeated use in her novels of a recurrent and interwoven theme, reaching a peak of emotional pitch, and sounding final chords in which the conflict is at last resolved. This musical structure is readily apparent in her three major works, *The Time of Man, My Heart and My Flesh,* and *The Great Meadow.*

Though I believe it is for these novels that she will be longest remembered, Messrs. Campbell and Foster have quite properly concerned themselves also with her outstanding work in the short story and in poetry. "The Sacrifice of the Maidens" is, I think, one of the finest short stories by an American writer, and the small body of Miss Roberts' poetry has a freshness and individuality which makes for regret that its bulk is not larger. It is especially unfortunate that she did not live to complete her projected long poem dealing with the life of Boone. This might well have become a major work in American poetry.

It seems to me that Messrs. Campbell and Foster have brought both sympathy and intelligence to their study of Miss Roberts. There is no aspect of her work which they have neglected, and their appraisal of the individual books strikes me as sound. For those who know her work their careful analysis should serve to heighten both appreciation and understanding, and their ability to convey the reasons why they estimate her writing so highly should interest such readers as their book may find, who know little or nothing of her work.

Any writer as gifted as Elizabeth Madox Roberts is certain to be rediscovered by both the critics and the reading public. Perhaps she must wait for a time, if we are to have it, when readers' minds are less bedeviled by the outward circumstances of our apprehensive world, and their insistent demands upon our attention. Meantime, a tribute to her in this form, so long overdue, may help to turn attention in her direction.

☆ x ☆

Contents

Foreword, by J. Donald Adams   vii

Acknowledgments   xiii

Introduction   xv

1. *Biography*   3

2. *The Relationship Between Earth and the Human Spirit in the Fictional World*   80

3. *Poetic Realism in the Fictional World of Elizabeth Madox Roberts*   96

4. *The Theme Stated : Major Motif :*
The Time of Man *and* The Great Meadow   122

5. *Variations on the Theme*   153

6. *The Allegorical Novels*   198

7. *Technique in the Short Story:*
The Haunted Mirror *and* Not By Strange Gods   230

☆ **xi** ☆

8. *Elizabeth Madox Roberts as Poet*   251

9. *Conclusion : Integrity in Life and Art*   273

Portrait of Elizabeth Madox Roberts   *Facing page*   32

Acknowledgments

Our greatest debt in the preparation of this book is to Mr. Yvor Roberts for his kindness in allowing us access to the Roberts Papers in the Library of Congress. Without these papers this book could not have been written. Special thanks are due also to Miss Mabel M. Williams and Mr. Edward Foster of Springfield, Kentucky, and Mr. Wallace Kelly of Lebanon, Kentucky, for valuable materials and suggestions. The libraries of the University of West Virginia and the University of Mississippi have given us constant assistance. Grants from our universities and from the Ford Foundation were most helpful. Still other aids are acknowledged at pertinent points of the text. For all such help, we are most grateful.

HARRY MODEAN CAMPBELL

RUEL E. FOSTER

Introduction

𝕭❧ The critical neglect of Elizabeth Madox Roberts during the last few years of her life and since her death in 1941 is indeed hard to understand. Her work was praised very highly during the late 1920's and early 1930's for its mastery of craftsmanship and significant content by eminent critics, none of whom it seems from various inquiries, has modified in the least his earlier judgment. Why then all the critical silence in the last two decades? Certainly her work has not dated: in both theme and technique, and especially in the happy fusion of the two, her novels and short stories should be absorbingly interesting to anyone who is concerned, say, with the work of Willa Cather, about whom several books have already appeared (though she died but six years after Miss Roberts). While Miss Roberts did not write so much as Miss Cather, her four best novels are on the whole quite as good as the four best of Miss Cather's; in fact, in some ways, especially in her poetic imagination and her gift for penetrating satire, Miss Roberts is decidedly superior to Miss Cather. Indeed, Miss Roberts' poetic imagination, or what E. M. Forster in referring to D. H. Lawrence has called "the rapt bardic quality," makes her best work worthy of comparison in this respect with the best of Lawrence and Faulkner.

Believing that it is high time to begin making amends for this neglect of Miss Roberts, we have made a detailed study of her life and her works—novels, short stories, and poems. With the permission of Mr. Ivor Roberts, Miss Roberts' literary executor, we have made extensive use of material, hitherto unpublished, in the very valuable Roberts Papers in the Library of Congress. Our studies have convinced us, and we hope that our book will convince others, that Miss Roberts belongs among the seven or eight best craftsmen in modern American fiction, and that her *The Time of Man* and *The Great Meadow* will almost certainly endure as major American novels.

HARRY MODEAN CAMPBELL

RUEL E. FOSTER

Oxford, Mississippi
May 1, 1956

Elizabeth Madox Roberts

AMERICAN NOVELIST

1. Biography

⁊※⁋⊙⁊※⁋⊙⁊※⁋⊙⁊※⁋⊙⁊※⁋⊙⁊※⁋⊙⁊※⁋⊙⁊※⁋⊙⁊※⁋⊙⁊※⁋⊙⁊※

ဦ In Springfield, Kentucky, we were accustomed to see her walk dreamily up the street in the quiet light of the late afternoon—an erect and patrician-looking person with a graceful carriage and an abstracted air. She bent distantly in occasional salutation to passersby and acquaintances.

By this time—the early 1930's—we all knew that she was a writer, and a celebrated one at that. We knew, also, that though she had spent most of her life in Springfield, she had yet gone a long way. We could never know all the details, but we wanted to know them. And gradually we began to learn about that long and difficult and in many ways unusual journey.

We knew, for instance, that Elizabeth Madox Roberts chose her ancestors carefully. Her father, Simpson Roberts, was descended from Richard Roberts, who came from Wales and settled in North Carolina or Virginia in the eighteenth century. Richard's son, Abram, emigrated to Kentucky and stayed. Miss Roberts' mother, Mary Elizabeth Brent, had been a beautiful woman, noted for her fine posture and graceful carriage. She traced her family back to Americans in the early eighteenth century and, towards the end of her life, set down a number of family memories in an interesting article on her childhood in Hart County, Kentucky, in the 1860's.[1]

Mrs. Roberts, Elizabeth's mother, remembered her grandfather, Valentine Garvin, who was tall, past six feet. He was of Irish, Welsh, and Germanic stock, and came to Kentucky from Rockingham County, Virginia, about 1804. He had been born about 1797. In his family were two legends of earlier times. His mother's grandmother had come to Kentucky over the Wilderness Road at a very early date. This woman was at that time a grandmother. The party was attacked by Indians not far from the fort to which they were going, either Harrod's Fort or Fort Logan or St. Asaph near Stanford. The grandmother and a small grandchild were killed. Her daughter-in-law, with a small infant in arms, was separated from the rest of the party during the raid, but she managed to keep herself alive and was found several days later.[2]

Another legend from the Garvins runs thus: The first of the name in America was David Garvin, who ran away from Ireland to escape being apprenticed to a tanner. He came to Virginia as a stowaway. Discovered on board, he was brought to Virginia as a captive of the captain of the ship and by him was bound out to six months' service to pay for his passage. With him was a cousin who shared his adventure, whose name is thought to have been Arthur.

---

[1] "Memories of Life on a Farm in Hart County, Kentucky, in the Early Sixties," *Filson Club History Quarterly*, Vol. XIV, No. 3 (July, 1940), 129–53.

[2] This is undoubtedly the prototype for a like occurence in *The Great Meadow*.

☆ 4 ☆

This David came to America about 1750, or earlier. One legend states that he served three years of indenture.[3]

And then, of course, there were Miss Roberts' parents. They were both strongminded, passionate, and imaginative people; they shaped the world which shaped their daughter's mind. The parents, in turn, were marked lifelong by the cruel events of the Civil War and the Reconstruction. Simpson Roberts, her father, was born October 31, 1847, in Henry County, Kentucky, into the tensions of the pre-Civil War period. Simpson, while still a child of fourteen, saw his father cold-bloodedly shot down for his refusal to join the national guard. At the age of sixteen, Simpson joined the Confederate troops of General Braxton Bragg, while they were camped at Perryville, Kentucky, shortly before the bloody battle fought there. Later he was captured in Georgia and sent to Louisville for confinement. But Simpson Roberts never forgot the brutality to his father, and although he lived to be eighty odd years old (dying in 1933), whenever he heard the name of Lincoln he spat with cold contempt.

Miss Roberts' mother, Mary Elizabeth Brent (born October 14, 1853, in Hart County, Kentucky), also remembered the Civil War with great clarity. Oddly enough Mary Brent's father, John D. Brent, began the war as an officer in the Federal Army, in which he served until he was badly wounded at the battle of Shiloh and honorably discharged. However, events occurring in Kentucky and in the nation caused him to shift his sympathies to the South. This change of heart was not lost on his daughter, and years later when she met Simpson Roberts, a Confederate veteran and

[3] These family legends have been summarized from Mrs. Roberts' Filson Club article. The story of David Garvin is the basis for Miss Roberts' poem, "Sailing for America."

struggling young teacher, she immediately shared his anti-
pathy for the North. Mary Elizabeth Brent was herself a
school teacher, teaching in Perryville, where the young
couple met and where, earlier, Simpson had begun his
military life. Their courtship was ardent and short. They
were married in Willisburg and began housekeeping in
Perryville, a quiet village still recuperating from one of
the bloodiest battles of the Civil War. Here Elizabeth
Madox Roberts was born in a small frame house on October 30, 1881.

We can see today that the ancestry lightly touched on
above is of great importance in assessing Miss Roberts'
talents. It gave her a stable, rooted, agrarian heritage and
it established her with strong southern sympathies which
she never lost. It was primarily north European, Anglo-
Saxon—a fact clearly demonstrated by her lineaments. Her
parents were spirited people of high intelligence, forced to
live rather meagerly through the hard days of the Reconstruction period. From them she inherited a great talent
and a stubborn strength of character. She never regretted
her choice of parents.

Years later, as a highly conscious literary artist, she turned
with an ever-growing interest to a study of this heritage.
The great web of family and interlinked flesh fascinated
her and became a growing theme in her novels. In her personal notes she made this entry about the fascination the
family past held for her:

Upon this inheritance the odors of old centuries continually
blow out of old books to join what is kept treasured thus within,
what is identical with the breath of life. These confirmations
of things held in family memory give a pleasurable sense of
one's own validity, as if, having known by the way of the senses,

one knew again by the way of the summaries of human experience that are on written pages. Thus one projects himself into more than one century and knows what it is to be alive in a reach and breadth of existence that transcends three score years and ten.[4]

Critical discussions in this book will point out the degree to which she pushed the theme of familial relationships in her novel. It can be said here that at the time of her death, she saw all of her novels as separate links in one vast familial chain; for instance, the people who live in the little hamlet of *A Buried Treasure* are descendants of the pioneers in *The Great Meadow*.

While she was still an infant, Miss Roberts caught the first glimpse of Springfield, Kentucky, the town which was to serve in its fictional prototype as the center of the universe of her novels and short stories. About 1884, her father moved his family from Perryville to Springfield, into a two-story frame structure immediately adjoining the new brick Presbyterian church. The building was in the block used as the business section of the little town, and Mr. Roberts made the first floor into a small grocery and used the second floor as the living quarters for his family. Since times were slack, he supplemented his income by working as engineer and surveyor for the county and such private firms as the Louisville and Nashville Railroad, which was then preparing to run a line from Louisville to Springfield.

A word is in order here about Springfield, since it is going to provide the major environmental influence on Miss Roberts. Springfield is located by a tiny rill which runs from east to west through a gentle valley. There are many natural springs, and in Indian days this area was used as a

4 Roberts Papers, Library of Congress. Hereinafter, references to and passages quoted from the Roberts Papers will be so indicated by an asterisk instead of a footnote.

watering place by both Indians and animals. In the 1770's and 1780's, when the first white settlements were being made in Kentucky, Springfield, being in the geographical center of the state, was frequently visited by trappers and pioneers passing from Louisville to Harrodsburg. This fact inspired some solitary but ambitious entrepreneur to build a log tavern here. By 1792, other taverns had appeared, as well as a few houses and that certain sign of civilization on the frontier, a log jail. Springfield was incorporated as a town in the 1790's, and began its long preparation as a focal point for the ranging mind of Miss Roberts.

By the time she was six years old and able to note its character, Springfield was a small town of about twelve hundred people. Its little business section clustered at the center of a great cross made by the intersection of the east-west highway with the north-south highway—the highways radiating out to the four points of the compass, extending through the rich, rolling farmland described in *The Time of Man.* The stores and homes of the natives were scattered along the arms of this great cross, with the exception of those of the Negroes, who spent their rich and riotous lives on a small street which led into one of the main highways.

In the countryside spreading out beyond this little town were farms, whose owners raised tobacco as their money crop, supplemented by wheat and corn and cattle and hogs. It was a purely rural, agrarian community whose big day came once a month with "County Court Day," when all the countryside thronged in to gossip, shop, and loiter about. This was also the day for horse trading, the center for this being a vacant lot on the alley behind the Presbyterian church. Here the farmers would bring horses, mules, and jacks they wanted to sell or trade, and here they would squat and discuss and haggle endlessly over the "boot." It is this scene, which she would see regularly once a month, that Miss Roberts put into *The Time of Man,* when Ellen Chesser runs away to Anneville. Springfield became the "home town" for the Roberts family, and here were born the remaining children (Brent, like Elizabeth, had been born at Perryville) William and Clifford the twins, Charles, John, Luellen or "Lel," and Ivor.

Elizabeth was soon a child big enough to help with the household chores and imaginative enough to devise ways to relieve the tedium. This combination resulted in what we might call her first literary creation—the Wilson family. Aided by the other children, Elizabeth created a fantasy family. They fashioned from their imaginations (a somewhat communal inspiration technique) a family consisting of Mr. and Mrs. Wilson and their children. The names of the Wilson children, and their number, were variable and depended on the whim of the moment. The Wilsons were fabulously rich and had everything the Roberts children lacked or desired. They fashioned also for the Wilsons comely dress and fascinating exploits. Mrs. Wilson, for instance, cleans with a gold broom and gold dust pan.[5] The Wilsons could be manipulated in any escapist manner desired. The imaginary family also gave the children a little secret world safe from the grownups. At the dinner table Elizabeth, for instance, could observe casually to her brother, Ivor, "I saw Mr. Wilson pass today."

This would elicit a puzzled glance from her father, who would say to Mrs. Roberts, "Mr. Wilson? Mr. Wilson? I don't know any Mr. Wilson around here." The children were delighted.

[5] Cf. Miss Roberts' poem, "The Richest Woman in the World," *Under the Tree.*

More of the escapist joy the Wilsons brought Elizabeth is apparent in this note from her papers: "They talked about him [Mr. Wilson] while they shelled peas or peeled potatoes. Eleanor's [Elizabeth's] tender hands shrank from a potato and from dishwater and strong soap. Perhaps it was because of these shrinkings and because of the narrow space in which they lived, the small yard closed in by the shadows of the church, that a race of men came out of the shadow."*

Mary Wilson became Elizabeth's alter ego in the fantasy family, and she equipped Mary with every grace and charm which Elizabeth thought she herself lacked. The fantasy children were always created older and more mature than their real life counterparts. Speaking of this fact later, Miss Roberts revealingly observed: "They wanted free people and children were not free . . . a terrible thing to be a child."*

More important to her than the imaginary Wilson family was the real and poignant figure of an old Negro carpenter, "Uncle" Wilse McElroy. She left an extended note on him which provides an illuminating insight into her own life at this period:

I see old Uncle Wilse McElroy going by . . . . He said he had been king in Africa.
Ah, his house.
Slowly with labor and pain and I cannot think what deprivation, he was building a house for himself and his family . . . . He helped build the villas with their observatories . . . and he dreamed of a house for himself. It grew very slowly, through years. I remember it first as a large frame, very gaunt and much weather-stained. Months sometimes went between the nailing of a board and board . . . . He liked to talk about his house . . . . It was his reason for being, his life. An old Negro, all Ethio-

pian, with a dream that reached through years. It was going
to have bay windows and porches and "zurbatory" .... The
house grew a little every year: every few pennies he could save
from his food and his clothes—he had little of either—bought
another weather board .... "When it is finished," he said,
"I'm going to live like a king."

It did have an observatory and it did have a bay window.
The king of Africa found himself in a villa world and he
rose to it.

.   .   .

The mansion was painted red finally. It was not finished
when he died of pneumonia—he was dressed in thin summer
rags that winter trying to save to buy the window sashes. But the
house had shape and color. Its pinnacle stood high and its
porch was floored. The roof was on.

And then she concludes with a personal application.

Myself a little girl trying to climb out of my sordid world by
the way of high towers and Uncle Wilse with his mansion
house rising above the shanties of High Street; I am glad we
knew each other. He was a better builder than I.*

The melancholy underlying these memories is what
almost any child of Miss Roberts' sensitivity might feel.
There was, of course, a brighter side to her childhood,
a side to which she often turned pleasurably in memory in
later years. She often spoke and wrote of her father's role
as a storyteller. He loved to gather the children about him
after the evening meal and spin tales to them. They would
crowd into his lap or hang on his arms and shoulders while
he recounted his version of the tales in Bulfinch's *The Age
of Fable*. He loved the savor of Greek and Roman names,
a taste he passed on to his talented daughter. Theodosia

Bell's pleasure in the repetition of "Mnemosyne" in *My Heart and My Flesh* is an example drawn from Miss Roberts' own life. Then the stories would branch out into tales of the Civil War and of the old days before the war, going on and on, while the children listened in warm and fire-drugged ecstasy. These moments were rich ones in her early life, and she never forgot them.*

Years later an interviewer[6] asked if she had read extensively as a child. She answered that she had not because her father's library burned before she was born, and her childhood was nourished on "phantom books." All that had floated away in smoke came back through the pervasive voice of her father, and his ultimate charm was greater than that of the printed page.

It was in this period of early childhood that the future writer displayed her first creative interest. At the age of eight, she turned out a little story—her first essay—and showed it to playmates whose aunt was her teacher. The aunt saw it and praised it, and Elizabeth felt gratified. But her major memory of the event was of the children's remark when they turned back the story, "Why don't you correct the misspelled word?" She didn't know which one and only later discovered that "ded" was supposed to have an "a" in it.

At eleven, she tried her first poem. She wished to show it to a close friend whose father wrote poetry. She yearned for the opinion of the father. So she put the poem in her sleeve and went to swing in the hammock with her girl friend. But her courage died, and she never disclosed it. No one else ever saw her first effort.[7]

On the bright side of her childhood also were the occa-

6 Interview, Louisville *Courier Journal*, February 24, 1929.
7 *Ibid.*

☆ 12 ☆

sional outings the family would take. The one she remembered most vividly was an all-day trip, made in a horse-drawn wagon, to the village of Frederickstown, some ten miles west of Springfield. It was a nice summer day, and the entire family went, even the current baby. Mr. Roberts at that time was engineer for a bridge being built over the small river at Frederickstown. He wanted his wife to see his handiwork. They drove through a pleasant agrarian countryside such as Ellen Chesser knew in *The Time of Man*. The children were good, and both parents enjoyed themselves. On the way down they drove two miles off the highway to Doe Run Trestle, a railroad trestle also built by Mr. Roberts. The lane led through a cool woodland which felt strange and attractive to Elizabeth. Later they reached Frederickstown and admired the new bridge and ate lunch. The children played apart from the parents, even taking over the care of the baby. This was a revelation for Elizabeth. She saw her mother suddenly and completely emerge as a "person."* Always before the mother had been engrossed in the care of a baby and had seemed almost a functional adjunct to the baby. Now, as her mother laughed apart from the baby, examined the bridge and river with interest, walked apart with Mr. Roberts, Elizabeth suddenly saw her as a distinct and individual being, unique in her own person. It was a joy to her. And it was a trip and a revelation she never forgot.

Gradually a rich texture of memory emerged from these childhood scenes. She remembered the long summer afternoons spent in play on the graveyard hill overlooking the town. This gave her a sense of apartness, of separateness from life; a sense of being over here and being able to look off and down on her home and town and regular routine of life. Through the town and behind her house flowed a small creek, a place for dams, tadpoles, and all the "water-play" in which children indulge. There was the nightly pageant of the cow being brought into the barn lot and the ritual of her father milking the cow and filling Elizabeth's cup with warm milk. There were memories of hot summer nights when the family sat in the yard and listened to the father's stories and looked at the summer stars and the drowsed lights of houses on Lebanon Hill. Memories of watching long baseball games on the school field at the eastern edge of town, where the young children sat perched on wooden fences while the young stalwarts of the town battled with teams from the neighborhood towns of Lebanon and Bardstown. The exciting, fearful memory of a lynching late at night, when a mob on horseback rode into town and battered down the jail door, haling forth a murderer to his hanging in Professor Grant's schoolyard. All this while the children cowered fearfully in bed. And the memory of the tense days of the tobacco wars and the "Night Riders" hastening through town in the first dark, threatening: "Put out those lights or we'll shoot them out." And the memory of her first visit to a Catholic funeral and the oddness of the vestments and robes on the priest and altar boys, thus strangely changed from their familiar selves.

By this time, also, Elizabeth had begun her schooling. There were no public schools, so the children of Springfield were educated in various private schools which were established from time to time. Elizabeth attended an academy known locally as "Professor Grant's," from the name of the proprietor and headmaster. There were some moments of sensitivity here, of course. Some of the girls whose parents were the well-to-do people of the town made unconsciously cruel remarks about her dress, which might be pieced or old. She shrank from such remarks, but had no difficulty otherwise. She entered into her studies with great fervor and enthusiasm, performing, as might be imagined, exceptionally well.

Elizabeth did make a lasting impression on many of her classmates. Mrs. Hettie Rudd Montgomery, a classmate during these years, recalls her manner with great clarity, even fifty years later. She writes:

Miss Roberts and I were in high school together and our desks were side by side. She kept so still and quiet that but for seeing her I would not have known she was present. I realized she was different from the average person, but I could not figure out just what the difference was. Her dreamy blue eyes and innocent expression made me wonder at her mystery.

She spoke only when called upon to recite in class. Here I envied her. She knew all the answers. These answers were given in a soft voice and gentle manner with no elaboration. I knew she could have said much more, but I never once realized what a great genius was hidden within her.[8]

It was during these years of childhood and girlhood that she formed what was to be one of the closest friendships of her life. A few doors down the street from Elizabeth's home lived Dr. Ray, one of the local physicians. Dr. Ray had two children, Nick Ray and Sue Ray. Elizabeth soon came to know them both. Sue was her own age and very talented. The Ray house was a large, rambling pre-Civil War home and a fascinating place for the children to play. Dr. Ray had a large collection of old Indian arrowheads and other relics which had been discovered throughout the county.

In a short time, Sue and Elizabeth formed a close friendship which lasted unchanged until the premature death of the former. They had a common love for music. Elizabeth

[8] From a letter to the authors, September 5, 1953.

often played the piano while Sue accompanied her with a guitar or mandolin. They were both sensitive, artistic. But there was a tragic conflict in Sue which increased as she matured. It manifested itself outwardly by a growing desire to flaunt the mores of the village. At a time when no lady smoked in private, much less in public, Sue would swing down the streets of Springfield dangling a cigarette from her lips, to the great scandal of the elders. She became more and more neurotic, eventually leaving Springfield and dying in Louisville, still quite young.

Elizabeth observed and sympathized with the tragic conflict within Sue. She did not condemn, and she never forgot. Years later she embodied much of Sue in the character of Theodosia Bell in *My Heart and My Flesh*. She never failed to defend Sue from the caustic tongues of gossip, saying, "The qualities I loved her for she still has." Years later she memorialized this friend in a small collection of books (about one hundred) which she gave to the Springfield Public Library. Each book had within it a one-paragraph printed inscription, which read as follows:

The Sue Ray Memorial Collection

This small collection of books has been placed in the Springfield Public Library in memory of Sue Ray. It will be called the "Sue Ray Memorial Collection." The books have been chosen with care by the giver, who hoped that each one might be of some use to the readers of Washington County and might be, at the same time, a small reminder, bringing Sue Ray back to the memory of friends who knew her, for she lived the greater part of her short life in Springfield. She was a musician of rare gift whose fine musical quality might have been a prized asset in any community. She gave her talent lavishly to her town and was a lover of all fine and lovely things.

Some years earlier, Elizabeth's mother's people, the Brents, had moved to Covington, Kentucky, where they had opened a boardinghouse. Elizabeth had already displayed genuine talent in school, and it was decided to send her to Covington to complete high school in the city school system. In 1897, she began her work there and completed it in May, 1899, when she graduated fifth in a class of nineteen. Covington seemed new and very big and somewhat strange to her. Later she set down an impressionistic picture of what this city meant to her as a young girl, in the picture of Mome, the fantasy city in the prologue to *My Heart and My Flesh*. It was a period of homesickness for her—homesickness not only for her family, but also for the town of Springfield and all the rolling land of the Pigeon River country.

She then returned to Springfield and spent a year at home, hoping to find the means of entering college. With some help from her father, she was able to enter State College of Kentucky (now known as the University of Kentucky) on September 17, 1900. She was admitted without examination as a freshman and was permitted to enroll in sophomore courses in English, mathematics, and foreign languages.

There comes now what might be considered a long interlude in the life of Miss Roberts. For various reasons—chief of which were ill-health and slender finances—she was unable to attend college again until 1917. Unquestionably, she viewed this long hiatus as a minor tragedy. She herself had no regard for the cult of "the college degree" (all of her stories express the superiority of "knowledge carried to the heart" over book knowledge), but there was much in college she wanted to learn about literature and art. She wanted, also, to associate with people who valued these things. Yet all this was to be denied her for fifteen years—until 1917, when she finally matriculated at the University of Chicago. Nevertheless, the period had its compensations. She made a number of fine, lifetime friends, and she absorbed the atmosphere, character, and folk speech she was to use in her later novels.

What is the character of her life in this period? She is a mature adult of twenty-one when it begins, and already the physical frailness which shadows the remainder of her life is apparent. In the photographs of this period, she appears as a shy-looking girl with a delicate, blonde beauty. Her voice was musical and well modulated and always remembered by those who heard it. She was a retiring person who made little noise in the outer world, but carried about with her an inner world rich in resources of the spirit—her true world was within.

Unable to return to college, she settled down in Springfield with her family, who had now moved into a large frame house on Walnut street—a house now known as the "Simns Home." She opened a private school, using the front room of her home as the class room. Miss Roberts, who was attending the local Christian church, had also begun to teach Sunday school there. She continued to do so for a number of years, in spite of the chagrin this generated in one of its staunchest elders—a grizzled veteran of the Civil War, "Uncle" Lytle Kays. He was chagrined because Miss Roberts had never made her profession of faith.

There are pupils still living in Springfield who studied under Miss Roberts at this period. Mrs. John L. Barber (nee Stella Simns) remembers her quite well as a teacher. Miss Roberts took part in a benefit play for the Christian church. Mrs. Simns (mother of Stella) attended the play and was greatly impressed by the beauty and clarity of Miss Roberts' voice. She asked Miss Roberts to take Stella as one of her pupils. Stella began her studies at sixteen under Miss Roberts, who was only four or five years older. Mrs. Barber has very keen and kindly recollections of Miss Roberts as a teacher. She particularly remembers the simplicity and candor of her manner. Her health was already rather poor, and she occasionally fainted while teaching. She taught usually from a rocking chair. It was rigorous work, and she was paid meagerly enough, receiving tuition of three dollars a month from each of her pupils.

To all intents and purposes Miss Roberts was now adopting teaching as her life profession. The next decade in her life (1904-14) was devoted to teaching. Uneventful enough on the surface, it yet brought her into close contact with the rural types which she was later to portray so skillfully in her novels.

Her family moved again, this time to another house on Walnut Street, which they were to occupy permanently. Here Miss Roberts opened a kindergarten and taught for a year. Then she taught for three years in the Springfield public school (newly organized). There was a clash of personalities between her and the superintendent, Mr. George Colvin, and she left to take a position at Pleasant Grove, a country school about five miles from Springfield, on the Willisburg road. It was past this school that Ellen Chesser was to take her fictional nightwalk in *The Time of Man*. While in Pleasant Grove, she boarded with Mrs. Lucian Gregory and entered into the life of the country community, noting all its details with great fidelity. She liked the rich, country food, the neighborly warmth, and the relaxed, country idiom.

Mrs. Hettie Rudd Montgomery, her former schoolmate, has left a fine and knowing glimpse of her in this period at Pleasant Grove:

> While she was teaching there [Pleasant Grove], the teachers of the county gave a literary program at her school. She recited "That Old Sweetheart of Mine." I have never been so impressed as I was when she gave that recital. The picture was so vivid; we saw and felt it all. What she gave in that is beyond me to express. As she stood there in her innocence and her deep feeling it seemed a bit of heaven had come upon us. I shall never forget her.[9]

After a year or so at Pleasant Grove, she moved to Maude, a community in a more remote section of the county. Here she met a reception as kindly as she had found at Pleasant Grove. She found further insights into the country people and a particularly rich source of ballads and folklore.

In 1914, Miss Roberts went to Colorado and remained with relatives for over a year, enjoying the bracing air and the drama of the huge peaks. She had begun writing poetry by this time and launched her first modest publication. A photographer friend, Kenneth Hartley, secured a number of striking photographs of mountain flowers. Miss Roberts composed a short accompanying poem for each picture. They thus had a thin, illustrated booklet which was privately printed for them with the title, "In the Great Steep's Garden." Sales were small, but Miss Roberts sent copies to friends and family and was glad to have launched something, no matter how modest, in print.

Her Colorado jaunt coming to an end, she returned to Springfield, anxious once again to actualize her dream of college. This meant a great deal to her, more in fact than

[9] Letter from Mrs. H. R. Montgomery to the authors.

many people realized. She once confided to a close friend that when her father refused her money for college, she had gone to her room and cried bitterly, knowing that he had given enough money to the church to send her through school. She began now to talk at length with her friend and neighbor, Mrs. Bosley, about college. With catalogs from a number of different schools, she would go to Mrs. Bosley's home and talk animatedly for hours over them. Encouraged by Mrs. Bosley, she eventually chose the University of Kentucky.

There were several reasons for this choice. She had already enrolled there years before. It was close to home and family, and it would keep her in her native state. This was important to as convinced a regionalist as Miss Roberts. Moreover, the University of Kentucky was relatively inexpensive. Most important of all, she had a friend there, James T. Cotton Noe, who taught in the school of education. Mr. Noe, a native of Washington County, knew the Roberts family well. He was also a poet well known in the state, and he knew of Miss Roberts' desire to write.

Miss Roberts spent a year at the university, and it was a relatively happy one. She concentrated on poetry and produced many poems that greatly impressed Professor Noe, who was moved to write Professor Robert Morss Lovett of the University of Chicago about her. As a result of this correspondence, Professor Lovett invited her to come to Chicago and study there. This she resolved to do.

On January 8, 1917, her long deferred hopes came true. She appeared at the University of Chicago and registered as a freshman, intending to take a degree in philosophy. This is a pivotal point in her life, and we can stop for a moment to observe her as she appeared then. What was she like at this time?

She was then thirty-six years old. She had an original, quiet intelligence with an inward poetic cast. Her sensibility was a complex one. There was in the world of her mind a long wind blowing out of the past, out of Virginia and Maryland and Harrodsburg, Kentucky, from the days of Daniel Boone and James Harrod: a wind bringing old phrases, old talk, and the personalities of long-dead ancestry to life. There was the memory of the little town in which she had grown up, the countryside stretching out around it and the rich, human relationships—comic and tragic—which she had witnessed or experienced. There was her feeling for the old South, imbibed strongly from both parents and never to be lost. And there was a feeling for place, for state, for the "Kentuckyness" of her life which was an integral part of her life, important in her art, and which never diminished. Some years later she phrased very perceptively this attitude toward Kentucky:

All young people wish to try the world and to find out adventures, but the young of Kentucky do not seem to look upon their region as a place from which to escape. A pride in the place where they were born stays with them when they go, if they must go, and often they return . . . . Kentucky has form and design and outline both in time and space, in history and geography. Perhaps the strongly marked natural bounds which make it a country within itself, are the real causes which gave it history and a pride in something which might be named personality.*

Important also in her thinking from this time on was her growing interest in the Catholic religion. Her family contacts had been firmly evangelical Protestant. She had Catholic friends, however, and through them she became interested in phases of the Catholic faith. Even before she

made her Colorado sojourn, she asked one of her Catholic
girl friends for a rosary and instructions on the saying of it.
Miss Roberts maintained that she said it faithfully and later
wrote her friend that she kept it on her bedstead in her
hall-bedroom in Chicago, which, she said, she called "my
cell." She was drawn certainly to aesthetic aspects of the
Catholic ritual and liturgy, and attended with her neighbor, Mr. Charlie McIntire, in 1922, the first mass of Father
Edward Russell, one of Springfield's native sons. Her observation was so keen that she was able to do the story. "The
Sacrifice of the Maidens," which describes Catholic nuns
taking the veil, after only one visit to this ceremony at
St. Catherine's Convent, located one mile out of Springfield. Later, when she had returned to Springfield and
begun writing, she made many visits to St. Rose, a Dominican priory located a few miles out of Springfield. She often
remarked, "There's beautiful art in Catholic ceremonies."

This interest in Catholicism seems to have been deeper
than a mere aesthetic interest. Around 1925, the same
friend who had given the rosary gave a Catholic missal to
Miss Roberts which she kept the rest of her life. This
volume, which the writer has examined, is extremely well
thumbed throughout, giving evidence of systematic reading in it. Mrs. Mary Sally Moran, who was Miss Roberts'
companion during the last year of her life, said that Miss
Roberts read in it every day during that final year. This
religious interest, which manifests itself in a number of
her short stories and in her novel *Black Is My Truelove's
Hair,* remained a pervasive one throughout all the remaining years of her life.

The Chicago period in her life, which was to last for the
next four years (1917–21), marked her transition from an
aspiring but completely unknown writer to a poet with a

number of publications favorably known nationally. It was also a period when she made some very close and lasting friendships, and a period when she gradually began to consider the novel as a medium.

There was first the period of getting set up in her hall-bedroom at 1007 East Sixtieth Street, of familiarizing herself with the city and the campus and her professors. It was a fairly drastic change from the environs of Springfield to the giant urbanism of Chicago, but Miss Roberts was malleable when necessary, and within a month (October 13, 1917) was writing a cheerful, matter-of-fact letter to Mrs. C. F. Bosley, the friend whose encouragement had meant so much to her:

My dear Miss Cile:—
Doubtless you think you are going to get a theme when you see theme paper coming out of the envelope. Not so, however, for I have done my share of themes this week. I did a paper for my History of English Language course today on my speech and the influences that went into the making of it. I called it "My Phonetic Autobiography," and had a very interesting time writing it. This course is a great deal of fun. I have two others, for I have a full program this quarter. French is one subject, and History of Greek Art is the other. I shall have to reconstruct my physiognomy and my mouth will take on a new and different shape when I achieve the tongue of "gay Paree." The instructor has the pronunciation to perfection for she is a part-French, part-English person. She requires all the conversation of the classroom to be French. But, alas, Greek Art, —a most delightful subject—is dispensed by a *Fossil*. Ah me! He is the typical college professor of the joke book. He is stuffed with chalk and maps and charts inside instead of the usual human stuffing of flesh and blood. His skin is made of papyrus found at the base of the Sphynx [*sic*]. His discourse

is so involved and obscure that I can not understand him. And worse and moreover, we use a text book—which he wrote! It is as obscure as his speech. He "hears our lesson," which he assigns in the text, just as if we were in high school. The subject is so interesting to me that I am sure I am going to like it, in spite of the instructor. (He, by the way, is the head of the department of archeology, and quite an authority.) Perhaps I shall like him better after a while.

I hope you are busy with your class again; it is so good to be busy. I think of you very often and send you many good thoughts.

Lel spent the day with me Saturday. She has actually gained weight under the stimulant of teaching small Bohemians and Poles. I visited her school one Monday about a week ago. She has such an interesting lot of youngsters. The little girls—none is any larger than Amelda or Hallie or Lum—all wear ear rings. They are clean little things, however, all in big up-standing hair ribbons (Americanisms they have learned; this last.) Lel sings in the local Methodist choir (at Berwyn) and wears a gown to do so, *a la* the Episcopal way. They are quite musical out at Berwyn and have a choral society, to which Lel has united herself. She enjoys this very much for it will afford her real vocal training. They are going to give some oratorios during the winter.

The Divine Sarah [Bernhardt] is here this week, also Lillian Russell, at the Coliseum, in some sort of benefit performance. I shall not attend but hope to hear some of the performances of the Chicago Opera Association. Madame Melba has arrived for the first performance. I wish you were going to hear her with me. I can not afford to hear them all but should like to hear Galla Curchi (I can't spell it), and Melba. She, Melba, is going to do *Fauste* and *Le Boheme* [*sic*]. The Chicago Symphony Orchestra Association is giving some concerts out here at the university. These will be quite inexpensive to students and convenient to attend.

I have three little musicians to instruct now, all in very primary grades of course. I should like to have one more to help balance this high cost of living thing we are up against. Milk has advanced to 13 cents a quart—from 10 cents. This is most deplorable, for the little children of the very poor will suffer. There is a rumor that it will go to 18 cts. soon. I shall have no difficulty in finding another student for there are so many children all about. The music teachers charge 75 cts. for a half hour lesson. I, being no professional musician, am willing to give the lesson for 50 cts. So you see I am a sort of *scab*—is that the word? The lure of the reduced price makes it easy enough to get students, but I must not take but four with my heavy university work.

I hope I shall hear from you some time soon. To say that "time will heal" is a platitude, and platitudes often annoy with their sermonizing; but time makes a difference and being busy and going on with the business of living makes a difference. I know a little secret that picked me up out of the almost-despairing place where I was and put me where I am now. I believe that each one can find the best way for himself; that is, the way one finds for himself is best; but I might give another hint of it. If only I had not been so selfish, so short-sighted, I might have helped Miss Mat. I believe one can correct any habit, or any mental pain, or state of mind, and can make over his character, can gain courage and calmness and just such habits of mind as he desires, by this little thing I know. If you ever want it I will give you the secret of it.

With very much love
Elizabeth

1007 E. 60th St.
Chicago, Ill.

She fitted unobtrusively into the student body and absorbed what she wanted from them without losing the strong independence she prized so highly. Professor Robert Morss Lovett of the University of Chicago English Department remembered her life in this period:

I remember Miss Elizabeth Madox Roberts . . . as an exceedingly good student of English Literature and a member of the Poetry Club. She wrote her first published book, a series of poems for children, while at the University. I do not remember that she had any difficulties except ill health, which has been a serious handicap throughout her career. Miss Roberts was often at my house, and needless to say was a great favorite with my family. She was, however, reserved, and told me nothing of her early life, surroundings, reasons for coming to the University, etc.[10]

She became associated also with a group of very talented students of whom Glenway Westcott, the novelist, is perhaps the best known today. He remembers her more dramatically: "There [at the University] was the young southern woman, alone absolutely original, unimpressed by the besetting evils and plagiaries, meek and insinuatingly affirmative, untouched by but kindly toward all our half-grown baseness."[11] Other students in the group were Janet Loxley Lewis, Monroe Wheeler, Maurice Leseman, Yvor Winters, Gladys Campbell, Vincent Sheean, and later Jessica and Sterling North and George Dillon. They were drawn together by a common interest in literature, art, and the problems of creative writing. Her friendship, once it was given, was strong, and the vigor of it can be seen in a note made by her after her Chicago period had closed:

[10] Letter from Robert Morss Lovett to Andrew J. Beeler, Jr., July 12, 1939. Quoted from Mr. Beeler's unpublished master's thesis, "Elizabeth Madox Roberts: Her Interpretation of Life," 1940, University of Louisville.

[11] Glenway Westcott, "Elizabeth Madox Roberts: A Personal Note," *The Bookman*, Vol. LXXI, No. 1 (March, 1930), 12–15.

Elizabeth Madox Roberts

"Glenway [Westcott] and Arthur [Arthur Yvor Winters]
off the Campus for good . . . were more of a force in the
club than any professor on the campus . . . ."*

There is a distinct impression among Miss Roberts' associates that her friendship with Glenway Westcott later
ripened into a romantic attachment. For various reasons
this never came to fruition. Apropos of this, there is a
note among her papers dating from this period; it is on the
back of an old music program:

Dear――

I came, and when I found that you weren't here, I paid attention to a sad sound there was in the remotest part of my head,
and knowing I should have little to give you but pain and my
love, I left the letter and ran off home.*

G.

Monroe Wheeler and Maurice Leseman were two other
members of this group who also became close friends of
Miss Roberts. Their friendship lasted beyond student days,
and they appear frequently in Miss Roberts' correspondence throughout the remainder of her life. It was with this
group of intimates that Miss Roberts began to substitute
the name "Elspeth" (Middle English form of Elizabeth)
for Elizabeth, and "Elspeth" remained the name by which
they affectionately addressed her in their conversation and
letters from this time on.

This little group was primarily a literary club, and they
met frequently to read and discuss each other's writing.
It was here that Miss Roberts began turning out the poems
which were published in *Under the Tree.* At the same time,
she was formulating her poetic theory, striving for a simple,
direct language, free of clichés, which would render exactly the clarity and pristine quality of childhood experi-

ence. The originality of this poetry soon drew attention, and she was awarded the Fiske Poetry Prize[12] in 1922. This recognition definitely helped her morale and encouraged her to submit her poetry to a publisher, B. W. Huebsch, who accepted and published it in 1922, thus launching her on her actual writing career.

There were, of course, her actual subjects going forward concurrently with the writing. Miss Roberts had registered on January 8, 1917, as Elizabeth Eleanor ("Eleanor" was added above the line as an afterthought) Madox Roberts, listing her birthplace as "Peryville [*sic*], Kentucky." (This spelling of Perryville illustrates the fact that Miss Roberts, like many other fine writers, was but an indifferent speller.) By June 20, 1917, she had completed two English courses with "A's" (in English composition she was limited to an "A-") and been awarded the David Blair McLaughlin Prize for excellence in writing English prose. She went steadily forward, taking work in philosophy and English literature. Her grades were high; and in the spring quarter, 1919, she received a Scholarship for Excellence in Junior College Work in English. In the spring quarter, 1920, she took a course in eighteenth century philosophy and concentrated on the idealism of Berkeley. She worked steadily and on June, 1921, was awarded a Ph. B. degree with honors in English and elected to Phi Beta Kappa.

Paralleling these surface events in her life were the events of her inner life which occasionally come through to us from the notes made in this period. In the fall of her first year at Chicago, we find her making this note on November 21: "I have found that there is a thing within myself to

[12] This began as a prize offered by Robert Morss Lovett to stimulate interest in poetry. It became permanent with the gift of one thousand dollars by Horace Spencer Fiske in memory of his father, John Billings Fiske.

which I can pray and unto which I can make an unbreakable vow." And later on the same page, she adds the optimistic afterthought: "I believe that everybody is trying to do right."*

We will never know what occurred within the next twenty-four hours to cause her to withdraw this statement for a bleaker view of human nature, which she expressed the following day, November 22. "I was perhaps unduly optimistic yesterday— I fear there is a streak—a trace of villainy in the human breed after all and it fills my soul with pain to have to admit it."*

Not the least of her personal concerns of this period derived from the affection she had developed for Maurice Leseman. She had grown very fond of him and yet felt that there was some social disapproval of this attachment since he was a Jew. The strongly idealistic note underlying this affection is apparent in the following short letter, presumably written to Maurice.

. . . . I have known you for a long time . . . . I saw this thing I am writing about in your poems from the very first . . . on this walk I expounded you to Eleanor.—and was very happy because I had found something real in the world.

. . . This . . . [her ellipses] I said is Maurice. It is the most real thing in the world—the Maurice that writes the poems. It is the most beautiful thing in the world, and later I expounded you to Janet, when I came to know her very well. I saw in you something very true and sincere and actual and all last summer this true thing about you was the surest hold I had on anything real at all and I loved it better than I loved anything else in the world."*

Miss Roberts might ignore public opinion with a bland nonrecognition, but she could not deny its presence in her consciousness. Springfield, in the manner of small towns where everyone knows everyone else, could make her feel its disapproval, as she clearly indicates in her letter to Janet Lewis, dated August 5, 1920. The following is an excerpt:

I can feel the pressure of the social mind here. People are kind and they of course do not know anything about me, but I can feel the social mind and its scorn of me because I love Maurice. From the social point of view it is all wrong for me to love him, and the social mind stands up and looks at me here . . . and that is part of why I wept.

But I do not weep any more, and it is beautiful for me to love him in the world of the inner reality. This is a beautiful world.*

In her Chicago period she began to make the acquaintance of some of the nationally-known literary figures of the day. Among them was Vachel Lindsay, whose profile she sketches rather acidly in the following letter. Reading it one catches a glimpse of the shy and retiring Kentucky writer being completely shouted down by this booming "Congo person." Our sympathies go to Miss Roberts.

Dear Monroe:
    . . . I went to dinner at Mrs. Moody's to meet Vachel Lindsay, whom I do not like, and Mollie Best, who happened to be there and whom I liked very much. Vachel is not a gentle man, or at any rate he gestures wildly with his arms and his voice in a General William Booth Enters Heaven manner. We sat together on the big floppy sofa that you know, and I was almost overturned by suddenness and gesture. Mrs. Moody had a General William Booth Enters manner too, borrowed or reflected from the great guest, I thought. They were very noisy and very gay and very robust. I felt like a skein of silk beside them, as if I might flutter into the fire any moment and never be missed. I could feel myself withdraw further and further

into the arm of the sofa, to avoid the gesturing arm of the Congo person whom I wanted to like. But he whispers in the ear and I do not like to be whispered in the ear by a stranger. I grew very still but I felt as if I must make some concession to the utter informality of the occasion and so I sat on my feet . . . . It was good of you and G. to drink to my book with champagne on the Heights. That is propitious. Ah, Bonn! Will I ever see Bonn? I'd be lost in Dutchland, I think . . . .

I read your article in the C. M. D. Magazine and I liked it. I think you could work over the same material into your *Sat. E. Post* articles and stories. The Business man loves to know how badly the other side of the world does it.

A few years later she emerged as a lesser rival, in effect, of Lindsay, as she and Janet Lewis planned a small trouba-douring tour of the West. She found that " . . . I should make a truce or a trust with Vachel . . . . Where my work is known, the reply is cordial, often quite warm—stating that Vachel Lindsay has been there and there is no more money. I want to get ahead of him next year if it is humanly possible"* This troubadouring, however, was not suited to her health and temperament, and the publication of her first novel, *The Time of Man,* in 1926, fortunately enabled her to forego it.

The Time of Man was a long time growing, and its roots go far back into her childhood memories, and particularly into her memories of the teaching years at Maude and Pleasant Grove. Her poetry had given her a keen interest in form which was greatly heightened by the literary dis-cussions she heard and engaged in at the University of Chicago. Her mind was awake to the problem and the challenge of literary form. The thrust of her interest is apparent in her following comment in a letter to Janet L. Lewis, August 5, 1920:

Photograph by Jay Te Winburn
Courtesy Miss Mabel Williams

Elizabeth Madox Roberts, about 1929

I will tell you why we continually go back to realism in art. Somewhere there is a connection between the world of the mind and the outer order. It is the secret of the contact that we are after, the point, the moment of the union. We faintly sense the one and we know as faintly the other, but there is a point at which they come together and we can never know the whole of reality until we know these two completely.*

By this time, she had become interested in the novel. The fact that her friends Monroe Wheeler and Glenway Westcott were both doing fiction increased the keenness of her interest. So during this same summer, 1920, she made her first essay at a novel, beginning a piece which she tentatively called "Sallie May." This was never completed, but the fragment which remains indicates that it dealt very closely with the people she had known in Springfield. At this time she wrote a letter to Glenway Westcott, telling of this initial attempt and of her neighbors, which provides us with a good insight into her mind and mood at this period.

Dear Glenway:

I am writing a novel too these days, or was last week and set upon it at once, and in less than thirteen days I had set 13000 words on paper. But then I fell ill for several days, and ah me, what a devastating experience. For two days through the pain and misery the story lived, an entity that I could touch with my mind and love with my heart, and then came convalescence and a weariness and apathy and my puppets are all dead. I can't make them get up and dance again . . . .

But before I lost her I made Sallie May march down life-ways, and Homer with her and the Stigalls—a family that live at a sort of Wuthering Heights place, and a phantasy named Blondetta, and a troop of old hounds that Judge Rowan left when he dies, old hounds that Miss Bell Rowan keeps on about

her, and the boy who pushed over a pillar one Hallowe'en
night and had to run away the next day because the village
wrath was on him. (He joined the army and then in the war
he was killed at Chateau Thierry, and now his picture enlarged
in crayon hangs up in the court house with the judges and his
body was buried last summer on the hill above the town with
all the people present and a bugle blowing taps. If the judges
could have caught him the day after he pushed over the pillar
that marked where Selectman Court was going to be he never
could have got away to war and there would be no portrait
of him in crayon hanging among the judges.)

All these I made march for me through headache and pain,
and now I can't make them go. But I will think of your story
and of Hannah and maybe they will live.

My garden is a joyous place. It is a little more of a garden
this year than last, when it was largely a vision and a plan.
This year I have a bench and a chair there, under a locust tree,
and along the fence—a high wire fence that looks into a neighbor's vegetable garden, I have planted cinnamon vines and the
flowering cucumbers and morning glories, to try to get a wall
of green to keep the neighbors on the side from seeing me
when I sit under the tree with my book. (They never sit under
a tree with a book, poor dears). They play songs on Sunday
that go:

tum tum tum—tum
tum tum tum—tum
call . . . ing to . . . day
call . . . ing to . . . day
Je . . . sus is ten . . der . . . ly ten . . . der . . ly calling
to . . . day.
all day long.

I am walled in on all sides except on the side of the primitive
tom tom hymns (the most interesting thing about them is
their primitive character) and I trust the vines to grow. And
so I sit under the tree and the ladybugs walk over me, and a

phoebe bird comes to the grape arbor and his mate sits on the fence, making little silver talk out of his throat, looking about with anxious searching head, feeling into the air for his presence. And the doves cry "do, do, do, do" all morning, a gentle imperative, musical and strange.

Sallie May, and her people, are less than an essence out of the soil. They are a word out of the clods.

I tell nobody of her but you and Monie . . . She may be only a dream-strife, a useless endeavor,—myself on endless stairs that hang over precipices, clutching.

The letter indicates that her efforts, though groping, have brought her close to her true métier. Still, her health is bad and she lacks confidence. Her mood is frequently low—" . . . myself on endless stairs that hang over precipices, clutching . . . ." Yet, the resources which will carry her through are already becoming evident. By this time she has accumulated a large number of ideas, phrases, symbols, patterns, songs, vignettes, etc., which will serve as the matrix from which she will construct the novel. Her problem, however, is complicated by a tense, dark mood which continually assails her. This mood is apparent in the following excerpt (letter to Janet L. Lewis, August 5, 1920):

The little country [this is her private name for Springfield and its environs as it lives in her imagination] is rather an intense little country this year . . . . I had to stop writing the poems because they grow so very intense. I felt that I must stop and wait. Except "The Sunday Bonnet" everything I have done since I came home has been tense and often tragic. I felt that I would break more hearts than I had a right to, and so I stopped and waited."*

In spite of this atrabiliar mood, the notes outlining gen-

eral plans and ideas grow more and more frequent. Some
are fragmentary and elliptical, like the following:

Admonitions for plan—
It is not to be autobiography. It must be higher art than that.
Myself, against the chaos of the world.
Art before chaos.
It must take shape in the end.
It must have form . . . .
Brief pictures suddenly cut as a reel.
Selecting out of consciousness a vein, a flow, which reveals the
whole flow.*

Again there is speculation on the nature of symbols, a
speculation which foreshadows her own practice in terms
of her novels:

Only large symbols are lasting
Hence the indestructible nature of the ancient Bible.
Noah's Ark. The Earth itself.
God made a covenant with all living flesh.
The Tower of Babel. Vain Sciences and isms.
They think they can thus climb out of the way of God's flood
of life and death.
How poor, how vain to tie spiritual truth to Science. The
Tower of Babel.
Eternal Truths. Yesterday, now and forever.
The void of illusion in which the mind floats.*

Then in November, 1921, appears a note combining her
determination to write a novel with a caustic repudiation
of the evangelical quality of her village world:

I wish to write one piece of prose. I can make no plan for it;
it seems to be written into the fibers of my being. I wish to
present myself against the background of my world, and that

is all that I shall ever be able to present. The difficulty is to choose material from the chaos about me and the apparent chaos that is myself. It would not seem to make much difference what one chooses, all things being equally important, but the *for what* is the vital problem . . . if I cannot trust the fibers of my being to make the pattern, to write it in its delicate traceries, there *will be no pattern.*

Tonight the winds run through stripped maple boughs— November . . . sometimes in these days of dreary wet and mud and the people . . . dreary . . . and the miles reaching out in every direction, close in upon me as the fabled rocks. . . . I am apart from the churchgoers with their poor imitation who- soever—will, apart from the Christmas bazaars with their passions over pincushions and dust-caps, apart from the rook- players who are holier than the bridge-players and the bridge- players who are scornful of the evasions of the rook-players . . . only artists go to heaven.*

Her mental state was complex. The creative springs were filling to the point of overflowing, and a definite plan was taking shape in her mind. A tension arose also from the paradox of her love and attachment to the physical world and many genuine people of Washington County and her active dislike of its village narrowness. Her ambition was tremendous, but her strength had severe limitations. She knew that there were hardened Philistines who dismissed her writing ambitions as mere falderal and dilettantism. She knew, too, that the serious writer must often work for long periods just this side of poverty. She had few illusions when she embraced with almost monastic fervor the holy orders of art. But she did know that for her art was *her* way of life.

I have laid out a hard road for myself; that I know; but no other is offered. I have only one way to go. I realize myself a little bit, and I can observe myself *a posteriori*. I find that I have tried for a poignant speech, as direct as a simple equation—$2+2=4$. And I have tried for great precision in rendering sensuous contacts . . . the points where poetry touches life.*

Later, she made this penetrating and poignant note: "I have known tragedy for a long time, and what it is to be marked, estranged and what it is to die over and over, and to be recreated from within, forever recreated."* This note of personal analysis establishes very early the motif which becomes the major motif of all her novels—the psychic death and rebirth of all her heroines.

Her mood, however was not always Olympian and elegiac. She possessed a shy but very real sense of humor, which bobs up occasionally in her notes. As in the following example: "I got out Woolly and read his rules, and Man Alive! My speech is rich not only in colloquialisms and provincialisms but actual vulgarisms."*

One gets a glimpse of the mildness of her revolt—she really wanted to hurt no one—in the following comment: "One encounters so much orthodoxy that one writes heresies in reaction, to laugh a bit. Higher criticism is the cult of the devil. One must not handle the things of the altar."*

We find, too, that her revolt against the evangelical style of religion in Springfield (as previously noted in this chapter) becomes much more marked now, presumably because of the influences of the Chicago period. One can never dogmatize on the precise religious beliefs of Miss Roberts, but we can pick up many strands of those beliefs and follow their general trend. As an artist, she felt the great importance of beauty to religion.

Our religion is a barren, treeless, flowerless . . . waste deriving from the reason of the 18th century. The preacher cannot

bring religion home to these hills. It is all platitudes and . . .
sayings. A woman sings—
> *"Let Jesus come into your heart."*
And what can this mean without reference to beauty?*

By autumn, 1922, her period of preparation was over.
She was forty-one years old, and her great creative period
was beginning; it was to continue without cessation, in spite
of disastrous ill-health, right up to her death in 1941. Her
first and greatest novel, *The Time of Man,* was begun in
the fall of 1922. The general plan—to show a girl's consciousness, beginning as an infant in almost nothing and
gradually coming to know all life, its flux and flow and
the spirit behind it—had been maturing throughout her
Chicago period. At this point Ellen Chesser, heroine of
The Time of Man, was born.

The entire following year was a busy one, most of Miss
Roberts' time being devoted to writing. She was now living
in the Roberts home on Walnut Street, at the very edge
of Springfield. She did much of her writing in the morning.
In the afternoon she would nap shortly and then walk into
the countryside. Her favorite walk took her out the Poor
Town Road, which began a short block from her home.
This was an old and poorly kept county road, execrable for
motorists but delightful for pedestrians in its serene rusti-
city. Miss Roberts had a very acute eye for the contours of
nature. She often returned from these walks to record in
her notes the particular birds, animals, and flowers observed, the cloud formations, ancient houses, and interesting people noted during her walk. Such passages as these,
often highly poetic in their phrasing, are very similar to
those used in *The Time of Man,* as Ellen observes the great
processional of nature around her. This road was seldom

traveled, so she enjoyed that solitude which was a prime pleasure to her throughout her life.

There was usually a short work stint in the late afternoon. After her evening meal and a brief rest, she would take a leisurely constitutional down Grundy Avenue to the handsome, parklike farm home of Judge Thurman which ended the avenue. She would pause at the stone gates leading into his place and look out into the pleasant fields of his horse farm. Then, with a grave and stately pace, she would return down the avenue to her own home. Those of us who lived on Grundy Avenue became habituated to this daily constitutional and the withdrawn, abstract manner in which it was carried out. Miss Roberts was courteous to anyone she met, but at the same time aloofly meditative. She gave the constant impression of having a very rich inner life to which she was devoting most of her attention.

In the spring and summer months, her routine was varied by her interest in her small flower garden. This garden was a source of great pleasure to her. She planted a hedge which grew to a point where it completely enclosed the garden and shut her in from the public gaze. She put out her favorite perennials and annuals until she had a rich, varied garden. Here she went from mid-spring to mid-fall for her sun baths. She was a sun worshipper, as it were, all the rest of her life, going to Florida in the winter so that she would not be deprived of daily sun.[13]

During all this time, she was keeping in touch with her friends of the Chicago period. Occasionally she would ask them down for a visit, bringing these Midwesterners into the very heart of her Kentucky. She enjoyed having people down who would appreciate the savor of the folk-

[13] Dena Janes, in *Black Is My Truelove's Hair,* shows the same love of the sun.

ways which still infused her county. At about this time
she wrote the following letter to Glenway Westcott:

Dear Glenway:

I hope that you can come home soon .... When you come I
will get a room for you in the neighborhood since we live in
a tiny house .... We can go to the country in our Ford car
and see lovely people who say "It ain't worthen" and "It's not
fitten" and in my own family you can hear . . . "ellum tree"
and "by yon bush." I hope you can run a Ford . . . .*

Mr. Westcott came, and together they drove into the
county—to Maude and Pleasant Grove, where Miss Roberts
had once taught. They heard the soft southern vocables
and looked at the scenes soon to be put into *The Time
of Man*. Visiting the convent and academy of St. Catherine's
and then driving over to the Dominican Priory of St. Rose,
they admired the Gothic stone church and walked through
the old cemetery where many pioneer Kentucky families
are buried under stones dating back to 1800. They stood
before the old stone gate with its rounded archway, which
her companion looked at admiringly, saying, "That's a
real gate. That's Romanesque." Other friends came—
Monroe Wheeler, Maurice Leseman and Janet Lewis.
These were kindred spirits, and they could understand
what Miss Roberts loved in this quiet pastoral world.

Although the novel which she had begun received the
greater part of her creative energy, she did not neglect her
poetry. Occasionally she gave poetry recitals locally. A few
times these were given on the front porch of her home to
a few of her intimate friends. One she gave publicly at
St. Catherine's Academy. She was a very accomplished
reader of her own verse, having a soft, well-modulated
voice which conveyed very accurately the nuances of mean-

ing in the verse. Nevertheless, these were trying times for her. She disliked public appearances, and her close friends could see that these performances left her very shaky. Consequently she kept them to a minimum.

While still writing poetry and trying to perfect her poetic idiom, she was also concerned with the practical means of promoting her poetry in the public eye. The following letter gives an excellent insight into these concerns at this period.

Dear Monroe—

I have been greatly grieved for Janet's disaster.

It pleases me that you like *A Child in a Garden*. Your warm phrases of appreciation were very kind, and your letter, all of it, together with your chance reference to Orpheus [the opera] was as a spark in the powder and I wrote *Stranger* the same night. It is not yet finished but I think I shall send it along . . . . I have been thinking of refrains for some time, wishing to incorporate the element in my Interlude in a small measure —but always in an organic and true relation to my material. Ballads are quite legitimate for me. My grandfather sang ballads with a great roaring voice that scared me half out of my life. He sang "Bangum and the Boar."

> *Bangum drew his wooden knife*
> *Dillom dom dillum!*
> *And swore he'd have the wild boar's life*
> *Qum qui quiddle quo qum!*

You perceive that this is a good roaring piece.

He sang the one about Sweet William and Liddy Marget.

> *Liddy Marget died like it might be today*
> *Sweet William like it might be tomorrow.*

It is a joy to find these being sung yet in the back countries and the hills. They came from England long ago, and it is lovely that I have them in the marrow of my bones and in my flesh. That they have marks of our country upon them makes them more precious. Liddy Marget is surely Lady Margaret and "like it might be today" is our own speech. Versions of these same ballads are found in scholarly English collections, Oxford editions, etc.

I have no wish, however, to copy ballads or ballad measures. That has been done, well and ill, for a hundred years, and is not my way. But I can be aware of all this matter as it lies in my own flesh, and then let come what may. And therefore *Stranger*. It has some lines which I shall work over. The sixth stanza displeases me. It is for the Interlude. Be as rough with it as you please.

I am compiling a small "anthology" of poems for children, thinking it may fill the need of gift-book and schoolreader at once, and bring in a little money.

Janet and I were planning to go west in the spring, myself troubadouring. I almost have some scattered engagements here and there—Rockford, Colorado Springs. I do not know now whether I can coordinate them and get others or not. It is difficult for me to get engagements for myself. I need a "manager." And I should make a truce or a trust with Vachel. My letter to the institution must necessarily be a mere statement that I will do this thing, and for how much and when. Where my work is known, the reply is cordial, often quite warm—stating that Vachel Lindsay has been there and there is no more money. I want to get ahead of him next year if it is humanly possible. But I shall have to have someone write the letter for me.

Her poetry continued, but more and more it was displaced by her growing concentration on her novel. She began to react to all events with a novelist's eye. A famous local personage, Colonel W. O. Reed, died. He was a regular army colonel who had experienced glamorous exploits in the Philippine insurrection and in World War I. Miss Roberts saw him as a person interesting both as a symbol and character, so she collected everything in print on his life and career. The material ran to some forty-odd news-paper columns, which she clipped and placed in her files. She also asked for and received copies of the letters of Gilbert Young, the young soldier who was the first Washington County man to be killed in World War I. He had figured as a character in her abortive novel, *"Sallie May,"* discussed above and had caught her imagination. She thus accumulated voluminous files, much of which she later used. This accumulation went forward through the rest of her life and included odd and archaic words, witticisms, names, folk-lore, thumbnail sketches of local citizens, old songs, and hundreds of minutiae[14] which in some way interested her. Much of this would make its way into pertinent scenes of her novels. This was her "ever-normal granary," on which she could always draw for local color and ideas.

During this fall of 1922 came also her first published volume (if the Colorado pamphlet be excepted). She submitted a collection of poems to Viking Press in May, 1922, and they were published in December, of the same year, as a volume, *Under the Tree*,[15] the title being taken from one of the poems included in the book. Her home-town paper, the Springfield *Sun*, took note of this, as did her friends in Chicago and New York. The publication did not, of course, advance her financially, but it gave her a small reputation and aided her morale enormously.

Most of the poems in *Under the Tree* were written while she was a student at the University of Chicago, many of the poems being composed in an old lodging house at Fifty-eighth Street and Maryland Avenue. Some of the pieces, however, were written in Kentucky, during summer

14 Such as the old folk saying, "All the jay birds go to hell on Friday."
15 This book was dedicated to her father, Simpson Roberts.

vacations, 1918–21. Many of them were offered as class work in Mr. Lovett's English course, and a few as daily theses in Mr. Flint's English composition class. They were also used as they were finished, a few at a time, at the small Poetry Club gatherings.

Miss Roberts worked steadily on her novel through the spring and summer of 1923 in Springfield, then left in October, 1923, for New York en route to Stockbridge, Massachusetts. She stayed in New York through October and November, visiting friends and working steadily at her manuscript. Then, going to Stockbridge, where she remained through the rest of the winter and part of the spring, she consulted physicians for the severe periodic headaches from which she suffered. Here, too, she pushed ahead on the manuscript.

In May, 1924, she returned to Springfield, writing through the summer and autumn. By this time, she had taken up hand weaving as a hobby. This required creative effort also, but it channeled off much of the nervous tension which accumulated during her writing periods. Consequently, she alternated writing with weaving to achieve a stabilizing schedule.

In February of 1925, Miss Roberts left for Chicago to visit friends and stayed until May, still working on her novel while she visited. By the summer of 1925, the novel was three-fourths complete. Back in Springfield with her family, she brought the manuscript of *The Time of Man* to a conclusion in November, 1925. A creative outburst sustained through a three-year period was over; it was to be the richest of her entire career. There remained now merely the mechanics of seeing the work through the press.

Miss Roberts had been in communication with the Viking Press since September of 1925, and they had agreed to publish the novel. So in February, 1926, Miss Roberts left for Los Angeles, California, to visit her sister, Lel, and incidentally to soak up the California sun and leave behind the disagreeable winter of Kentucky. While in Los Angeles, she requested that the manuscript of *The Time of Man* be sent back to her for certain minor changes. It was printed and proofread in May and published in August, 1926,[16] exactly four years after it had been begun.

In a sense this date marks an important dividing line in her life. Up to this point she had been a private person; after this date she became a public personage. Before this date, she had been striving to articulate an artistic pattern from her own life. Now the pattern had been set, and she had to work variations on it. Writing this novel had been a long, hard trip and had cost her more woe than we can ever know. Looking back, she could see that she had come a long way—a very long way.

Waiting on the California coast for the hungry critics to decide about her book, she was understandably nervous. But she need not have been. The book was an immediate success. It was widely reviewed, and the reviews were uniformly excellent. *The Time of Man* appeared in an era when the stale posturings of James Branch Cabell were the vogue, and her novel was a breath of fresh air through the overly perfumed literary atmosphere of the period. It was praised by critics and professional writers alike, Sherwood Anderson saying of it: "A wonderful performance. I am humble before it." Fortunately for Miss Roberts, it was more than merely a critical success; it was a financial success, also. Chosen as the October, Book-of-the-Month Club selection, *The Time of Man* was later published for an

[16] It was dedicated to her good friends Arthur Yvor Winters and Janet L. Lewis.

enthusiastic audience in England and, still later, in German, Swedish, Spanish and Dano-Norwegian editions. The Modern Library also published an edition of it.[17]

This success was immensely gratifying to Miss Roberts, who had worked hard and waited a long time for recognition. She was frail; she still had to watch her health; she lived quietly. Much of her mood of guarded happiness is contained in the following letter written to a friend, Miss Stella Simns (now Mrs. Stella Simns Barber), at the time of the first success of her book:

> Purser Apts.
> 1659 Ocean Front Blvd.
> Santa Monica, Calif.
> Oct. 20, 1926

Dear Stella:

Lel and Carl were just here to see me and brought your letter. I am staying in an apartment in a hotel at Santa Monica looking out on the sea .... I am at Pursers Apartments which is on the Ocean and I am never tired of watching the waves and speculating about the tides, matters of which I am not any too well informed. I have a small steam heated apt. living room, kitchen, and bath, with a large window toward the water. I find it much more invigorating here than in Los Angeles where the days were often very hot and I found it difficult to walk. Here it is always cool and breezy and already I am walking more.

I was ill all spring. I had a hard spell of grippe and a lung cold when I first arrived here and that left me with a slight lung moisture. The Dr. had me lie in bed or on a couch all spring and thru the early summer, and pronounced my lung dry by the middle of July. Since that time I have been slowly regaining strength and I am now about as fit as I was when I left

[17] Robert Morss Lovett, in his memoirs, *All Our Years*, records that he unsuccessfully urged the Pulitzer Prize jury, of which he was a member, to give the Pulitzer Prize for the year to Miss Roberts for *The Time of Man*, which he thought was the best novel of the year.

home. And my weight is better, nearer to my supposed normal. I hope to gain a great deal of strength down here where the air is fresh and fine and the sea a constant delight to me. I am at work on another book, a matter I started in the spring, long before I was healed. It is well along and I expect to have it finished by spring. If I finish it as I now expect to do, it will be published next autumn.

It was very lovely to hear from you. I think of you often. I hope you will like my book when you read it, and I am glad that you saw some of the reviews. They have been splendid. I hope you saw that of Robert Morss Lovett in *The New Republic,* and that of Krutch in the New York *Saturday Review,* or of Harry Hansen in the *New York World,* or of Smith in the *Dallas News.* I have not seen all the reviews myself. One has appeared almost everywhere I suppose. The publisher is going to start a large advertising campaign for my book next month. It has already paid me a large sum of money, much more than I anticipated for it altogether.

I am glad if Mrs. McElroy liked my small achievement if she remembered me and was glad. I thought of her often when things began to go my way for she was very gracious to me when I first began to study the art some years ago and was my first encouragement.

I have no plan beyond the immediate future. I shall probably stay here several months. When I am strong enough again I hope to make a visit to Ky., but I shall have to wait for that until after the winter is over.

Your mother delights me with the beauty of her mind and spirit. I always delighted in talking with her. Please give her my kindest regards and affection. I feel sure that she will sympathize with the strong, elemental, spiritual quality which I tried to symbolize with my story of Ellen.

You will surely write to me again. Please do so soon.

With much affection
Elizabeth [script]

Writing was now her life, and she turned to the completion of her second novel, *My Heart and My Flesh*. She had begun this work in the spring of 1923, and carried it along as a foil for *The Time of Man*. With much more time available, she was able to bring the novel well along by working through the winter of 1926 and spring of 1927 at Santa Monica. This novel in its plan and execution is the opposite of *The Time of Man*. *My Heart and My Flesh* presents a well-born heroine from whom everything, except the breath of life itself, is taken. Theodosia Bell, the heroine, is an extremely somber and melancholy character, much given to introspection, and this melancholy marks the book up to its closing chapter. It is quite possible that the reaction from the strain of the first book and the bad health which dogged her through the winter of this year worked its way unconsciously into the tone of the book. Much of her early life in Springfield came back as she wrote this novel, and it became to some extent a minor *Remembrance of Things Past* to her. (Psychologically, Miss Roberts herself seems much closer to the temperament of Theodosia Bell than to that of Ellen Chesser.) The old Negro carpenter, Uncle Wilse McElroy, came back to her, and she wrote a fine chapter on him. Anneville is simply Springfield at the turn of the century. Theodosia Bell and her grandfather embody Miss Roberts' memories of Sue Ray and Dr. Ray. The ghosts of old scandals in Springfield rise and walk through the book. She drew on her knowledge of early Springfield citizens and took some of them bodily into her book with very little alteration. Among the Negro characters, Moll Peters was based on Moll Hundley, and Stiggins on an actual mulatto stableboy, Stiggall. The farm of Tom and Doe Singleton was a fictional rendering of the locally famous "Grundy Home," the farm of Mr. and Mrs. Sam Grundy. Americy also had a prototype well known locally. The prologue of the novel shows us in "Mome," the city of Cincinnati as it appeared to Miss Roberts as a child, and also the Presbyterian church in Springfield beside which she lived many of her childhood years. Thus, nearly every scene in the novel occurs in a milieu familiar to any Springfield resident who remembers the town as it was in 1900.

This novel was three-fourths completed by the spring of 1927, so she took it with her to Chicago and finished it as she listened to the rough dash of the waves of Lake Michigan. She returned to Springfield in September and read proof, then rested for a while. *My Heart and My Flesh*[18] was published late in 1927 and received a mixed reception. Some critics felt that it was too "mentalized" and introspective; others praised it very highly for its lyricism and beauty of phrasing. Miss Roberts listened to the critics, but was not disturbed by them. She was busy polishing off the manuscript for her third book, *Jingling in the Wind*.

Jingling in the Wind was something of a safety valve for Miss Roberts. She began it some years earlier while her two other novels were being written, turning for relaxation from these two serious works to the light satire of *Jingling in the Wind*. The book had been suggested to her by some remarks Maurice Leseman, who had become an advertising executive, had made to her about modern American advertising. So she contrived a satirical fantasy which threatens always to break into broad farce. She took an immense pleasure in the writing of this book. Her friend, Mrs. Bosley, recalls Miss Roberts reading the manuscript aloud to her and laughing so hard she would have to stop reading.

[18] Dedicated to her sister, Lel (Mrs. Carl Bernhardt).

This book was a catharsis for the nervous tensions which accumulated as she wrote her more serious work.

She took this manuscript with her to New York City, where she spent the winter of 1927–28. Glenway Westcott saw her again during this period and left a somewhat baroque word picture of her which captures a good bit of her manner and appearance:

I saw her . . . in a darkened, hot, but never warming room, seated with her yellow-crowned head almost between her knees as are certain Blake drawings; now signalling from the windows with a towel when she had need of human attendance, now like royalty in a convent drawing apart in an arrogant and pious self-communion; abstractions forming out of the tedium, the shadows of past persons becoming the flesh of future characters—thinking, thinking, remembering, biding her time, uttering extensive dreamy theories and troubling witticisms, with an occasional incorrectness of folk-songs in her speech. Or later still . . . her thought clear to countless people but her person a riddle still, in a decorous skyscraper suite . . . she ignored the hour and the date for long periods while she wrote, often more than half of the twenty-four hours at a sitting; then . . . ventured forth with a brother or a devotee into the common city, finding it as delicately bizarre as if she had invented it also; and about twice a year met critics and practitioners of her art, but in a corner or an alcove, one at a time, preferring (and with reason) to tire her mind by speaking rather than her heart by listening, with something blue-blooded, almost Russian, in her bearing. For the South is another of those lands of antique gentry brought low.[19]

The patrician aloofness of her manner, which remained with her till the end of her life, was partly protective and

[19] Glenway Westcott, "Elizabeth Madox Roberts: A Personal Note," *The Bookman*, Vol. LXXI, No. 1 (March, 1930), 12–15.

partly innate. It in no way detracted from her humanity
and kindness of outlook. And *Jingling in the Wind* demon-
strates the diversity of mind covered by this manner. This
book appeared late in 1928, to the great bewilderment of
the majority of the critics and the complete chagrin of
her townspeople. The critics found the pastoral beauties
of the book and the fun and gaiety of it, but they were at
a complete loss to determine its intent and meaning.

If the critics were lost, Springfield was completely be-
fuddled. To begin with, most of Springfield was not quite
at home with novels such as Miss Roberts produced. In
1928, the novels in the Springfield Public Library which
had the best circulation were those of Bess Streeter Aldrich,
Gene Stratton Porter, and others of that ilk. The reading
ladies of the town preferred these. When they heard that
Miss Roberts had a first novel in progress, they hoped for
something of the Porter vintage. When *The Time of Man*
was published, the Springfield paper gave it a small item
on the back page, using the front page for the story of a
local hen which had laid some tremendous number of
eggs. The Springfield public was dismayed at the book. The
ladies were a little upset by Ellen Chesser; she was not
genteel, and the fact that she discovered "lice" in her hair
gave the whole book an off-color character that was shock-
ing. Surprised that Elizabeth would describe such a low
person, the ladies believed that such an improper book
would give people a bad opinion of Springfield. To people
who had never heard of Theodore Dreiser, all this was very
upsetting. They were still a little dubious when *My Heart
and My Flesh* was published. Many of the Presbyterian
ladies thought the prologue was a sarcastic portrayal of
their church—though this was certainly not so. Even more
disturbing were the themes of incest and miscegenation

and the shades of ancient scandals. Then came *Jingling in the Wind,* and they were completely at sea.

Miss Roberts was aware of all this and decried it with a wry humor, realizing it would take some time for her home town to become aware of the real meanings and excellences of her work. She was intensely local and wanted her work to be understood at home. Before her death she did have the satisfaction of seeing a growing public among her own people.

By this time (1928), she was well launched in her writing career and had established the technique of her composition. One of her basic ideas involved keeping several projects going at once; this provided a change of scene and rhythm for the writer, as well as affording insurance in the event one of them was unsuccessful. In keeping with this idea, Miss Roberts was already in the note taking stage on *The Great Meadow* before *Jingling in the Wind* was published. Note taking was a laborious "stage" and included the core idea of the novel, the skeleton structure of it, thumbnail sketches of characters, long lists of tentative titles, examples of folksayings and folkidioms, and lines from ballads remembered from her childhood. These notes accumulated in great profusion and in a most haphazard fashion. They were scribbled on old envelopes, handbills, scraps of wrapping paper, backs of musical programs, and whatever was at hand when the ideas came to her.[20] When the totality of the novel "set" in her mind, she arranged the notes in chapter order and began composition. From this point on, no further notes were added. Able to compose quickly and easily, she wrote the first draft of *The*

[20] One of Miss Roberts' eccentricities was her great frugality in the use of writing paper. For instance, one manuscript copy of *My Heart and My Flesh* was typed on the back of a carbon copy of *The Time of Man.*

Time of Man in long hand, then typed it. After this novel, she typed all the rest. She believed more or less in inspiration, waiting until the mood for a certain scene struck her mind, then sitting down and typing it off in a spurt of passionate impetuosity. The plan and structure of a novel she labored over, the style and phrasing of particular scenes never. Her style came with the flow of her thought, and despite its perfect patterns and intricacy, required no conscious strain and artistry on her part. It is this great facility with language which explains her phenomenal output. Within a fifteen-year period, she produced all of her novels and short stories and a great portion of her poems, did extensive reading, and carried on a fairly large correspondence. This output becomes remarkable when we remember that she was never free of ill-health and that, during the last six years of her life, there were weeks and months when she could do no work at all.

Thus, in 1928, with her technique well established, she turned her mind to the composition of *The Great Meadow*, the novel which was to become the favorite of her fellow townsmen. In a material sense, things had improved for her. The success of *The Time of Man* had given her sufficient money to build a handsome brick residence. Since her mother and father could not be induced to leave their old home, Miss Roberts built her new house as an adjunct to the older frame residence. The central room of the new house was a spacious, book-lined study and library. There was still the large, tree-studded front lawn, still the simple, sunny flower garden in the rear. It was an admirable spot for writing—quiet, spacious, and comfortable, and it was here that most of *The Great Meadow* was written.

Miss Roberts had scarcely settled down to her work when an announcement arrived from *Poetry* magazine, notifying her that she had been awarded their John Reed Memorial prize for poetry. She had published frequently in *Poetry* since her Chicago period and was happy to get this mark of recognition from them. She then turned back to shaping the plan of *The Great Meadow*.

In terms of its conception, this was her earliest novel. As early as 1913, the idea for this novel had come to her. The germ of the novel went all the way back to her childhood, back to her maternal grandmother's wonderful recollections of the past. "I used to sit near my grandmother to hear her tell of the wonders of her youth and to hear her thrust her memory back into the memories of her fathers and mothers."[21] The grandmother, with a fine gift of language, would tell how her Virginia ancestors came over the Wilderness Trail, past Indians and through forests to "the great meadow" of Kentucky where they founded forts at Boonesborough and Harrodsburg. The little girl listening was fascinated. She questioned her grandmother again and again about these adventures and about the people who made the journey. Then, years later as an adult, the vision of these pioneers returned to her.

I saw these people coming over the trace, some of them coming early when there were hundreds of miles of scarcely broken forests to be passed. The drama was brief, but it was full and picturesque. I thought it would be an excellent labor if one might gather all these threads, these elements into one strand, if one might draw these strains into one person and bring this person over the trace and through the Gateway in one symbolic journey.[22]

21 Elizabeth M. Roberts, "Over the Trace to the Great Meadow," *Wings*, Vol. IV, No. 3 (March, 1930), 6. Published by the Literary Guild of America.
22 *Ibid.*, 9.

With the central idea of her novel clearly in mind, Miss Roberts set about doing sufficient research to "flesh out" the story authentically. She made occasional trips to Louisville, where she worked in the files of the Filson Club[23] and the Louisville Public Library. She also drove frequently to Harrodsburg and studied the rebuilt pioneer fort which now stands there. This fort and the authentic furniture, firearms, and equipment with which it is furnished proved of great aid to her in visualizing the fictional milieu of her novel. There were also old records, dating from the founding of the Fort, which were helpful to her in giving an air of verisimilitude to the Kentucky scenes of her novel. She made no effort to examine exhaustively the tremendous amount of accumulated historical material (diaries, commonplace books, county histories, etc.) available. She carried her research only to the point of capturing the atmosphere and validating the detail of the individual scenes.[24]

Once this necessary research was done, the actual writing of the novel went forward rapidly in 1929. In addition to the unique lyricism of her style, this novel was distinguished from the usual historical novel by its motif of Berkeleian philosophy, which added measurably to the tone and depth of the story. By the end of 1929, the writing was done, and she went to New York in January, 1930, to supervise the publication.

As she prepared the manuscript for the press, she dedicated it to her friend, Glenway Wescott, knowing his great interest in the pioneer life of his own state, Wisconsin. Then, one day to her hotel came Carl Van Doren, editorial

[23] The Filson Club is devoted to research into Kentucky history. Miss Roberts became a member on January 7, 1929.

[24] Her brother, Will Roberts, gave her considerable help in assembling this historical data.

head of the Literary Guild, to announce that the Guild
had chosen her novel as their March selection. She was
greatly pleased and wrote a letter to Mrs. Bosley, confiden-
tially informing her of the choice, which had not been
made public as yet. The Guild choice more than doubled
her income from the sales of her book.

The Great Meadow was immediately popular on its publication in March. It was published abroad in England,
Germany, and Spain. Grosset and Dunlap brought out a
cheaper edition in 1932. Metro-Goldwyn-Mayer bought
the movie rights and made a movie which added nothing to
the luster of the original book. The novel got excellent
reviews from the critics and became that rare exception, a
work which was both a critical and popular success. More
than that, it appealed to Springfield readers,[25] who ignored
the Berkeleianism and read it as a good historical novel.

As for Miss Roberts, she had returned to Springfield and
was taking a momentary rest. In the four years which inter-
vened between the publication of *The Time of Man* in
1926 and *The Great Meadow* in 1930, she had quickly
achieved the status of one of America's greatest living novelists. She had plans already on paper for new novels, new
short stories, new poems. Although she felt no diminution
of her creative powers, she paused for a moment to enjoy
her laurels. She cast a retrospective eye over the way she had
come, recalling her early problems, hardships, defeats, and,
finally, success—a death and rebirth pattern similar to that
experienced by her heroines. She was experiencing the joy
of this recreation. Relishing the feel of the four novels behind her, she talked about them a little to Mrs. Frances

[25] Although Miss Roberts had to make arrangements herself to induce
a local drugstore to carry copies of her novel. There were no book retailers
as such in Springfield. The public library had copies which were soon well
thumbed.

Schultz, one of her close friends in Springfield. She seized on an analogy from Shakespeare and, thinking of how her own life had worked its way into the fabric of her novels, phrased it succinctly thus: *"The Time of Man* was my *Hamlet, Jingling in the Wind* was my *Midsummer-Night's Dream* and *The Great Meadow* was my *Romeo and Juliet."*

Shakespeare had always been her mentor, and she read him now more closely than ever. She knew that reading aided that rightness of phrasing on which she prided herself. "Now my masters are Hardy, Shakespeare, Synge, Beethoven—with symphonies[26]—Dickinson, Hopkins. I am still a musician, deeply within, along with what ever else I am. *The Time of Man* is a symphony brought into words, for I believe that it is, whatever its failings, complete in itself. At its roots, its inception, it might have taken musical form."* She had discovered Gerard Manley Hopkins in the 1920's, and liked him more and more. By the middle of the 1930's, he was to become her favorite poet and exert more influence on her poetry than any other single writer.

Her reading was extensive enough, but its especial characteristic was its intensity. She went very deeply into whatever book caught her interest. She was buying books for the library of her new home at this time, and a memo among her papers lists representative works she was purchasing at this period. Among them were the poems of Hopkins, the works of Henry James (a list of about twenty had been recommended by Ezra Pound), of Walter Savage Landor, Benedetto Croce, Sir James Frazer's *The Golden Bough,* and Jessie Lee Weston's *From Ritual to Romance.*

As Miss Roberts rested during this summer, she carried on a few activities. She drove to Lebanon, nine miles from Springfield, and read her poems to the ladies' club gathered

26 The Fifth, Seventh, and Ninth were her favorites.

in the public library. They were impressed by her national reputation and wanted her to talk about her novels. But she read from *Under the Tree* instead, and her low, carefully modulated voice soon satisfied her audience and gave them some of her own feeling for the pristine world of childhood.

Soon after this came the notice that she had won the second prize for the best short story of the year in the twelfth O. Henry Memorial Prize Award, 1930. Her story was "The Sacrifice of the Maidens," based on the ceremony of the taking of the veil by Catholic nuns. She wrote this story after a single visit to the veil ceremony at the local convent of St. Catherine's, one mile from Springfield. She used the native locale and a native family—the Barbours—in the story, involving through the title an association with religions more primitive than the Christian.

About this time the women of Springfield decided that it would be an appropriate gesture to give a public reception in honor of their famous writer. The clubwomen of the town assembled, made arrangements, and then approached Miss Roberts. They were considerably chagrined when she thanked them very warmly but refused absolutely to appear at such a reception. As an unknown she had longed for fame and its enchantments; fame came, and she turned away from certain aspects of it. This is an anomaly not unknown among other writers. William Faulkner, to a considerable extent, has in the past exemplified a similar attitude. Miss Roberts, of course, was a shy and reticent person, and public appearances of any kind were ordeals for her. So the public reception was dropped.

Miss Roberts had other ways of keeping herself a part of the community in which she lived. She was a charitable person and rarely turned down an appeal for help. Her help was always unobtrusive and unheralded. She gave for the joy of giving. One of the foremost women writers applied to her for a loan in time of financial trouble and was immediately and quietly accommodated. To the limit of her poor health, Miss Roberts gave also of her time. A young girl, a local telephone operator, who aspired to be a poet, came to Miss Roberts with her verse and asked advice. Miss Roberts gave it unstintingly and encouraged her in every way she could. Although she avoided the public eye, there was a rich and buried life of sympathetic assistance to those who needed her.

By now the rhythm of relaxation and concentration was ending its passive phase, and the need for undertaking a new work was growing on her. So she turned, toward the close of the summer of 1930, to the composition of a novel later published as *A Buried Treasure*. The story had its inception in a newspaper clipping from the Springfield *Sun* about a local farmer finding a pot of gold coins. This clipping had gone into her files. A year later she made this note. "Last year far back in such a farm, at a place that can scarcely be reached by any wheeled conveyance whatever, a small farmer owner found a buried pot of silver and gold, a kettle of old Spanish money."* This incident teased at her imagination and grew gradually into a light parable or allegory in which the treasure took on more metaphysical meaning. This allegory was set forth in a long short-story published in two parts by *Harper's* magazine in December, 1929 and January, 1930. But since the story seemed to demand fuller treatment, she started to expand it into a short novel in the fall of 1930. The work went quickly forward and was completed and published as *A Buried Treasure*,[27] in 1931. The Literary Guild made it one of

[27] Dedicated to her brother, Ivor Roberts, a very great favorite with her.

their selections, and it was later published in England. All in all, Miss Roberts was well pleased with its reception since it was basically a story whose deepest appeal would be its poetic overtones and language.

The years from 1931 to 1935 represented a period of comparative peace in the life of Miss Roberts. She now had status as a writer, a competent income, a pleasant place to work, the companionship of her family and of a diverse group of friends. The only real discord was her health. She was still forced to husband her strength, and she was suffering more and more from the skin irritation which was to dog the remainder of her life. A letter to Mrs. Bosley from Louisville (where Miss Roberts spent her winters during this period) gives a suggestion of the tempo of her life and some of its daily concerns and pleasures.

My dear Miss Ceil:

Louisville is much as usual except that the people feel the local depression and money losses. About every third house out in this district is for rent or sale, but among the lower priced neighborhoods things are not so bad. I have been occupied with trying to get my hands and feet cured of the rash that continues to distress them. I am taking the ultra violet ray treatment and there is some small improvement, but the disease is nervous in character and is very slow to yield. One of my friends here was obliged to take so much of the light and saw such marked benefits when she kept it up, that she bought one of the machines. I may come to that myself. They cost from $270 and upwards.

I went to the arts club last evening to hear two musicians, one a young man who played the piano well and the other a girl who played the violin. There was dinner too, and so the evening was long and well filled. I was much pleased with the Brahms sonata which the young man played. I went with

Barbara Tunnell and Mrs. Embry and Miss McGill, and there were a number of others present who were known to me, among them Mrs. Cooper and Mr. Stewart.

I am told that *The Great Meadow* is showing in Harrodsburg this week. I had a telephone call the night before last from somebody there inviting me to be her guest during the performances. It is not announced as yet for Louisville but is expected any week now. Friends of mine have seen it both in New York and in Hollywood. Lel wrote me in much detail of it. She said there were many changes in the story, some of them she found hard to accept, but that, as a picture, it was very dramatic.

I was glad to know that the rain was so general and so steady throughout the state. The water here was wretched and the doctor thought the water—treated as it is so heavily with chlorine—was causing the difficulty with my skin, wholly or in part. I changed to Anita Springs water which is splendid. I do not know what I will do when I come back there. I do not think I can endure the water if it is as it has been for the past two years. I wonder if it is necessary to put all that stuff into it. I sometimes think that a chemical company has simply "sold" all the towns this chlorine,—created a need, as they say in business. I had as soon risk the germs as have the nervous and skin ills that follow the chlorine.

I shall have to find out where my drinking water is to come from before I can venture out there.

Let us hope for more good rains.

My best wishes to yourself and Mr. Bosley.

Elizabeth

The letter indicates her growing concern with her health. The extremely acute sensitivity which was one of Miss Roberts' principal artistic assets was in another sense a disadvantage to her. This sensitivity increased her nervousness and, in turn, led to an almost morbid preoccupation with her health, which in her last years verged on hypo-

chondria. She became a passionate devotee of the sun, thinking it might be a sovereign cure for all her ills. Also she
began to carry her own drinking water with her. In Springfield she would call the office of her dentist and check the
temperature of his office. If the temperature was above a
certain point, she refused to make an appointment. The
extraction of a single tooth was magnified into a great
ordeal. This tendency grew more acute as she neared the
end of her life.

During these years, she turned more and more to weaving as a means of relaxing her nerves. It served partially
as physical therapy and partially as creative expression.
In addition to the weaving, she did frequent pen and ink
sketches, evidently for her own enjoyment. The great
majority of them which remain among her papers are
sketches of women and are essentially satirical in spirit.
They are competently done, with an exaggerated flowing
line, and in some subtle manner conveying an immense
laughter at the women. Much of Miss Roberts' very real
and deep sense of humor worked itself into these sketches.

Although her life settled into a quieter mood, her writing
went forward with its usual vigor. Throughout the summer of 1932, she was preparing the manuscript for her first
volume of collected short stories. She had nearing completion three short stories, the last of which was finished in the
early summer of 1933. To these she added four stories
which had appeared earlier in separate periodical publication. Among these was "The Sacrifice of the Maidens,"
a story which had first appeared in *Letters,* the literary
magazine published for some years by the University of
Kentucky. Doubtless Miss Roberts smiled ironically as she
prepared this story for the collection. Years before, in the
early 1920's when she was struggling for recognition as a

writer, her friend and neighbor, Miss Thelma McIntire, had called on the senior members of the English department at the university and asked them to consider Miss Roberts' work. Some notice of a general sort from them would have encouraged the young writer. But not one would take the time and trouble. So ten years elapse, and Miss Roberts becomes a leading American novelist. And all, all is changed. The faculty adviser of *Letters* writes a fulsome letter asking for material. Other members desire interviews and, on receiving them, write their accounts for local newspapers in glowing terms, basking in the reflected light of glory. How easy, she must have reflected, to acquire the aid after the aid is no longer required. But though ironical, Miss Roberts was never bitter.

The seven stories were arranged in a volume entitled *The Haunted Mirror* and published by the Viking Press in November, 1932, with a second printing in February, 1933. The reviews were not long, but they were uniformly favorable, noting particularly the overt primitivism of the stories and the prominent emphasis on style. The stories gave further proof that Miss Roberts had great potentialities as a poetic dramatist, although she never published in that particular genre. Such stories as "Children of the Earth" and "Death at Bearwallow" have so lyrical a beauty of concept and language that they could easily be altered into poetic drama of distinction.

When Miss Roberts had dispatched *The Haunted Mirror* to her publishers, she turned to research on what has proved to be the most obscure of her major novels. It was her custom to keep in close touch with the historic past of Washington County, for it was in terms of this past that her mind moved most effectively. This past came to her from many sources, from old records and journals, from the memories of her family and relatives, and from occasional articles about historic families of Washington County which ran for several years in the Springfield *Sun*.

Among the bizarre accounts dredged up from this background was the story of Basil Haydon (the Stoner Drake of *He Sent Forth a Raven*). Basil Haydon[28] had lived near Woodlawn, a little village in Nelson County just across the Washington County line. He had disliked Abraham Lincoln, the rising Middle Western leader of the newly formed Republican party. Haydon was an ardent Democrat and a confirmed apostle of the doctrine of State rights, and he vowed that if Lincoln were elected he, Haydon, would never set foot on God's green earth again. He was a man of his word and never left his home, though he lived into the twentieth century. This story from the region of Fredericksburg (later to be the scene of *Black Is My True-love's Hair*) fascinated Miss Roberts with its symbolic possibilities. It had been in her mind for some time when she decided definitely to develop it into a novel. She devoted most of the summer of 1933 to accumulating material, local color, and background at Woodlawn. She stayed there for a good part of the time, soaking up the atmosphere and setting down voluminous notes. With this material, she returned to her home and began work on *He Sent Forth a Raven,* which continued through the fall of 1933 and much of 1934. The novel was completed and published in 1935. The critics were puzzled by the book, and the reviews were critical of its obscurity. Miss Roberts was not particularly perturbed by the adverse criticism, but felt that the critics got off on the wrong track by trying to equate the Raven with some one character in the book. "The Raven,"

---

28 Basil's brother, R. B. Haydon, attained a degree of fame as the originator of one of Kentucky's finest whiskeys, Old Granddad.

she says, "is the dauntless spirit of that poor weakling man trying to go his way alone."[29] She felt this novel to be closer to *My Heart and My Flesh* in mood and tone than to any of her other novels. Stoner Drake, the protagonist, with his indomitable but twisted will, displays many analogies to the demoniac Captain Ahab of Herman Melville. This parallel was undoubtedly a conscious one, since Miss Roberts ranked *Moby Dick* near the top in her hierarchy of great novels. She even devised a melodramatic ending in which Stoner Drake perished in fire when he refused to leave his burning home and break his oath. Although this is an obvious parallel to the death by drowning of Ahab, it doesn't seem as fortunate in its context, so she abandoned it for the less melodramatic conclusion the novel now bears. Miss Roberts herself had no misgivings about the quality of the novel, but she put it behind her and turned to another and far more pressing concern—her health.

Through the three or four years preceding 1935, her general health had been growing worse. The skin condition had increased in severity, her periods of weakness were more frequent, and definite signs of anemia had appeared. She became worried about her condition and consulted her Louisville physician, Dr. Humphreys. Dr. Humphreys, a general practitioner, was unable to isolate the real nature of her difficulty. He sent her in 1936 to Dr. Morris Flexner, a specialist, who ultimately diagnosed her disease as Hodgkin's disease and told her that there was no known cure for the disease, that its progress was slow, and that she could be assured of a few years of life and work yet.

Miss Roberts received this grave disclosure with great incredulity and refused, at first, to speak of it. Within the

---

29 Andrew J. Beeler, Jr. (unpublished thesis), 1940, University of Louisville, "Elizabeth Madox Roberts: Her Interpretation of Life," 10.

same year (1936) she went to Chicago and placed herself under the care of Dr. Pusey Brown,[30] an internationally known skin specialist. She remained in contact with him for the rest of her life.

It is, of course, impossible to describe the influence of this knowledge on the inner life of Miss Roberts. That it affected her profoundly her friends are sure. She wanted no pity, however, and spoke of her disease to no one but her most intimate friends. Undoubtedly, though, it contributed much to her growing nervousness during her last years and to the occasional periods of deep depression.

At this period began her friendship with Miss Mabel Medora Williams,[31] who was to become her dearest friend and companion and to whom she dedicated her last book, *Not By Strange Gods.* Miss Roberts' life now entered its ultimate stage. Everything which happened from this time on was shadowed by the consciousness of her fatal disease. It was fortunate for her that so understanding and congenial a friend as Miss Williams appeared at this crucial juncture in her life.

Miss Williams was congenial for a number of reasons. She was a native Kentuckian, having grown up in what was known as the "Old Conner place"[32] in Fredericksburg, and she had much of Miss Roberts' love of state and place. She had studied art extensively and had a very keen artistic and literary sensibility. Most important of all was Miss Williams' insight into the complex inner life of the writer and her quick sympathy for the disguised sufferings of her concluding years. As a sophisticated and intellectual per-

[30] Mr. Otto Rothert, secretary of the Filson Club in Louisville, was instrumental in bringing Miss Roberts to the attention of Dr. Brown.

[31] A niece of Mr. Joe Conner, mentioned earlier in this study.

[32] This appears fictionally as the home of Bob Wheat in *Black Is My Truelove's Hair.*

sonage, she became an oasis in what Miss Roberts sometimes felt to be the intellectual Sahara of Springfield.

Miss Williams had met Miss Roberts in Louisville in
1935, and as their friendship grew, she occasionally visited
the writer at her Springfield home. In June, 1936, Miss
Williams drove with Miss Roberts to Centre College, where
Miss Roberts received the honorary degree of Doctor of
Letters.[33] Miss Williams remembers that the writer was very
composed and beautiful as she stood up to receive the degree. But she was also making a great effort to appear effortless, and they left as soon as the ceremony ended, declining
the many luncheon invitations pressed on them. Such
public appearances were always trying for Miss Roberts,
and they became even more difficult during the last few
years of her life.

The summer was a relatively quiet one for Miss Roberts.
She received occasional visitors who came to talk of literature and the problems of writing. The visitors varied and
usually were interesting. Women from Lexington and
Louisville were often anxious to visit. Aspiring but unknown young writers sometimes wrote for permission to
call. Miss Roberts received as many of these people as her
health would permit.

In August, Miss Williams returned for a very pleasant
week's visit. She remembers that at night Miss Roberts
would frequently turn through favorite poets and read
them with some interpolated commentary. There would
be Housman's *Shropshire Lad* or Hardy's *Poems,* old English ballads, Robert Frost, contemporary lyrics from *Poetry*
magazine, and occasionally there would be some of Miss
Roberts' own poetry read quietly in the soft light of her

---

[33] The degree had been issued in 1935, but she had been too ill to
receive it.

comfortable library. And there was always Gerard Manley Hopkins, who had become her favorite poet. On one occasion she picked up *A Buried Treasure,* which Miss Williams had just begun, and read passages from it to illustrate what she called the two pivotal points—the little knowledge and the big knowledge (Ben Shepherd).[34] These were quiet relaxing sessions for Miss Roberts, and she undoubtedly had them in mind when she dedicated her last book, *Not By Strange Gods,* "To Mabel Medora Williams."

In the winter of 1936, Miss Roberts went to Louisville and stayed in the Puritan Apartments. She was there when the great flood—the worst in Louisville's history—struck the town. The consciousness of an immense city completely overwhelmed by massive natural force was very unsettling to her. As day followed day, and the flood situation grew worse, Miss Roberts became more and more impressed with the sheer brute power of the flood. It assumed the strength of a vast symbol for her. She collected newspaper photos and accounts for her files and began a novel on the flood, which she was working on at the time of her death. And till her death she carried a "flood fear" with her.

Although the last five years of her life were difficult ones, there was little real slackening in the program of work she laid out for herself. She thought of herself as one who must husband her fires, yet she continued to read extensively, contemporary material as well as the classics. Miss Roberts received a prepublication copy of *Gone With the Wind* and read it without any particular enthusiasm. She predicted, however, that it would become a runaway best seller. Her mother, who remained an unreconstructed rebel until the end of her life, liked it immensely and felt

---

[34] Cf. the discussion of *A Buried Treasure* in Chapter V for an explanation of these phrases.

somewhat chagrined that she could never convince Elizabeth of its worth. James Joyce, Miss Roberts read also—and admired. Thomas Mann was much liked, especially *The Magic Mountain*. And, then, her favorites among the "classics" she still perused—Chaucer, Shakespeare, and the Greek dramatists. Hopkins and Dickinson among the modern poets were always with her. She came also to rely more and more upon music in these last years. Her love for music was a profound one, and it now assumed a more mystical cast as she voyaged more and more deeply into her own being. When J. Donald Adams of *The New York Times* visited her in 1939, she told him that Bach and Mozart were used frequently to set the mood for her writing.

Miss Roberts conserved her strength also by remaining aloof from many of the fashionable literary causes and reforming groups of the day. Her attitude here is suggestive of Emerson, who also adopted a protective aloofness partly to conserve his limited strength. The following excerpt from a letter, written somewhat before this period, illustrates well this attitude on her part:

You are wrong about my joining causes or taking up beliefs, more than a little there. I do not join myself on to things. I am free deeply within. I seldom write into a letter anything that greatly concerns me—although now I am so doing. I am concerned now, being frank now. I have preferred to skirmish not in the inner citadel, but rather out in the meadow beyond the wall and moat.*

During this period she occasionally recorded her dreams, some of which seemed to be anxiety dreams. At other times her dreams would present beautiful aesthetic structures, as a vast range of mountains which appeared more real and beautiful in the dream than in actual life. On one occasion she took gas for a tooth extraction. A dream of great clarity and beauty emerged, and she set it down later with satisfaction over its aesthetic purity. She dreamed running motion, then a great, beautiful modern city, a sense of great pageantry, man functioning splendidly while she looked on with an extrahuman gaze. The dream had perfect form —like a sonata. "I had," she wrote, "been in a world of pure and abstract thought and design."*

A new problem arose. As her health grew worse, her medical expenses greatly increased. Since her writing time was declining, her income was going down. She began to worry about finances and applied for a Guggenheim Fellowship on September 21, 1937. She spoke of her plight, citing the fact that though she had approximately eight or nine books in print, her income from her books had been only $253 in 1936 and $124 in 1937. She spoke in somewhat disillusioned tones of the rewards of the artist in this country, and said that the young writer should think twice before entering writing as a profession. She then requested aid on the basis of her ill-health and declining income. Mr. Henry Allen Moe, director of the Guggenheim Foundation, was very helpful and sympathetic. However, technical stipulations in the Guggenheim charter prevented him from awarding her a grant, and she was forced to drop this inquiry.

She now turned her energies to the writing of another novel. As it always did, this preoccupation with work brought a rise in her spirits. Back in February, 1933, she had begun a sketch which she completed in May of that year and titled "Tamed Honey." She told Miss Williams that this sketch had been suggested by John Jacob Niles' singing of an old ballad, "Black Is My Truelove's Hair." In the summer of 1936, she expanded this sketch to a five-part form. Then, in 1937, she rewrote and expanded this material into a complete novel, finishing the writing in July, 1938. She tells us, "I was very tired . . . . The title was being considered slowly but suddenly was resolved as inevitable. The pages . . . were sent away. After that I slept many hours. Each night and much in the afternoon. When rest was accomplished I began to write the story which soon became "Holy Morning."*

The title which she chose was *Black Is My Truelove's Hair,* and the novel was so called on its publication, October 14, 1938. On the whole it was favorably received, most interviewers complimenting it highly. There were only a few adverse criticisms. One reviewer felt that the characters were not sufficiently massive to carry their portentous roles. Several remarked that it was good, but not so good as *The Time of Man.* This last criticism moved Miss Roberts to write, "Would I want to write *The Time of Man* over and over, or even once again?"* She felt in general that the reviewers had read the novel cursorily and missed the symbolic intent almost completely. Any reader giving the novel a careful second reading will probably agree with her here.[35]

She had used as the locale of the novel the little town of Fredericksburg, seven miles out of Springfield. She felt very close to the scene and the people of the novel; it possessed that reality which was more real than actuality to her. One day while driving on the Fredericksburg road, Miss Roberts pointed out to Mrs. Frances Schultz the stretch of highway down which Dena James walks in the opening scene of *Black Is My Truelove's Hair.* The novel was like another life to her.

By this time the winter hegira to Florida had become a fixed element in her routine. Her anemia made the cold

[35] The symbolic meaning of the novel is discussed in Chapter V.

weather of Kentucky winters extremely disagreeable; the cold also seemed to accentuate her skin disorder. So each autumn she followed the sun south. In the winter of 1937–38, she went to Orlando, Florida, where her friends Mr. and Mrs. Bosley were staying. She liked the town so well that she wintered here the rest of her life. During these winter sojourns she lived quietly. Rollins College invited her on one occasion to read her poems to an assembly there, but, not feeling up to it, she declined. She was gradually withdrawing from the world.

By 1938, Miss Roberts had begun to turn over in her mind her last big project—an epic which would have as its central figure Daniel Boone and which would be written either for the radio or the stage. She hoped to realize a good sum of money from this work, and she thought Boone was a big character who could carry the necessary weight of symbolism. An examination of the notes left by Miss Roberts indicates that she got no further on this project than the initial stage. It was evidently to be epical in tone and scope. Daniel Boone was to be the protagonist of a cycle of poems which were to combine both lyric and dramatic qualities. The theme was to sweep across all modern man and treat the effect that skepticism deriving from a materialistic science has had on him. It broached the familiar theme of the fragmentation of the mind of modern man— the dissociation of his sensibilities. In her manuscript notes there are poems on Boone in which he practices all trades —blacksmith, herbalist, hunter, and others. The intent was to show that Boone was the "complete man," before dissociation had begun. So the poem would cover all modern religious and spiritual ideas and values and plans; it would have a universal reach. Boone said he was never lost (and would be at home in physical matter—protons, photons, etc.); therefore Boone would be the leader to take us through chaos. Evidently Boone was to be a clearly realized physical figure in his own time and milieu and was to extend his presence symbolically throughout the chaos of the present time. This would be a difficult artistic problem, and she left no indication of how she would solve it. Possibly it would have suffered the fate of Hart Crane's *The Bridge,* but Miss Roberts' grasp of her regional background was so close and intense that she might have mastered this difficult problem and turned out something which would have been unique in American poetry. However, her increasing ill-health kept this plan from ever maturing.

Miss Roberts did find the energy, however, to continue her poetry, and in April, 1940, she published *Song in the Meadow,*[36] a well-balanced volume and the last book of poetry to be published in her lifetime. At the time of her death, there were numerous unpublished poems among her papers which the family will presumably publish when they think it fitting.

In these last years, Miss Roberts kept up her weaving and her interest in her garden. Her concern with her immediate personal world knew no deterioration in spite of her failing health. Visitors still came, among them Jesse Stuart, her fellow Kentucky author, and J. Donald Adams of *The New York Times* literary staff. Townspeople still visited her, aspiring writers still asked her advice. To these inquiries she returned brief but courteous answers, as in the following note to a teacher of creative writing:

It would not be possible for me to undertake much of the problems of writing here . . . . But always to present the matter and not simply to tell it . . . . Regarding one's work as an art:

[36] Her poetry will be treated in greater detail in Chapter VIII.

the purpose to bring order to the chaos of life as we confusedly perceive it: to experience the returns and rewards that float back from the inward stream of the unconscious when the mind is continually absorbed with these quests.

I do not know of any books which would adequately discuss writing as an art. There are many helpful textbooks no doubt. The notes and practices of certain eminent practitioners might be studied.

To yourself and your students I send greetings—
Sincerely
E. M. Roberts

Knowing that her remaining life span was very short, she became interested in having a good portrait of herself to leave to her friends and family. Her favorite for several years was the Ullman portrait, made in Louisville in the 1930's. It is a handsome, somewhat austere portrayal. In the early 1930's, she had met Wallace Kelly, a photographer, in Lebanon, Kentucky. Mr. Kelly, who was a writer himself and greatly admired Miss Roberts' work, made a series of portraits in 1939 which pleased her greatly. One of these, a youthful-looking photograph, became her favorite among the many pictures done of her. At the time of her death, Mr. Kelly and Miss Roberts were planning a series of interpretive portraits that were to bring out visually some of the salient aspects of her personality. These, unfortunately, were never completed.

By 1940, the strain which the disease imposed on her sensibilities was beginning to show itself in a number of ways. Her manner sometimes became curt and edgy. She had always insisted on her right of privacy from public inquiry. Thus, as early as 1929, some irritation had showed in her peremptory answer to biographical questions raised by John W. Townsend: "My life is my own property. I put whatever of it I desire into my books and the rest is of no interest to the public."[37] There would be times in Louisville or Lexington when she was attending a dinner party in her honor when she would lapse into a profound and continuous silence. This could make a difficult time for the hostess, who had no inkling of the inner problem which Miss Roberts carried about with her. But these dark moods were undoubtedly exceptional, even in the last year of life. For instance, the present writer called on her at her home in Springfield in the summer of 1940, and had an interview whch lasted for some two and one-half hours. She talked at length and very animatedly on her own work, on modern poetry,[38] and read extensively from her poetry. It must have been a tiring experience to a person with her limited strength, yet she gave no sign of irritation and was both kind and gracious.

The winter of 1939–40 had been spent in Florida. But as soon as March came, she began to yearn for Kentucky and dispatched a letter to Mrs. Katherine Mayes in Springfield, demonstrating her pleasure in Florida but, perhaps, even more her love of Kentucky:

Down here we have a delicious May weather that verges upon June. . . . The flowers have been lovely for a month. We have pansies, roses, snap-dragons, sweet-williams, sweet peas, and azaleas all about us, and the heavy scent of orange blossoms . . . .

Orlando is a sweet little city . . . . In easy walking distances I have the shopping center, the favorite lake, about twenty churches, a good skin specialist, a fine dentist, a garden for sunbathing and several friends.

[37] Quoted in John W. Townsend's "A History of Kentucky Literature Since 1913," *Filson Club History Quarterly,* Vol. XIII, No. 1 (January, 1939) , 29.

[38] She disliked, for instance, the private symbolism in the poetry of T. S. Eliot.

I think though of the sweet little blooms that come early at Elenores [her Springfield residence] and wish that somebody were there to enjoy them. I never see them anymore. Down the fence row are many little bulb things, and beside the front door is the shrub of the sweet odors, the sweet viburnum, I think it is. Often one sniffs a sweet whiff of it as far as out on the road . . . . Do walk up to my place and sniff the sweet smells of it—if it lived through the winter, for alas it may not have done so.

Remember me to Frances, and to you a Happy Spring!

Elizabeth

Another month passed, bringing warm weather definitely to Kentucky and Miss Roberts home from Florida for what would be her last visit to "Elenores." She opened her home and, joined by her mother, spent a quiet summer in Springfield, still receiving friends and well-wishers. Her wasting illness now showed clearly in the gauntness and emaciation of her face. Writing was immensely exhausting for her, but still she pushed ahead at it, putting together the stories which would be published in March, 1941, as the volume *Not By Strange Gods*. She made further plans for the Daniel Boone material and carried forward the writing on two novels, none of which she would be able to complete. She must have thought often of the prognosis of her physician in 1935. According to this prognosis, she was now concluding her allotted span. She was sometimes sad, but she was never afraid. Twenty-five years earlier she had written, "I have known . . . what it is to die over and over and to be recreated from within, forever recreated."* She could still say and believe this.

Her thoughts turned more and more to religious consolations. An old Springfield friend who had presented her with a Catholic missal in the 1930's (knowing her interest in the Catholic liturgy) called on her one day during this last summer and found her reading the "Litany of the Saints." "It is very beautiful," the writer said, "very beautiful."

During the course of the summer, Miss Roberts' debility became so great that she felt it necessary to employ Mrs. Mary Sallie Moran to serve as her nurse and companion. Mrs. Moran served faithfully during the entire last year of Miss Roberts' life. The fall soon came, and "Elenores" was closed. Miss Roberts took a last look at the fall flowers blooming so profusely in the garden she had loved the past thirty years, and departed for Orlando, Florida, with Mrs. Moran. Undoubtedly she felt this was her valedictory.

In Florida, the winter began badly for her. Suffering from the ravages of the disease, she had to spend much time in bed. Music was a continual and long solace to her, and she read each day from her missal. She wrote to her family, particularly to her brother Ivor, a very great favorite. A few friends were received for very short periods. It was clear to her that she would soon be leaving.

On January 18, she was made a member by proxy of the National Institute of Arts and Letters. She was too ill to attend the reception. Her writing ceased, but her mind remained clear.

In early March, her condition grew markedly worse, and she was removed to Orange Hospital in Orlando. Here there were periods of consciousness in which her mind could sweep back over the long way which she had come since the childhood memories fashioned "under the tree" on the cemetery hill overlooking Springfield. Her brother Ivor, who had been often with her as a child "under the tree," arrived and watched with her as she dreamed her life away in the afternoon of March 13, 1941. Her body was returned to Springfield and buried in the cemetery on the hill, the same one in which she sat as a little girl.

"And while I was there I looked all down,
Over the trees and over the town."

2. The Relationship

between Earth and the Human Spirit

in the Fictional World

ꙮ We turn now from the solitary, intense personal world of Miss Roberts to her less solitary but equally intense fictional world. Her fictional world is an extension and prolongation of her personal one; but her fictional world is molded nearer to her secret desire. It is an arranged world, ordered and disciplined from the chaos of daily life to the form and pattern which art can give. It is a world constructed of two entities—external nature and the spirit of man—whose harmonious relationship is indispensable to human welfare and happiness. All of her work, both prose and poetry, is an attempt to present this relationship in all of its rich particularity and overtones. From this relationship grow the structure, style, and pervading tone of her work. Moreover, this relationship is a highly conscious one on her part, one frequently stated explictly by her. "If I can, in art, bring the physical world before the mind with a greater closeness—richer immediacy—than before, so that mind rushes out to the very edge of sense—then mind turns about and sees itself mirrored within itself."* In her most successful works she succeeded in doing this very thing—portraying the mind as it "rushes out to the very edge of sense"; and this success gives a unique savor to her work. This chapter will attempt to examine briefly three major elements of this world. The hope is that this examination will establish a point of vantage from which to view the detailed presentations of her novels and short stories. It will, therefore, be preliminary and impressionistic rather than detailed and exhaustive. We will treat, as the three major elements in her fictional world, man's spirit, the earth, and the resultant state when spirit and earth are mutually interacting. Obviously, in the novels these three elements are mixed together in that organic complexity which we find in real life. But for the sake of analysis and clarity, we will here present each in a separate discussion.

In those remarkable personal notes, now in the Roberts Papers in the Library of Congress, Miss Roberts returns again and again, in that lifelong intimate dialogue she carried on with herself, to statements of the sorrows, permutations, and final triumph of spirit. The following comments are from her notes on *Under the Tree.* They have almost the tone of a manifesto as they address themselves to an analysis of mind and its strength:

I do not know how poems are made . . . .
But observing the mind in its conscious and unconscious functions—a posteriori—I find these observations to be true.

. . .

I believe that the total mind is greater than any of its attributes in a sum total.

. . .

I believe that it is the high function of poetry to search into the relation between mind and matter, into the one-ness of flesh and thin air . . . Spirit. Into the wedding of grass, intellect, instinct, imagination.

There is an intense seriousness evident here, and it is sincere. In her personal life, this reliance upon the force of the spirit is manifest. It emerges clearly in the following excerpt from a letter written in 1917 by Miss Roberts to a close personal friend who had suffered a tragic death in her family:

I hope I shall hear from you some time soon. To say that "time will heal" is a platitude, and platitudes often annoy with their sermonizing; but time makes a difference and being busy and going on with the business of living makes a difference. I know a little secret that picked me up out of the almost-despairing place where I was and put me where I am now. I believe that each one can find the best way for himself; that is, the way one finds for himself is best; but I might give another hint of it. If only I had not been so selfish, so short-sighted, I might have helped Miss Mat. I believe one can correct any habit, or any mental pain, or state of mind, and can make over his character, can gain courage and calmness and just such habits of mind as he desires, by this little thing I know. If you ever want it I will give you the secret of it.[1]

"This little secret," as her art and her life clearly demonstrate, is the great strength of the human spirit, which, though it cannot change the physical universe, "can correct any habit, or any mental pain, or state of mind . . . can gain courage and calmness . . . ." This secret of innate spiritual strength is carried directly into her novels. We can see it emerging as each of her fictional heroines awakes

[1] Letter from E. M. Roberts, Chicago, to Mrs. C. F. Bosley, Springfield, Kentucky; envelope dated October 12, 1917.

to a consciousness of spirit and then gradually and painfully discovers its primacy over the external world. This is essentially a spirit of Christian stoicism, realized so intensely and steadily in her own life that she is able as an artist to make it appear naturally in the consciousness of her characters, thrust up from their inner tensions and resolutions, a quiet inner awareness of the realms of spiritual being. We see it with great clarity, for instance, in the person of Ellen Chesser *(The Time of Man)*. Ellen, in the following scene, torn by the infidelity of her lover Jonas Prather, becomes keenly aware of spirit:

. . . but in her dreams in the night she often arose to a great quiet beauty. There a deep sense of eternal and changeless well-being suffused the dark, a great quiet structure reported [*sic*] of itself, and sometimes out of this wide edifice, harmonious and many-winged, floating back in blessed vapors, released from all need or obligation to visible form, a sweet quiet voice would arise, leisured and backward-floating, saying with all finality, "Here I am."

Somewhat later, Ellen, going off through the country on one of the Chesser's frequent moves, looks out upon a range of mountains and is stirred inwardly to a subtle feeling of the inner topography of spirit.

The mountains grew more definite as she looked back to them, their shapes coming upon her mind as shapes dimly remembered and realized, as contours burnt forever and carved forever into memory, into all memory. With the first recognition of their fixity came a faint recognition of those structures which seemed everlasting and undiminished in herself, recurring memories, feelings, responses, wonder, worship, all gathered into one final inner motion which might have been called spirit; this gathered with another, an acquired structure, fashioned out of her experience of the past years, out of her passions and the marks put upon her by the passions of others, this structure built up now to its high maturity.

This consciousness of the life of spirit is identified in *The Great Meadow* with the life of reason. For example, Berk Jarvis speaks to the Indians who have captured him and desire to eat him:

"When life goes outen me the strong part goes too. You couldn't eat ne'er a bit of it. Whe'r I go to heven or whe'r I go to hell or whe'r I go no place at all, whenever I go from here my strength goes along with me. I take my strong part and you'll never get it inside your kettle and you couldn't eat it into your mouth."

In a sense, Berk Jarvis and Daniel Boone, the two dominant male characters of the book, are symbolic representations of the power of spirit, through reason, to subdue the dark, lawless impulsive side of the universe. And Diony Hall, who is herself a powerful exponent of spirit's ultimate force, comes to a clear realization of this symbolism in the final scene of *The Great Meadow:*

Diony put the bar across the door and made the house ready for the night. But she sat in the dim light of the last candle, sitting beside the table . . . . For a little while she felt that the end of an age had come to the world, a new order dawning out of the chaos that had beat through the house during the early part of the night. Her thought strove to put all in order before she lay down to sleep. She felt the power of reason over the wild life of the earth. Berk had divided the thinking part of a man from the part the Ojibways would have put into their kettle and into their mouths . . . . Boone had said that he was never lost, she reflected. Boone moved securely among the chaotic things of the woods and rivers . . . . The whole mighty frame of the world stood about her then, all the furniture of the earth and the sky, she a minute point . . . . Boone, she contrived, was a messenger to the chaotic part, a herald, an envoy there, to prepare it for civil men.

"The power of reason over the wild life of the earth." This sentiment could in effect become a fitting epigraph to any of Miss Roberts' novels, because it suggests the basic pattern of these novels. In each novel we have a young girl whose existence is threatened by the "wild life of the earth" —usually the lawless passions of men. And always the girl triumphs by discovering within herself the ultimate power of spirit over all external circumstances. And just as Boone brings order and harmony into the wild and chaotic frontier, so the Roberts heroines bring order into their own lives through spiritual discipline and, in a manner, into their very milieu. Jocelle, for example, emerges as the source of order at the close of *He Sent Forth a Raven* while Stoner Drake declines into senility, and Ellen Chesser as the source of order for her family amid their tribulations at the close of *The Time of Man*.

It becomes apparent that each novel portrays a spiritual cycle in the life of its heroine; these cycles are similar. They have that universality which suggests the emergence of an archetypal pattern—loosely a death-and-rebirth archetype —spiritual death-and-rebirth. This archetypal pattern is a very conscious one (it will become evident in the discussion of individual novels which follows), a very ancient one, and a very personal one with Miss Roberts. In a sense, it is a projection into each of her novels of a phase of spiritual experience through which she herself had passed.[2] Conse-

2 See page 38.

quently, her imagination moved naturally into a spiritual death-and-rebirth cycle.

Thus, in quick summary, we can say that spirit is the fundamental entity in her world. It is a great womb from which springs reality, knowledge, and that ultimate courage which enables man to endure. It is the cornerstone on which her fictional house will rest.

The second great theme in Miss Roberts' fictional world is the earth—earth as physical nature and as the life that arises from but clings closely to the ways of this nature. The whole aspect of her work here is virtually primitivistic, but it is not the kind of primitivism which is often equated with a foolhardy ignoring of harsh reality and an escape into a mythical golden age. Miss Roberts shows us ugly and mean people and actions in her world. They are not glossed over. The spirit wins by meeting and surmounting these evils through the strength it draws from the earth and nature. Thus, in all of her books, the characters move in a deep awareness of nature. Nature is made physical and palpable. The atmosphere of *A Buried Treasure,* for instance, is drenched with the weathers and elements of the earth. We are as aware of this rich, sensuous medium as we are of the characters themselves. It thickens the fictional world. This earthiness permeates every aspect of her work. The very people who move through her novels are children of the earth. Consider her heroines: They are either country girls or small-town girls who are close to the earth and, like Theodosia Bell, draw strength from it in moments of great crisis. Miss Roberts' most striking creation is Ellen Chesser, a child of an itinerant farm couple. Ellen's knowledge is from the earth, her life is measured by the rhythmical seasons of the earth, and the very consciousness of her soul comes to her in earthy symbols. Theodosia Bell of *My*

Heart and My Flesh is crushed by the knowledge of evil and almost perishes until she comes to teach in a small country school and dilates under the rich sun and friendship of the countryside. In *The Great Meadow,* Diony Hall sees the earth as the great projection of the eternal mind and lives in close consonance with the soil and the forests of eighteenth century Kentucky, a brave new world. Dena Janes (in *Black Is My Truelove's Hair*), seemingly wrecked from a callow affair with an irresponsible truck driver, wins back her integrity and happiness on a small Kentucky farm. The richly symphonic closing of *A Buried Treasure* brings together the farmer folk of a small Kentucky hamlet in an ancient ring dance, reminiscent of twelfth-century England. There is no single novel, short story, or important poem in which the earth does not figure as a significant and healthful influence. Her characters are drawn, then, from the countryside, from the soil. This is not to say that they are hermits and hate society. All of her major characters—except Stoner Drake, in *He Sent Forth a Raven*—have a sense of their community with man, but they mingle this with a constant awareness of the abiding and enduring land. Thus, their consciousness manifests always a healthy balance between society and nature that is characteristic of Miss Roberts' primitivism.

The pervading earthiness of her work is manifest also in the settings of her novels. The characters of her novels and short stories people a three- or four-county segment of central Kentucky, an area Miss Roberts calls the Pigeon River country. Pigeon River is a name used by the pioneers for a stream called Salt River today. To the south and east of Salt River extend the streams flowing into it. These streams drain a gently rolling section of bluegrass land which moves to the knob land of Marion County on the south, where the foothills of the Appalachians begin. It is a country of small farms interspersed with wooded patches, a country where spring and autumn are idyllic, equally poised between the temperature extremes of north and south. There are no cities here, only small towns and farms. It is a beautiful land, bearing, as late as 1900 (the time-period of most of Miss Roberts' work), occasional evidences of the primitive world which confronted Daniel Boone a scant century earlier. Washington County is typical of this area; and in this rural—but not degraded—county, Miss Roberts has set the locale of *The Time of Man, He Sent Forth a Raven, My Heart and My Flesh, A Buried Treasure,* and *Black Is My Truelove's Hair.* This is Miss Roberts' native county, and the natural background so beautifully and evocatively realized in her work is that of Washington County. The scenes of her fiction are country scenes; her world is a country world. Community life in her fiction centers about Anneville, which is Springfield in real life.

In 1900, Springfield was a small town of some one thousand people, where a boy could stand in the court square and toss a rock into any business house in town. Its life was hardly more than an extension of the farm life which surrounded it; it depended completely on the prosperity of the county farmers and rose and fell with their changing fortunes. The farm life in 1900 was still essentially simple. In the distant hills and by the remote creeks of the county were farms with people whose way of life had not changed since the Civil War. The entire setting is agrarian.

The transition from Springfield to Anneville is a simple one. For Anneville is Springfield set in an aesthetic frame, moved into the realm of art; Anneville is what Miss Roberts the artist saw as she looked at Springfield. At the same time, it is a complex transition in the sense that art is complex. In Anneville, the setting is agrarian; and here the drama of Miss Roberts' fictional world is played out in a lonely farmhouse, either a fine spacious one befitting the landed gentry or a small tenant cabin. The heroine may run into the uplands where the cattle graze, or work methodically through the tobacco field, or find delight in the formal patterns described by turkeys rushing toward the scattered corn. Thus we are never allowed to forget that the setting is the earth, and the people who act herein are of the earth; and these rustic people, unlike the swarming metropolitan hordes, have nothing to separate them from Mother Earth. Note, for instance, this scene from *A Buried Treasure*:

Lying about, beyond his sight now, but realized, were the more level farms that rolled away through the central Kentucky plain, and these would be planted or left in pasture . . . . This earth itself, Terra—the first, the earliest, the most ancient oracle, the most profound deity—showed herself here in the beginnings of lesser mountains and little rivers.

This passage projects the earth-presence into the forefront of the reader's consciousness. And this earth-presence is never absent from the novels—it is always there, solid, omnipresent, weathered, strong, a part of God's covenant with man. No other American novelist has kept us so skillfully aware of our real setting—Mother Earth.

Still another primitive element in the Roberts world is the attitude toward knowledge. Book knowledge is not scorned, but the most important knowledge for both Miss Roberts and her characters seems to be a traditional knowledge that is compounded equally from the communal wisdom of the folk and the rich stoicism engendered by direct contact with nature. It is this amalgam which guides Diony Hall and Ellen Chesser and, to a lesser extent, Dena Janes and Theodosia Bell. And it is this knowledge—not that of the schools—which brings Philly Blair at the close of *A Buried Treasure* to the realization that the real "Buried Treasure" is the human heart in friendship with others of its kind. Allen Tate, in "Ode to the Confederate Dead," speaks of "knowledge carried to the heart," by which he seems to signify this very traditional knowledge of which we speak here. And where else in American fiction can we find a character whose life is a more convincing exemplar of "knowledge carried to the heart" than Ellen Chesser of *The Time of Man?* A clear-cut and moving statement of this theme is made by the Hawthornesque mountaineer in her short story, "On the Mountainside":

"I was a plumb traitor to my God when I left the mountains and come to the settlements.

". . . I reckon you relish learnen, young man, and take a heap of delight in it and set a heap of store by the settlements. But the places you knowed when you was a little tad, they won't go outen your remembrance. Your insides is made that way, and made outen what you did when you was a shirt tail boy, and you'll find it's so. Your dreams of a night and all you pine to see will go back. You wont get shed so easy of it."

Finally, this theme of primitivism is made especially memorable for the reader by the striking conclusions to her novels. These endings are remarkably similar. They are, without exception, quiet, serene, pastoral endings, occurring after a kettledrum burst of violence. The closing scene is usually a night scene. Always the setting is a richly pastoral one where the earth overwhelms the senses with the power of its opulent elements. The ending of *The Time of Man*—cited already in a different context—is a case in point. Even more sensuous in the evocation of the *feel* of the summer night, the earth, and the earth-sounds is the last scene in *My Heart and My Flesh*. Theodosia has been saved from death and from death-in-life by her farmer lover, Caleb Burns. It is night, and Theodosia lies in bed awake far into the night, hearing outside the steps of Caleb Burns walking up and down the earth.

Outside the purity of the night spread over the cut fields and the cows were laid down on the open pasture-top near the ragged tree. Steps came off the farther slope, man's steps, sublimated and hollowed by the distance, feet walking through the grass, about the barns, off to the farther end of the pasture . . . .

The leaves of the poplar tree lifted and turned, swayed outward and all quivered together, holding the night coolness. The steps returned to the pasture, going unevenly and stopping, going again, restless. They went across the hollow place and came back again toward the rise where the cows lay. They walked among the sleeping cows, but they did not stir for it was a tread they knew.

This is the last sentence of the novel, and it leaves us with a clear-cut, simple picture in which there are three entities —Theodosia, Caleb, and the earth—all blended quietly into a serene night pastoral.

Thus, at every major point in her novels, her work is fastened firmly and unyieldingly to the abiding substance of the earth. And this attitude toward the earth is genuine and lasting on her part, an attitude fixed in her early childhood and lasting till her death.

In the foregoing discussion we have seen that the earth and the spirit are the twin nuclei of the Roberts fictional world. They are the irreducible core about which all else revolves, and their relationship sets up the third important element in that world. To examine this third element one must understand that in her fictional world all things flow, all things are moving, happening, occurring, emerging, becoming. It is a verb world, a world of the progressive tense, an "ing" world. The quality of that world is the quality of fluidity, of merging and emerging—a cosmos of endless flux (there is, however, nothing of the ethical relativist about her work). This flow represents the relationship of earth to spirit—a relationship originating in perceptual knowledge. The spirit is subject, and earth is object; when they are conjoined, perceptual knowledge arises and sweeps across the mind. This flow of perceptions fleshes out her world, providing it with density and movement; and very markedly it shapes and informs her narrative technique. The language itself moves in an undulating flow which produces a muted, murmurous quality infusing all of her best work.

This flowing quality is organized in terms of the personality of the protagonist, who is always, in the novels, a girl or woman. The protagonist, through a growing self-consciousness, becomes aware of the fixity of her innate spirit and thus establishes the basis of reality. This stable entity then serves as a point of reference in terms of which the protagonist (and we through her) can gauge and judge the flow of perceptual experience. Miss Roberts is careful to set up this point of reference at the very beginning of her work. Here, for instance, is the opening sentence of *The Time of Man.* "Ellen wrote her name in the air with her finger, *Ellen Chesser,* leaning and writing on the horizontal plane." Thus, with a direct, primitive, pointing definition, Ellen concentrates on name as symbol of the immortal part of her, her spirit. And again and again in the course of the story, the mystery of the identity of self fascinates Ellen, as in one scene she shouts to the sky, "I'm Ellen Chesser! I'm here!" Or turn to *The Great Meadow* and read the first two sentences: "1774, and Diony, in the Spring, hearing Sam, her brother, scratching at a tune on the fiddle . . . placed herself momentarily in life, calling mentally her name, Diony Hall. 'I, Diony Hall,' her thought said, gathering herself close, subtracting herself from the diffused life of the house that closed about her." Then the protagonists, secure in their own reality, yield to the rich flow of sense experience building up a changing, evolving picture of the world about them. This sense experience always contains for Ellen Chesser and for Diony something elusive, vague, and a little unreal. It is mentalized in the sense of being projected by the mind and thus less real than the mind. It is this attitude which gives a somewhat contextualistic[3] cast to the Roberts world. Ellen's world is never static. The detail is movement, and the movement is unending, projected from the matrix of mind from which it springs. Turn to almost any page of *The Time of Man* and one finds this characteristic flow, as if time were made palpable. Here is a typical example from *The Time of Man*:

. . . It was early spring now, the lean time of the year, the cold spring. There was little to eat but bread and bacon. Some farm bell rang, far off over the hard hills, a faint sound beating thin against the air. It was after eleven o'clock, then, time to prepare the food. Jasper would come across the meadow, bent, stiff. She could feel the noon reaching over the entire country,

---

[3] Contextualism. The theory that reality is not fixed and stable, but a flux of interpenetrated parts unseizable by the intellect. Cf. S. C. Pepper's *The Basis of Criticism in the Arts*.

valley and stony hills, the farm bell leaving faint echoes in the mind together with hunger, a feel of the approach of food, bacon and bread and grease.

She felt the noon on her skin, and she heard it in her ears and tasted it in her mouth. It lay on her seam like a load and dragged at her needle. It was imperative; it could not be set aside.

In her poem, "Conversations beside a Stream," Miss Roberts speaks of "sitting beside the stream of life. Beside the multiple flow of human onward-going being." And, thus, she herself coins the best designation for that phase of her world which we have been treating here. Whether we are in the world of her short stories, *The Haunted Mirror,* or the pioneer world of *The Great Meadow,* or the child's world of her poems, *Under the Tree,* we are most markedly in a "multiple flow of human onward-going being." Yet the flow is not all, for she also reminds us that, "Life is from within, and thus the noise outside is a wind blowing in a mirror."[4]

These three aspects—spirit, earth, and the phenomenal flow—are the salient entities of her fictional world. Later chapters will take up these and other aspects in greater detail. All of these aspects appear in a sonnet Miss Roberts composed in the 1930's, a sonnet full of man's spirit, the earth, and the "protean weltering" of man's "onward-going being." She made it the dedicatory poem in the volume entitled *Song in the Meadow.*

Sonnet of Jack

I give you day, our day, any day, for entering
Man's time on the earth, his world for cutting
aslant through his track.

4 *Jingling in the Wind,* 256.

Earth and the Human Spirit in the Fictional World

At the crossroads here, bearing his heave-ho aback,
At the point where his damned-to-perdition sin
    and his sheltering
Spirit join his throat-throbbing, bird-singing
Joy,—here, stubble-wise and tool-handed, into the
    day comes Jack,
Jack Plumber, Jack Plowman, Jack Scrivener,
    dowered with much or the lack
Of it, man-willed, washed up as beach drift out of
    protean weltering.

His friends, then, with him, one to pull, take,
    hand, fetch and carry,
Come with himself, no less in the reckoning—
    Bob, Dick and Harry.
Or woman-formed, dainty in dalliance or
    strong in her childings,
Kate, Mug or Prue. They, all, giving God
    praise, sown thus as wildings,
Spread free of the bony house toward heaven,
    their joy, his or theirs, say
What you will,—dead Friday and born again
    already on Thursday.

3. Poetic Realism

in the Fictional World

of Elizabeth Madox Roberts

Even as early as 1927 (in his *Aspects of the Novel*), E. M. Forster was not justified in calling D. H. Lawrence "the only living novelist in whom the song predominates— the rapt bardic quality as contrasted with the furniture of common sense." For one thing, Faulkner had already published *Soldier's Pay and Mosquitoes,* but, more important for that period, Elizabeth Madox Roberts had already published *The Time of Man,* and *My Heart and My Flesh* appeared in 1927. If so challenged, Mr. Forster might reply, with some justice, that the lyrical flights in Faulkner's first two novels were usually structural digressions and that such rhetoric could hardly be called "bardic." But he certainly could not justify a similar statement about the first two novels of Miss Roberts. This is not to say that the works of Miss Roberts are as important as those of Lawrence, but her inferiority is very much less than the critical neglect of her, and the world-wide attention to Lawrence, might indicate. To be sure, the poetic quality in her work is not so intense as that in the work of Lawrence, but it is very strong and very deep, and it avoids the excesses of both form and content into which Lawrence's "raptness" frequently leads him. Her bardic quality is not to be "contrasted with the furniture of common sense"; on the contrary, she achieves the very difficult combination of high poetic quality and common sense, a true balance between the romantic and the classical.

The most specific evidence of the remarkable poetic quality in the fiction of Miss Roberts is in her diction and her sentence structure. She uses a number of rhetorical devices for making language poetic—subtle rhythms, consonance, assonance, onomatopoeia, inverted syntax, euphonious names, archaic expressions—but, unlike Wolfe and unlike Faulkner (in some of his works), she never fails to make her rhetoric structural in the story. This difficult combination was no doubt somewhat simplified for Miss Roberts by the fact that, for her, basically the spirit of poetry is not different from that of prose (just as, philosophically, the realm of spirit seems quite as vivid to her as the realm of matter): the simple characters in her stories frequently sing traditional folk songs, and in her two delightful volumes of poetry (which, though original, preserve the spirit of folk songs), there are several poems about characters found in her fiction: "Ellen Chesser's Dream of Italy," "Diony in Albemarle," "Philly in the Kitchen," and three on Daniel Boone, who appears here and there in *The Great Meadow*. But in spite of the close relation which she feels between imaginative prose and poetry, she carefully avoids the confusion of the two, and she always maintains in any poetic prose passage the exact degree of poetic intensity appropriate to the character from whose point of view it is presented. Only one example will be given here, since these same poetic devices will be illustrated (though not discussed as such) in the later treatment of the more complicated aspects of her imagery.

Ellen Chesser—an uneducated but sensitive and imaginative country girl—is already beginning to feel both the loneliness and the beauty of life. In the following passage she dreams of being happily married to Joe Trent, who is above her socially but is obviously attracted by her beauty and charm:

> The trees spread upward into the blue air and were lost, and far away some geese, disturbed, were crying, the tones coming as high thin music flaring upward into the dark. She would have something pink to wear, or fair blue, a bow or a ribbon somewhere on her body. Blue cloth could go trailing over wide stairs, down white steps . . . herself spreading and trailing through blue cloth, gentle and sweet-scented . . . all her enduring life . . . .

The poetic thoughts here are Ellen's, presented with just enough assistance from the author to outline the beautiful natural background. The simple, appealing rhythm (appropriate to the emotional imagination of a young girl falling in love for the first time) is partly the result of a parallelism of phrases: for example, "over wide stairs, down white steps," with assonance in the repetition of *i* and alliteration in "wide" and "white." The progress of the language, like that of music, is restrained by the repetition of rhythmical units—here words like "upward," "trailing," "blue"—and by appropriate pauses (corresponding to musical rests) indicated here at intervals by three contiguous periods. Consonance runs through the passage with a prevalence of liquid *r*'s: "trees," "spread," "upward," "air," "were," for example, all in one line (as the passage appears in the book). The archaic adjective "enduring" is used in this grammatically redundant fashion by simple country folk (who call it "enduren") to mean "whole"; the *ing* form here, as part of the simple but heightened (poetic) realism of the diction, embodies the emotional climax of the passage and is functional rhythmically in being parallel with the four other present participles in the passage (part of the prevailing falling rhythm). The passage as a whole, considered structurally, is important in the emotional development of Ellen, from whose point of view nearly all of the story is presented.

The structural implications of Miss Roberts' poetic prose can be seen also in the close connection between her imagery and the philosophical and religious attitude underlying her art. Her early, simple religious faith (of the frontier Protestant evangelical type) was considerably refined by a training in philosophy at the University of Chicago, where she took her Ph. B. degree, Berkeley being her favorite philosopher. All this was grafted on to a strong artistic instinct, or perhaps imagination, through which she took an almost pagan delight in expressing the sensuous beauties of nature. The result in her art is a rich (occasionally ambivalent) combination of a perfectly natural and sincere mythopoeism with Berkeleian idealism modified by elements of a Protestant evangelical religious faith.

The mythopoeic projection of her characters into each other, or into nature, or of nature into them—an almost pantheistic merging—seems absolutely uncontrived, almost as if she literally believed in the primitive identification of word with thing, and a very earthy thing at that. But the teaching of Berkeley led her to say, and to believe, that language and physical objects are unsubstantial veils to conceal reality, which of course is purely mental or spiritual. For Miss Roberts, indeed there was no contrast between the earthy and the spiritual; epistemologically the two are the same for her, as they are for Berkeley, but the emphasis of the artist and her philosophical master, as might be expected, is different—to such an extent that Miss Roberts at times seems to be engaged in a kind of reverse Berkleianism: Whereas Berkeley as a philosopher is engaged in transforming what is called the physical into the spiritual, Miss Roberts as an artist expresses the spiritual in terms of the physical, the sensuous. Indeed, the sensuous richness and the idyllic glow imparted to realistic scenes of rural life remind one of the Dutch masters in painting. Her scenes, however, reveal very little of the coarseness to be found in the work of some of the Dutch masters (as, for example, in Van Ostade's "Peasants Merrymaking"); in her work we have the artistic counterpart of the religious word made flesh. There is, to put it another way, in her metaphorical language an interpenetration of the abstract and concrete in which the abstract is always invigorated by being given concrete qualities, while the concrete is given more general significance by being associated with the abstract.

Consider one of the most charming examples of the abstract made concrete in Miss Roberts' presentation of an imaginative little girl (Theodosia in *My Heart and My Flesh*) reflecting on the dreariness of the Calvinistic theology to which she is constantly subjected, this time in a formal sermon:

The words would be confused with drowsiness and weariness, and the foreknowledge of God would settle to the odors of the yarn carpet and the dry melancholy of the village Sabbath . . . Want-of-conformity-to took Transgression-of into a great stale book and closed flat the covers . . .

☆ 100 ☆

This concretizing of theological abstractions is simple and direct like the allegorizing of Bunyan, and seems appropriate for the imagination of a sensitive and intelligent little girl like Theodosia, who had no doubt read *Pilgrim's Progress.* In one respect Miss Roberts here had a more difficult task than did Bunyan: Bunyan had the benefit of a full allegory to make his individual metaphors credible; Miss Roberts had to establish the metaphorical illusion here in two or three sentences that fit the psychology of a little girl. Of course, she has included this in the fantasy about the mythical city of Mome (soon to give way to the sleepy little southern town of Anneville), which forms the introductory chapter of *My Heart and My Flesh.* But she does not need such a framework. Consider Jocelle's reflections (towards the end of *He Sent Forth a Raven*) following the birth of her child: "Sleeping, and waking, she saw within the act of seeing, as if the brain itself were a prism, a crystal-clear design, a mathematical form, and as such common to all men. Common-to-all-men drowsed over her and brought Logan from the garden where he now rested from the long night of sharing with her the coming of the child . . . ." The phrase "common to all men," part of the predicate of the simile in the first sentence, is transformed, as subject of the next, into an abstract substantive, which is personified by being given the active predicates, "drowsed" and "brought." As an important part of Miss Roberts' philosophy (which will be treated in more detail later), this personified abstraction is at the same time made to symbolize the force which binds all mankind into a kind of cosmic and primarily happy unity.

Again like Bunyan and the dramatists of the medieval Moralities, Miss Roberts personifies a sin—more specifically, by synecdoche, transforms the sinner into the sin, as

☆ 101 ☆

in the following sentence (in *He Sent Forth a Raven*), in which Catharine is deserting her little daughter, Jocelle, for an amour that will be sordid even if it results in marriage: "The woman receded as a blue breath of cloth going into a doorway among closing shadows, a restlessness bogged in passion and clothed richly in a temporary envelope of soft blue cashmere cloth made on the style worn in the parlors and churches at that season." There is, of course, a subtlety of imagination here not to be found in *Pilgrim's Progress* or the Morality plays: first, the literal woman moving so rapidly that, impressionistically, she "recedes as a blue breath of cloth going into a doorway among closing shadows"; then, because of the impatient intensity of her desire, she becomes the quality that drives her, "a restlessness," the abstraction giving emphasis to the concrete, as if to say, "She has become restlessness itself"; the abstraction is immediately concretized, as is the next powerful abstraction applied to the woman, "passion," by the very physically expressive participle "bogged." The speed toward gratification caused by passion is ironically slowed down, even "bogged," in the heavy coarseness of that very passion, which is further concretized by being "clothed richly in a temporary envelope of blue cashmere cloth." The adjective "temporary" may suggest (without being a specific symbol) that the restlessness will in time be completely bogged in a quicksand more powerful than passion.

Another, more direct, aspect of Miss Roberts' artistic word made flesh is her "physicalizing" of the very word *word* or *words,* as in this explanation of the effect of a rural sermon on the young audience (in *The Time of Man):*

They heard the voice of the preacher as it broke and parted

among the corners of the room and flattened against the ceiling—Rehoboam and Jeroboam, kings, and the kingdom divided, never again to unite, Rehoboam and Jeroboam, great words striking the wall, great words with jagged fringes of echoes hanging from each syllable, and the lonely kingdoms . . . the great sadness of the lonely kingdoms settling upon them as they sat, Elmer, Dorine, Ellen, Maggie, and even Sebe.

It is interesting to notice in this passage the climactic effect of the structural metaphor. The attractive young hearers are first impressed by the forceful voice of the preacher, "as it broke and parted among the corners of the room and flattened against the ceiling"; they then begin to notice the words uttered by that voice, not so much for their meaning as for their physical impact, "great words striking the wall, great words with jagged fringes of echoes hanging from each syllable." They finally begin to feel the emotional effect of the actual meaning, which becomes so vivid that they feel "the great sadness of the lonely kingdoms settling upon them . . . ."

Miss Roberts not only concretizes the word *word* or *words* as in the above passage and in many others, like the one characterizing Ellen's reflection upon her own "loveliness" as "thought spreading itself wide with words," but she even physicalizes the word *spirit*: for example, she characterizes Jocelle's love for Logan as ". . . a spirit within flesh crying out by way of words and eyes and trusting devotions." The *spirit* here physicalized by being made to "cry out within flesh" retains a portion of its abstractness because "trusting devotions" is one of the modes of its "crying out." "Devotions" is a richly ambivalent word connoting in part the physical acts that indicate affection and in part the quality of character exhibited by these acts. For Miss Roberts the spirit and the flesh are not merely co-operating as in Browning's, *"Nor soul helps flesh more now than flesh helps soul;"* they are in truth different only as two aspects of one unified reality. She would agree with Berkeley in calling this monistic reality the ideal, but as usual the artist in her cannot resist invigorating the spiritual by physicalizing it instead of spiritualizing the physical. For Ellen, to consider another example, the sight of mountains is the objective correlative which elicits "recurring memories, feelings, responses, wonder, worship, all gathered into one final inner motion which might have been called spirit . . . ." Miss Roberts does not need to trace *spirit* back etymologically to its source in *breath*. In her imagination spirit is still physical and, to the reader, unusually convincing because this imagination is not a literary one. We are not dealing here with sophisticated, self-conscious symbolism. Whether or not we have what Maud Bodkin calls "archetypal imagery" is a question that ought to be considered, and will be after we have examined other varieties of it in Miss Roberts' work.

Another type of Miss Roberts' mythopoeism seems at first to be quite different from the physicalizing of the spiritual. This is the almost pantheistic merging of her characters with external objects in nature. Sometimes the character encompasses a portion of nature, as in Theodosia's reflection upon the tragedy in her life:

She was aware of herself as the residue of disaster . . . . As if the bandage had been removed from a recent hurt or fracture, she spread painfully out through the hills and fields, through the ways to go.

Sometimes nature encompasses, even oppresses, the character, as in Ellen Chesser's reflection, as a little girl, on the suffering of Artie Pinkston while her baby is being born:

The hills gathered closer in and Artie Pinkston helped to wind them tight and wind them close . . . . After a while [during the delivery of Artie's baby] the hills would open up and send out great cries.

And as Ellen thinks of the mystery and repulsiveness of sex on this hot summer night:

The stars were out, very low, and very near, pushing down, falling of humid weight. The air scarcely moved at all, but now and then a warmer motion spread down from the higher places, pushing through skin and lying along the inner threads of nerves, fiddling on delicate quick with familiar searching hands.

For Ellen, as she grows older, however (and for other characters in Miss Roberts' works) the intimate relationship with nature often becomes a happy one—sometimes with a sensuousness reminiscent of passages in Whitman's "Song of Myself":

The weather, with its winds, snatched at her [Ellen's] hair and tore at her garments; it wet her face with its rain and laid wet hands on her arms and shoulders, or warm amorous hands on her back and loins.

Sometimes nature seems even to become alive in the characters. Ben Shepherd (in *A Buried Treasure*) is so close to nature that it seems, "As if the land had in him become conscious, as if it would ask these things." Ben and other simple people who live very close to the rhythms of "the earth itelf, Terra—the first, the earliest, the most ancient oracle, the most profound deity," attain a kind of cosmic significance as incarnations of this deity, without any loss of the simple realism of speech and action. Cosmic implications in the imagery might seem to indicate a truly Berkleian spiritualizing of the physical instead of the reverse, a rendering of the spiritual in physical languages that we have so far noticed—but for the fact that the cosmic itself, though ultimately spiritual, is always concretized: thus for Ben the configurations of these Kentucky knobs on the horizon become "a great god lain down to sleep at the edge of the sky," and Philly and Andy, who find the money in the old stump as he watches them, become "two drab, mythical shapes bending to take a vessel out of the earth."

Another example of the metaphorical merging of a character with nature appears in Ben's sexual dream of his sweetheart, connecting her with the earth in a relationship as old and as natural as primitive fertility rites:

It was pleasant to feel the delicate heat that she engendered . . . . It seemed to him, dreaming, that it would be a pleasant thing to load risk upon her, to put upon her, to lavish, to spend, to take, to pull up, to make her the earth itself, to give to her, to plow her deep, to plant her with a harvest, to fertilize her with rain, to fling himself down on one of her cool hills in the shade.

By no means all of Miss Roberts' merging-with-nature metaphors indicate that either the human who is merging or the nature with which he merges is good. For example, the old hen sucking her own eggs becomes vividly identified in Philly's imagination with the miserly Cundy:

Soon afterward the hen came from the nest in a wide arc, flying and fluttering, throwing out a great broken bleat of joy and fright that brought all the other hens to a cackling chorus. Philly had a momentary sickness spread over her . . . . She saw

Cundy pressing his large mouth into the egg to sup out the sweet inner part . . . . The old pullet had eaten a hole into the morning . . . . She had made a crack in time itself and in the illusions people hold together.

This, of course, is the psychological effect on Philly, but at another level the passage is connected with Miss Roberts' philosophy of life. She believes that the whole organization of life in the universe is primarily good, but evil, too, has implications far beyond its immediate vicinity. An evil life, or even an evil deed, just to that extent does interrupt the cosmic unity, or "make a crack in time itself."

Besides the mythopoeic projection of her characters into nature, and of nature into them, there is often an imaginative merging of the characters with each other. Again and again the very word *merge* is used in these metaphors: As Jasper approaches Ellen shortly before their marriage, ". . . she was merged with him in the deep moments of his last approaching steps . . . ." "She felt herself merge with Jonas" when she was in love with him and he with her; then, when he jilted her,

She would tear him out of her mind. She would tear him out if she had to tear out her very entrails, if she had to gut herself, brain herself with her own hands.

She could never do it; he had run in very deep upon her life. She would kill him with her terrible hands. She would strangle him with one strong grip. He had run into her blood and into her very breath. She hated him. She would take him out of herself if she had to tear him out with a gun or with a knife. She would kill him where he stood when she saw him again.

Certainly the "blood-togetherness"—the dynamic tensions —in the relations of D. H. Lawrence's characters to one another is never conveyed to the reader with more intense empathy than that of this passage in its context. Although Miss Roberts' narrative technique (to be considered in later chapters) is primarily plastic rather than dramatic, in the sense of physical action, the psychological (emotional) tensions in her characters are always powerfully dramatized. Her very language indeed is dramatic, but it is a representational, not a linguistic, drama; that is, the poetic language is never used for its own sake.

At a more complicated level of concrete-abstract merging, Miss Roberts sometimes has the character merging with the temporal process: ". . . herself [Theodosia] subtracted from the content of the walls . . . and extended as continuing in a running movement through history, past and future." Or, as a variant of this type, the magnificent metaphor (towards the end of *Jingling in the Wind*) in which the spider unrolls for Jeremy and Tulip (in love with each other) the whole panorama of history. The spider begins by advising Tulip not to answer Jeremy's question of whether, in winning her love, he "played St. George or Theseus, whether I rescued a maiden from a dragon or subdued an Amazon."

"Do not tell," said the spider, speaking softly with her soothsaying hands as she walked quickly away, having finished the fly. She leaned a moment against a romantic age and walked then across Egypt and a theory of time to sit quietly down upon an old war, and she began to speak again, making a sort of whisper speech with her long fingers as she plucked lightly at the war and moved then to settle at last over cause and effect. "Never tell him," she said.

Here, as always in the imagery of Miss Roberts, the language of imagination, even fantasy, seems perfectly realistic because it is so closely connected with one of her most cherished convictions—that a simple life close to the rhythms of earth is, in the pursuit of happiness, the climax of all history. The spider does not take very seriously her spinning of the big events in history; she "leaned a moment against a romantic age" and "plucked lightly at the war"; what she considers really important is the practical advice she gives the young lovers (who, at last, have escaped from the evils of our industrialized society) for happiness in their married life.

An example of one other type of mythopoeic merging will connect with another important element in Miss Roberts' imagery, music. Often the characters become identified with some form of music. Consider this description of the evangelistic frenzy of the rural preacher, Hez Turner (in *A Buried Treasure*):

Hez Turner was beating the time with his own hands, himself riding on the power of the song, and he began to admonish with a loud voice, his phrases thundering with the rolling song and making terrible warnings and judgments that seemed to be falling from the leaping music.

And now the influence of music on her style must be considered in some detail. The influence of music is omnipresent both in content and form—in musical phrases used as vehicles in her metaphors, in the subtle rhythms of her sentences and paragraphs, and in the general tone of her work, which seems to find what Havelock Ellis would call the dance of life a reflection of the cosmic rhythms of the universe, not unlike the old Ptolemaic "music of the spheres."

Sometimes, to be sure, musical language has no more serious function than to help her capture with precision a gay mood, as in the following passage from *My Heart and My Flesh*.

The song was always heard to the steady fall of the pick or the rise of the shovel, syncopated so that it set the shovel apart from itself and but half owned its rhythms, or rather as if it accepted its confines and then escaped from them by the witty loop-hole of a quarter-beat.

The human significance of music (even when there is no literal music) is of course clear to young lovers—if they, like Dena and Cam in *Black Is My Truelove's Hair*, are already in tune with nature:

The broad light of a sunny day spread over them and the fitful music hummed in and out of the air. It was the new world, a new day. Music anywhere at all, out of the hill, out of the briers, but nobody made it or sang it. It was the human world beating over the inanimate world.

In times of distress, human music, co-operating with the rhythms of external nature, may provide a temporary escape, as in Theodosia's turning to her violin when she is suffering from the loss of Albert's love:

. . . bending the tune to the outspread fertility of the fields and the high tide of summer with herself apart, insulated by the waxlike softness of her flesh and dispossessed by the penurious withdrawals of the house . . . she would surround herself with thin spectral music from which passion had been withdrawn.

But, in another mood, the music of this same violin may express Theodosia's feelings of the tragedy of all life: ". . .

a distressed lack-melody that mounted with a perpetual question toward the constellations . . . [as if to say] woman's life is short and full of peril."

The close association of the spiritual and the physical, in St. Paul's sense, considering the body as the temple of the spirit, is often strengthened by music:

. . . remembering that the music must come out of the spirit, the soul she Theodosia would search inwardly for some token or glimpse of this shadowy substance, this delicate eidolon.

But with all her love of music, Theodosia never makes the mistake of thinking that it is spiritual reality, or a substitute for such reality, just as Miss Roberts never considers that her art *is* religion, that a symbol *is* the reality of which, in less sophisticated ages, it was thought to be symbolic. Theodosia, instead, reasons that if music comes from spirit, it should lead back to spirit, be one means of understanding God: "I want to go to the end of music," she says, "and look over the edge at what's on the other side . . . . I'll look over the last precipice of music and say, 'God!' I'll say, 'Where are you?' "

Again, music becomes part of the cosmic unity: a happy solution to the problem in *A Buried Treasure* brings together at the end these simple rural folk for a celebration. In spite of certain human frailties exhibited earlier in the book, such are the innocence and integrity of their motives and the joyous vigor of their closeness to "Terra, the most ancient of oracles," that their singing and dancing in a circle in the moonlight, the beautiful "powdered air," becomes a convincing symbol of the happy rhythms of the rotating earth:

The throng, set in a circle, made a great wheel that turned about a little thorn bush and sang a game-song:

> *Here we go round the mulberry bush*
> *On a cold frosty morning . . .*

When this was sung once through another song arose from another part of the wheel, all of the boys and girls catching hands and turning . . . . The great wheel turned, making ready a world, a world of mankind turning all together, Philly and Andy and Ronnie Rudds and old Bonnie, with all the girls and boys of the farms. As the earth itself the wheel turned under the moon . . . . The girls were giving their prize to the boys who in turn gave to the girls, this way and that, and chased each other around and around on the outer rim of the world, or the great wheel would be turning, making ready.

Up to now in our discussion of Miss Roberts' imagery, we have considered various types of interpenetration of the concrete and the abstract, including the physicalizing of spiritual language, the merging of characters into external nature (or of external nature into them) in various ways, the merging of characters into each other, the merging of characters (more abstractly) into the temporal process, and the various uses of music in both the form and the content of all this poetic language. We must now consider in some detail what has been implied as basic in her treatment of all these various types of imagery—the quality of abounding vitality, which never failed her in all the physical suffering of the last decade and a half of her life.

The intensity of this feeling for, and love of, life is communicated emphatically with such force that a further comparison with D. H. Lawrence suggests itself. In her book entitled *Archetypal Patterns in Poetry,* Maud Bodkin quotes E. M. Forester's description of the poetic intensity in Lawrence as, "an irradiation of nature from within, 'so that every colour has a glow and every form a distinctness which could not otherwise be obtained,' " and she adds: "Such 'irradiation' seems to me an instance of what I have described as 'glory' transfiguring those objects that assume for us the character of archetypal images, reflecting in some special degree the life within and beyond us." Without calling such irradiation of nature from within "archetypal"[1] either in Lawrence or Miss Roberts, one can recognize the same quality in the imagery of both writers. Both are truly, in language applied to Wordsworth, "priests of the wonder and bloom of the world." There is in each an almost pantheistic merging of their characters with nature and, at times, of nature with them—a quality like the prephilosophy, primitivistic identification of word with thing.

[1] One may disagree about calling such images "archetypal" or, in Jung's language, "primordial." Even the emotional patterns corresponding to such transfiguring images, for both author and reader, need not be inherited in the structure of the brain, what Jung calls *"a priori* determinants of individual experience"; they need not be due even to what Miss Bodkin calls "predisposing factors present in mind and brain." Miss Bodkin thinks she is modifying Jung when she says that in poetry, "we may identify themes having a particular form or pattern which persists amid variations from age to age, and which corresponds to a pattern or configuration of emotional tendencies in the minds of those who are stirred by the theme." These "forms are assimilated from the environment upon slight contact only" by the aid of some "inner factor." But Miss Bodkin, no less than Jung, is certainly implying an inheritance of some mysterious kind of "racial memory" in the structure of the brain, since this "slight contact" with the environment is at the time when the "forms are assimilated." She does not seem to realize that the assimilator has been making emotive and cognitive contacts with the environment from birth, the accumulation of which, and the selection from which at the time of the contact with the poetic theme, could sufficiently account for the response. If we may believe competent biologists, we do not inherit even emotions; we inherit a body capable of emotions and cognitions. This, of course, does not prevent effective contact with the most ancient themes in poetry. It means simply that each generation *learns,* and does not in some mystical sense *inherit,* these *"archetypal"* images from previous generations.

The blood in the characters of each author does not merely flow; it leaps and bounds, as, for example, in the famous passage toward the beginning of Lawrence's *The Rainbow*:

So much warmth and generating and pain and death did they know in their blood, earth and sky and beast and green plants, so much exchange and interchange they had with these, that they lived full and surcharged, their senses full fed, their faces always turned to the heat of the blood, staring into the sun, dazed with looking towards the source of generation, unable to turn around.

And the following descriptions of Miss Roberts' Ellen: Thinking, while she is young, of a potential lover, her "blood leaped before her up the canyon"; and even after she is married and the mother of several children, living the hard life of a tenant farmer's wife,

She felt the vigor of her being as she stood in the sharp cold of the morning where all tender living things were withered, herself in her richness and vigor the most living thing in the whole sight, her skin kindled by the cold, her eyes bright, the child within her hidden yet but alive, her throat, her step, her standing figure even and firm . . . . She felt the moon on her skin, and she heard it in her ears and tasted it in her mouth.

There is the same mingling on equal terms of physical-istic and spiritualistic language in the two writers, but at this point the differences begin to appear: the vision of the transcendent in Lawrence is more intense than in Miss Roberts but also considerably less steady. There is nothing in the work of Miss Roberts which can compare in inten-sity to the description (in *The Rainbow*) of Will's religious experience in the cathedral when Anna is with him:

His soul leapt, soared up into the great church. His body stood still, absorbed by the height. His soul leapt up into the gloom, into possession, it reeled, it swooned with a great escape, it quivered in the womb, in the hush and the gloom of fecundity, like seed of procreation in ecstasy . . . . There his soul remained, at the apex of the arch, clinched in the timeless ecstasy, consummated . . . . Then again he gathered himself together, in transit, every jet of him strained and leaped, leaped clear into the darkness above, to the fecundity and the unique mystery, to the touch, the clasp, the consummation, the climax of eternity, the apex of the arch.

But such ecstatic experience of course cannot last, and Will's "passion in the cathedral" makes Anna jealous and angry. Lawrence's characters, apparently like him, have moments of ecstasy followed by intervals of intense depression. F. R. Leavis is correct in saying that Lawrence's characters do not revel in sex for the sake of sex. They strive to attain a perfect sex relationship, through which they hope to transcend the "close intimacy of farm kitchen" in marriage and to reach the "beyond." The intensity of this search for the "beyond," in Leavis' opinion, puts Lawrence in the great tradition of religion. But apparently neither Lawrence nor Leavis can distinguish true aspiration from romantic and pathological straining. For example, Leavis admits the "abnormal intensity" of Will's relation with his little daughter, Ursula, caused by the emotional failure of his relation with his wife, Anna (since Anna too often exhibited the "feminine dominance that must defeat the growth of any long-term relation between a man and a woman"). Yet Leavis thinks such a father-daughter relationship between Will and Ursula, like a similar one in the previous generation, an example of the "beyond" and the "rainbow." This, says Leavis, "is no mere romantic yearning."

There is a "beyond" quality also in the characters, expressed in the poetic imagery, of Miss Roberts, but they are not always trying to fly off into what T. E. Hulme (in referring to romantic writers) calls the "circumambient gas." Her main characters find the beyond in the beauty of the present—they do not try to transcend the "close intimacy of farm kitchen," because in domestic happiness, which for them is predominant in spite of suffering and tragedy, they find that the transcendent has become immanent. And this close human intimacy is reinforced by, often absorbed into, the very heart of nature itself. Consider the following passage, as offering a quieter, more normal, but still intense and (for many readers) more moving kind of transcendent quality than Lawrence was capable of expressing (Ellen and Jasper are spending the night in the open before they are to be married on the following day):

"Your fingers on my neck and on my throat, they are soft, Ellie, like feathers, and they rub gentle-like up and down . . . ."

"Or our own house sometime, that belongs to us and all of our own stock in the pastures. Three quick taps on the farm bell to call you to dinner. A rose to grow up over the chimney. a row of little flowers down to the gate."

"Your skin is soft under the coat, and warm, and you are a fair sight to see. Your mouth is sweet to taste and your hair is sweet, and under the cloak is sweet . . . ."

"A strong house that the wind couldn't shake and the rain couldn't beat into."

"I will slip your arms outen the cloak and fold it around you. And me and you will sleep wrapped in the cloak."

"And I will never leave you, Jasper, forever, but I will stay with you all my enduren life and I will work for you all my days."

"It's sweet under the cloak . . . ."

She began to dream. Jasper was in her own body and in her mind, was but more of herself. She sank slowly down to the stone and to the leaves lying upon the stone, and the great bulk of the rock arose to take her. Dolomite stones shut over her and she was folded deeply into the inner being of the rock and she was strong with a strength to hold up mountains. Far away, as if it were beyond the earth, she heard a dog bark, a strange voice, none she had ever heard before, and long after that the sour odor of a fox came up from below the cliff and a little step went off in the leaves. Then Jasper whispered something that was lost in the substance of her dream, but she remembered a little of the sweet odor of the fox and the barking of the dog, but after a while they were mingled with Jasper's unheard whisper and went when she sank more deeply into the stone. After a while the stones were still again, and when she waked from sleeping daylight had come over the small valley that lay beyond the cliff.

This is a rural-Kentucky Song of Solomon, simpler than the Biblical and without its allegory, but in the same exultant, sensuous, and yet spiritual tone. This passage, and indeed all of Miss Roberts' work, is indicative of a wholesome aspect of part of our country (still present and too often overlooked)—the will to live and to enjoy simple, innocent living—that may be more important for our survival than any other. And those of us who have been reared in a rural environment can testify that, though the language and the actions of the Ellens and the Jaspers in Miss Roberts' works are somewhat heightened for dramatic purposes, the artistic rendering is a poetizing but not an exaggeration. The spirit of our rural folk is essentially like that of the characters in Miss Roberts' fiction rather than like that of the Joads and the Jeeter Lesters. Miss Roberts is indeed a realist, but a poetic, not a photographic, realist.

By way of summarizing the qualities of Miss Roberts' style considered in this chapter, it may be well to quote a passage (there are many such) combining all of them and to analyze it in some detail:

Her [Ellen's] laughter with Elmer was carried from one meeting to the next, always near the surface of their being, and for his leading she stepped wantonly in the quadrille and beat the rhythms with her head and shoulders. Or for Mr. Townley, who was identified with his music, her manner was an extension of the ripple of her dress, and when she went dancing down his guitar notes between their eyes passed the flash of all laughter, music and dancing made one in the moment, each chord a thread or a ribbon on which she walked with light feet as she twinkled down the dancing floor. His wife with their many children would be standing along the wall. Dorine on her side would tell the confidences of her liking for Elmer, dwelling on each to relive its significance, so that their two likings and wishes, Elmer's reticent and unformed, Dorine's eager, unshy, realized, flowed over her and around her as if she were its musical core. With Elmer she made laughter, each complementing the other, each playing a little with the fountain of his own need. In their kiss the froth of the high tide of summer arose and frayed. It was as if they sang a come-hither-come-hither to all the summer and all the country side.

In the first place, the lively and sparkling rhythm of the sentences is appropriate for the gay music of the country dance. Then, musical language is woven into a series of metaphors, in which the characters merge, in varying degrees of completeness (each degree subtly defined) with each other, with the music, with nature, and with the idealized essences happily incarnated (and thus effecting a kind of cosmic unity) in this innocent merrymaking. Ellen and Elmer are united in their laughter and dancing only

"near the surface of their being." Ellen's merging with
Mr. Townley is far more nearly complete, because (though
they could not express their feeling) music is for both of
them a vital medium of aspiration—that is, in the sense
of their yielding themselves to it until they become inseparable from it. Mr. Townley "was identified with his
music," for both himself and for Ellen, and Ellen, too,
becomes so identified through dancing to it that "she went
dancing down his guitar notes." This mutual identification
with the music enables them (at a higher level) to appre-
hend, indeed to become united with, "the flash of all
laughter, dancing, and music made one in the moment."
This centainly must be something like the Platonic essences, genuinely apprehended, even if Plato would have
condemned this festive type of approach. The phrase,
"made one in the moment," implies that the essences—
through the purity, innocence, and perfection of the festivities—have been both ideally apprehended and temporally
illustrated. In other words, there has been (figuratively,
but in a sense more than figuratively) aspiration upward
and a return incarnation, both "made one in the moment."
But that is not all; the incarnation is specifically elaborated.
Miss Roberts never leaves the nature of the relation between the supernal and the mundane in a "misty mid-
region of Weir," as Poe always did. To be sure, an attempt
to make explicit the exact details of the incarnated essences
involves the risk of failure; it is much easier to evoke the
mood and leave it at that. But Miss Roberts is never afraid
to elaborate: for her, as for Berkeley, there is no dichotomy
between the physical and the spiritual, although, as an
artist she seems to reverse Berkeley by transforming what
is called the spiritual into the physical, the physicalizing
which we have called the artistic word made flesh. In this

identification with Mr. Townley's music and, then, with the essence of "all laughter, music, and dancing," Ellen "dances down his guitar notes . . . , each chord a thread or ribbon on which she walked with light feet as she twinkled down the dancing floor." So complete is Ellen's immersion in the music that even the memory of previous conversations—Dorine and Elmer telling her of their love for each other—"flowed over her and around her as if she were its musical core." Then, as in a musical composition, a note is repeated and developed. In her laughter with Elmer (already mentioned), each was "playing a little with the fountain of his own need." This fountain, their own buoyant youth and fertility, becomes identified with the abounding fertility of nature ("the high tide of summer"). The equation for defining the significance of their kiss, then, might be arranged in this way:

their human fertility: fertility of nature=their kiss: "froth of the high tide of summer."

That is, their kiss is a genuine but light expression of their fullness: "near the surface of their being." But for Miss Roberts, in that part of her philosophy which approaches a kind of pantheism, the fertility of mankind and the fertility of nature are really one, so that when she says, "In their kiss the froth of the high tide of summer arose and frayed," she is uttering what is for her a truth that goes far deeper than a pretty metaphor. Whatever his own philosophy, the reader feels the emotional impact of this whole passage.

This is the festive expression of nature, but implicit in it is a complete and very serious and ethical philosophy of life. The final sentence relates this whole scene to Shakespeare's Forest of Arden: the rural-Kentucky Arden has much of the same kind of magic enchantment to be found in Shakespeare's, but seems more realistic and, in relation to the rest of her work, seems to say something like this: As human beings we don't have to go to a never-never-land to find the poetry of true happiness; it can be found in reality—if reality is kept simple and wholesome and close to the rhythms of nature, and, above all, if we really understand what she says in the concluding sentences of *Jingling in the Wind*:

Life is from within, and thus the noise outside is a wind blowing in a mirror. But love is a royal visitor which that proud ghost, the human spirit, settles in elegant chambers and serves with the best.

✦✶✦✶✦✶✦✶✦✶✦✶✦✶✦✶✦✶✦✶✦✶✦✶✦✶✦✶✦✶✦✶

4. *The Theme Stated: Major Motif:*

The Time of Man *and* The Great Meadow

✦✶✦✶✦✶✦✶✦✶✦✶✦✶✦✶✦✶✦✶✦✶✦✶✦✶✦✶✦✶

1. *The Time of Man*

As Miss Roberts says in her unpublished notes for *The Time of Man*:

Two ways seem always open to me as one having such environmental influences as mine, and such mental and physical equipment. One way the way of satire, the other the way of symbolism working through poetic realism.*

She was indeed to demonstrate in *Jingling in the Wind* and *He Sent Forth a Raven* her mastery of satire, but even these contain elements of poetic realism, and all her other books are primarily devoted to this very difficult combination, a true blending, of poetry and realism; though she always succeeds when she uses this difficult method, she manages it most skillfully in her two greatest books, *The Time of Man* and *The Great Meadow,* which are to be considered in this chapter. Such a method, of course, is possible only to one who believes that poetic beauty is the most important aspect of reality without ignoring undeniably sordid and ugly facts. Though Miss Roberts acknowledges that tragedy is an important and real part of human existence, she believes also that it can be transcended in the no less actual and immanent realm of spirit. She would have scorned the belief (widespread in modern literature, criticism, philosophy, and theology) that spirit is as subjective as emotion—an imaginary realm deriving its reality solely from its therapeutic value in "organizing" our lives. Spirit for Miss Roberts is just as clear a fact as matter, and, as we have seen earlier, much of her imagery is devoted to physicalizing the spiritual, not as a linguistic exercise after the fashion of the logical positivists, but as an expression of the real nature of spirit, which is too often hidden from us by the vagueness of our spiritual language. She did not have to trace the word *spirit* back to its etymological source in the word *breath;* for her, spirit, the eternal, is as close and as natural as breathing. It has seemed necessary to recall this much from earlier discussions in this book to introduce a detailed study of *The Time of Man* and *The Great Meadow*.

Although these two books were not written or published consecutively (*The Time of Man* was her first book of prose and *The Great Meadow* her fourth), they are treated together here for two reasons: (1) in them we find her two most memorable characters, Ellen and Diony, and the most intense and fullest expression of the theme—the primacy of the human spirit—that prevails in all her work; (2) this power of the human spirit is expressed in these books in a manner that approaches the epic. Each book indeed is a kind of Odyssey of the human spirit—the wanderings of Ellen and Jasper and their children in *The Time of Man* and of Diony, Berk, and their company in *The Great*

Meadow exhibit an endurance and heroism comparable to that of Ulysses, and in the same noble spirit, although the modern wanderers (except for a little philosophy learned from her father by Diony) are uneducated country folk. And the refreshing quality in Miss Roberts' modern variants of the *Odyssey* is that she gives no ironic parody to indicate modern degeneracy, after the fashion of Joyce, Pound, and Eliot; instead, the comparison is suggested by the beautiful poetic language in which the tale is told, the elemental vigor and heroism of the characters, the emphasis on their closeness to the Earth-Mother, the Goddess Terra, from contact with whom their vigor is derived and their simple dignity enhanced even against this vast cosmic background. The heroic suffering and endurance of Berk Jarvis during his long captivity among the Indians and his successful escape and return are especially Odyssean in character, but there are various other specific parallels which will be discussed later. Miss Roberts' unpublished notes indicate that the analogy suggested in this paragraph was intentional. Of *The Time of Man* she says:

It was, I think, in the summer of 1919 that I began to think of the wandering tenant farmer of our region as offering a symbol for an Odyssey of Man as wanderer buffeted about by the fates and the weathers.*

Of *The Great Meadow*:

It was a mythical country into which they went . . . . Their farewells in Virginia were known to be final or epic farewells.*

But "mythical" means simply poetic, never exaggerated. The characters are never sentimentalized or made faultless. Though the realism is heightened poetically, these characters appear as we who have lived among them know country folk are, and certainly must have been as far back as the early pioneers of *The Great Meadow:* men of flesh and blood with strong senses and a passionate love of life, but a life in which spirit is just as real as flesh—spirit in them, as one of Miss Roberts' characters says, "crying out of flesh," at times with extreme weariness but more often with the joy of living—always indeed in joy or sorrow, with a strong will to live.

Convincing characters, of course, are made so not only by being true to life, but by the technical skill with which they are presented in a convincing plot structure, from a dramatic point of view (or perhaps various points of view), and by all the other devices of technique that contribute to a successful story. Such craftsmanship Miss Roberts always provides—in *The Time of Man* and *The Great Meadow* better than in any of her other books, although her standard is high in all of her work. Her mastery of diction and imagery has been discussed in an earlier chapter and is mentioned here only incidentally, as it contributes to the understanding of other broader aspects of the technique in these books.

The general structural organization of these books is somewhat in the nature of a pageant. In fact, Miss Roberts frequently refers to a series of scenes as a pageant. Since the main characters—Ellen in *The Time of Man* and Diony in *The Great Meadow*—like their author, are Berkeleians, it is to be expected that life would appear to them as a kind of spiritual drama (a moving pageant) deriving its substance (since Spirit is the eternal substance) from the Mind of God. And, of course, these characters, through whose points of view in the main the stories are conveyed to us, are not spectators but the most important actors in the drama, being, from the Berkeleian standpoint, actors quite as much in their extensive and intricate reflections as in their physical actions. Because of this subtle and intense blending of philosophy and religion with point of view in these novels, the reader's pleasure is enhanced by a double pageant: (1) the simple but very dramatic life in which the heroines are involved, and (2) the rich psychological and spiritual drama of their reflections on this life. One can complain of the scarcity of action (the deliberate pace) of Miss Roberts' work only if he considers intense mental and spiritual drama inferior to physical. We are, to be sure, not without physical action, and when it occurs, it is presented in terse and vivid language—the barn-burning scene and the nocturnal whipping of Jasper in *The Time of Man* and some of the Indian fights in *The Great Meadow*. But these books are primarily studies of the main character in each, and physical action is appropriately subordinated.

The pageant of life in *The Time of Man* appears as a series of dramatic scenes, some idyllic and some tragic, the cumulative effect of which is very powerful even though there is no definite climactic organization in the tradition of the well-made novel. That the whole story is very carefully planned, however, is clear in the work itself and in her very explicit notes, which deserve quotation here:

It did not seem much longer than necessary as I contemplated it when I made it. The whole is not a plotted story in any artificial sense, though I follow form—a musical form, perhaps, a felt form, and in that view of it I and II form a sort of overture, containing, as they do, all of it in the end. All the incidents have not been chosen for the latter half of it, but there is to be no "return" except in a sense of art—no "return" in the externals of circumstance. The most that I care to do is to present the

sweet soil, the dirt of the ground, black earth, bitter and foul
of odor, full of worms, full of decay which is change, not evil
—black earth, ground, soil . . . and the other one, white sun,
light . . . these two forever mingled and mystically braided
together in life form, all life, which is Ellen . . . . Life is a
slender thread running like a ripple through the brown crust
of the earth.*

Life or spirit, then, as concentrated in, symbolized by,
Ellen is the main concern, but this symbolism, through
Ellen as the symbol, is made as solid and rich as the "sweet
soil" and as clear as the "white sun." The story, therefore,
is focussed on (presented through) Ellen's consciousness,
and the external events and the other characters (though
interesting in themselves) remain subordinated to her.
These events and characters, though subordinated, are perfectly clear, but they derive their clarity, and their dramatic
quality is intensified, from their being presented to us
through the point of view of one so intensely alive as she.
Even the trial of Jasper for barn-burning—something
which Dreiser might have stretched into most of a volume,
as he did the trial in *An American Tragedy*—is treated very
briefly, and we get news of the trial only as the report
reaches Ellen, who stayed at home while it occurred, the
significance of the trial in the story of course being her
reactions to it. The "musical form," then, follows the gradual maturing of Ellen's personality (her spirit), the "overture" being the presentation of her childhood through
adolescence, and the later "return" her reflections on this
early life as her own children are growing up.

It is in this way that content and form (theme and embodiment of theme) are so closely welded together in the
work of Miss Roberts, and never in any of her other books
quite so much as in *The Time of Man*. The vitality of

Ellen's spirit, of course, is that of Miss Roberts herself. Miss Roberts was born and as a child lived in poverty almost as oppressive as Ellen's, and overcame this and many later difficulties with the same kind of spiritual self-assertion. Ellen's shouting her joy in living to the hills—her "I am Ellen!"—and her recovery from sorrow by this strong awareness of the mystery and glory of self-identity—all this, if we may believe those who knew Miss Roberts, was a reflection of a similar exultant and unconquerable spirit which made her continue to write beautiful and important fiction and verse as long as she lived, although she was in constant pain from an incurable disease during the last years of her life. But this closeness to her characters never means, as it too often means in the work of Thomas Wolfe, an uncritical autobiographical absorption into the content of the story. As she says again in her notes for *The Time of Man*:

Through an identity of myself with the actors, goes still and always a condition of aesthetic detachment, aware and unaware —at once within the action, and aware of the tragedy and beauty of all-enclosing form.*

Miss Roberts' skill in handling point of view is exhibited from the very beginning of the book. Ellen's father, having broken away from the caravan of nomadic country folk, has settled down to work for a farmer; Ellen, separated from her closest friend, Tessie, thinks that her father has stopped for only a short while, and reflects thus: "She would have something to tell Tessie when her father's wagon overtook the others. She recited in her mind the story of the adventure as she would tell it." Since Ellen is eager to interest Tessie, this recital is very naturally and dramatically given in

Ellen's own language, including bits of imagined conversation between her and Tessie. In this way the necessary exposition for the situation at the beginning of the story is given.

Similarly, all the other exposition in the story comes economically and naturally through conversation or through Ellen's thoughts, which are dramatized by being presented usually in her language interspersed with bits of remembered conversation. Ellen thinks of what has happened, sometimes looks forward to what will come (or to what she hopes will come). As Miss Roberts says in her notes, this story "could never be an analysis of society or of a social stratum because it keeps starkly within one consciousness, and that one being not of an analytical nature or a 'conscious' consciousness. There is a tryst here, a bargain, between two, and two only, and these two are Ellen and Life." But Miss Roberts certainly does not make a fetish of the limited point of view and does not hesitate to assist the characters' thoughts with omniscient-author explanations when they are necessary for clarity. The omniscient-author explanations, however, never take the subject as a text and wander off into vaguely moralizing digressions; they are limited to a presentation of psychological processes which the character is experiencing but could not express in her own words or is perhaps unaware of. In other words, such explanations are most frequently a rendering of the poetized essence of Ellen's thoughts, in harmony with the poetic realism that is the tone of the whole story.

Thoughts of certain parts of the past appear repeatedly in Ellen's memory, but the method is never repetitive because the past is always recalled under different circumstances, which throw new light on the events themselves and on the development of Ellen's spirit. In fact, the double drama mentioned earlier is for two reasons especially impressive in these scenes unfolding new and significant details that have occurred but are revealed only in the recollection: (1) the dramatic interest of the events themselves is enhanced by this gradual revelation, and (2) the mental drama of Ellen's reactions to an event at the time of its occurrence may be enhanced by its being later recalled in her suffering mind as identical with some crisis in her own life. Such an event is the suicide of Ellen's neighbor, Miss Cassie MacMurtrie, when she (Cassie) became aware of her husband's infidelity. When the terrible event occurs, we are not given many details; the main point is that when, at the coroner's inquest, Ellen is asked whether she could give any reason for the suicide, her truthful answer in the negative is dictated by her deep love for Jonas, who is her first serious sweetheart.

Jonas enveloped her mind stirring in the farthest corners of her being and she could not think why one would quit life. A great will to live surged up in her, including the entire assembly— the coroner, Squire Dorsey, Henry, Miss Tod, Mr. Al, all of them. They would all live. She was living. Only life was comprehensible and actual, present. She was herself life. It went with her wherever she went, holding its abode in her being. She was alive, she was alive.

Then, after Jonas jilts her and she has worried until she hates him passionately enough if he were present to kill him (with the butcher knife which she is using to cut meat for supper),

a great strength came to her that made her hands tremble under their grip. Then words that were printed into her memory long ago began to run forward, and this hour lost its identity before the force of another, long past, until she swam back into the past as if she were an apparition, without presence of its own. The voices spoke aloud, voices of men, filling the room with their terror, speaking sharply, speaking with authority or fright.

"How to get 'er down . . . ."

"Cut the rope . . . ."

"No, don't cut the rope. She might be still a-liven."

"Bring up that lamp, Ellen."

Then follows a much fuller account of the discovery of Miss Cassie's body than was given at the time when the suicide occurred, bits of conversation like the above and Ellen's agonized attempt "to free herself of the specters, to push aside the old event and disentangle her own" appearing alternately; the speakers (as often in Miss Roberts' impressionistic rendering of crucial scenes) are not identified, apparently to increase the dramatic concentration on the center of interest. The recurrence of this tragic episode in Ellen's memory in sharp detail (and the revelation to the reader of details not given earlier) is especially appropriate here because Ellen's grief-stricken condition (in the intensity of her love for Jonas) is now almost as desperate as was that of the betrayed Miss Cassie:

Jonas had been in her thought too long so that her very breath had grown up around him. He was even then tearing a pain through her breast. She saw even more vividly the face on the floor, two men leaning over it, one preparing it for life and the other for death; and then the coroner, "Yes, she tied the rope herself, that's plain" . . . . She was leaning over Miss Cassie as she lay on the floor—Ellen and Miss Cassie and no other. She leaned over the dead face until she was merged with its likeness, looking into the bulging eyes, the blackened mouth, and the fallen jaw. She went down the stairs and out the door of the house . . . . She was still merged with the face . . . . She wandered over the rise of the pasture hill; there was a turmoil in the fog of the earth, in the dew of the soil, in the sweat of the planet. Her feet wandered to the old barn and over into the edge of the marsh.

But to attain the dramatic, Miss Roberts can, if the portrayal of Ellen demands it, dispense with both reality, either tragic or idyllic, and Ellen's reflections on such reality. Ellen's occasional indulgence even in light fantasy can be kept dramatic. One of the most charming passages in the book is that describing Ellen's reverie (during the happy days before Jonas jilts her) as she rides in the buggy with the faithful but homely Sebe, who courts her with only the vaguest of hope but with as much ardor as his bashful nature can muster. Sebe has been describing the prosperous little farm they would have; we get the picture as it comes out in Ellen's reverie:

Ellen saw in her mind the little farm beyond the creek with ducks floating out in a stately procession on the water holes and the hens cackling their high barbed songs in the bright mornings, and a quick woman, herself perhaps, gathering in the eggs and selling them for coins and spending them for a disc plow or a binder or a horse rake, and the wind blew brightly, sprightly in clear mornings, cool and bright mornings, and the little house would stand off in the bottom among cornfields, crisp cornfields . . . . She seldom went inside the house, her life moving outside among the poultry and the shifting coins, viewing the clock-work of the barnyards and the plenty of the cribs. If she went inside the house it was Jonas who came there. Sebe kept remote in the picture as the mere organizer and mover of the pageant, for she could not endure the sight of his ears . . . if they persisted in holding a place, then she smote the pageant with light words, tore away hencoops and barns with gusts of laughter . . . and sent the geese and ducks scurrying with her hard scorn. But most often Sebe's offending members kept out of the picture or retreated humbly, having been caught overstepping, and then she helped build back the barnyard she had demolished by asking the price of ducks or the annual yield of feathers.

This passage maintains with great skill the exact relation of fantasy to reality that would be appropriate to Ellen's maturing personality. The prosperity in this brightly definite but easily dispelled "pageant" of her imagination is quite different from the poverty of her actual experience, but the imagined farm is only an idealization of the kind of locale and life that she knew, in contrast to her dreams as a little girl of faraway places that she had seen pictures of and read about in Tessie's geography. Even in this light, witty passage, we are reminded of the intensity of Ellen's personality, as when Sebe's ugly ears appeared in the picture, she "tore away hencoops and barns with gusts of laughter . . . and sent the geese and ducks scurrying with her hard scorn."

Ellen's memory is at times aided by her imagination, so that she may recall portions of the past which, though they occurred, she has never actually experienced. Her mother has told her so often of her six little brothers and sisters, all dead before she was born, that at several points in the story she recalls them, mentioning their names as if she had known and loved each one individually. She lives in imagined memory most intimately with their tragically brief lives towards the end of the book as, with her own children about her—after the death of one of them and her father—she recalls her own life compounded (according to the human lot) of joy and sorrow.

Or hearing Hen's foxhorn, a hoarse note without music, a rough throaty call, she would wonder that the swift cry of a horn had once gone into her like a glad spear, and she would penetrate her own history, into memories long habitually forgotten. It had seemed forever that she had travelled up and down roads, having no claim upon the fields but that which was snatched as she passed. Back of that somewhere in a dim darkened dream like a prenatal vision, she saw a house under some nut trees, a place where she lived, but as clearly seen as this she could see her brother Davie and the others, the more shadowy forms of the older children although all of them were dead before she was born. So that this house with the odor about it of nut shells was all imbedded now in the one dream that extended bedimmed into some region where it merged with Nellie's memories. Life began somewhere on the roads, traveling after the wagons where she had claim upon all the land and no claim, all at once, and where what she knew of the world and what she wanted of it sparkled and glittered and ran forward quickly as if it would always find something better.

All of Ellen's reflections upon the past help to unify the story; this one especially, since towards the end of the book it gives a retrospective summary of her life and emphasizes once more the theme of the story, life, now as when she was a child, "running forward quickly as if it would always find something better." Remembrance of things past here is never an escape but an incentive to go forward ("To strive, to seek, to find, and not to yield").

And so at the end of the book as at the beginning, the wanderers are on the road seeking something better. After Jasper has been cruelly beaten by the hooded group of men (under the mistaken assumption that he has burned a barn), he, Ellen, and the children pack all their belongings that they can get on the wagon, leave the rest behind, and drive down the road, not knowing their destination. Some of the children talk about the mystery and beauty of the stars on this clear night, and Dick, the studious one, tells them that they can learn all about this subject and everything else, as he intends to do, in books. Dick is the child in whom, as we have learned earlier, Ellen "felt her own being . . . pushed outward against the great over-lying barrier, the enveloping dark." Ellen's feeling toward Dick, indeed, may be taken as a symbol of the courage of this whole family, facing what at best for them could be only a formidable unknown. And, just as truly, the universal appeal of this whole book (and almost all Miss Roberts' other work) should be its artistic availability as a symbol of the courage which enables most of the human race unceasingly to "push outward against the great over-lying barrier, the enveloping dark."

2. *The Great Meadow*

In *The Great Meadow* as in *The Time of Man,* the great pageant of life is rendered dramatically through the consciousness of the heroine. The material in *The Great Meadow* could have been exploited, after the fashion of almost all historical novels, for a great deal of physical action. The setting of the story is just prior to and during the American Revolution, and it deals with the early settlement of Kentucky and brings in historical characters like Boone, Logan, Harrod, Major George Rogers Clark, and others. All this material is used mainly to throw light on the spiritual development of the heroine, Diony, with the physical action usually presented in swift, impressionistic sketches, but the concentration on Diony is not so great as that on Ellen (in *The Time of Man*), because the minor characters in *The Great Meadow* contribute more to the great theme of the primacy of man's spirit than do those in the earlier book. Diony's husbands, Berk Jarvis and Evan Muir, are men of a heroic mould no less great than that of the great historical character—superior to Ellen's tenant farmer husband, Jasper, though Jasper, except for one errant period, was a good man. And Diony's mother-in-law, Elvira, belongs among the truly great pioneer women. The fictional characters, indeed, are hardly to be distinguished from the historical ones because they are all true to the spirit of that great age and equally vivid as Miss Roberts portrays them. Of the compelling origins of this book, she says in her unpublished notes:

I saw these people coming over the Trace, some of them coming early when there were hundreds of miles and scarcely broken forests to be passed. The drama was brief but it was full and picturesque. I thought it would be an excellent labor if one might gather all these threads, these elements, into one strand, if one might draw these strains into one person and bring this person over the Trace and through the Gateway in one symbolic journey. The names of the persons I have projected were not written on the census taken at Fort Harrod in 1777 although I placed them there, as present at the time. They are the spiritual consummation of all who came the way they came . . . . *

Except for a brief section entitled, "An Interval," to tell of those who lived at Fort Harrod when Diony and Berk arrived there, all this wealth of background material never delays the swift progress of the story. In this book, even more than in *The Time of Man,* may be noted the swift and inexorable flowing of time referred to in Chaper II. Especially is this evident as Diony is growing up. These two statements, for example, within three pages:

Diony felt the year go past and once, for a moment, she heard the great ticking. There was war in Boston, the colony fighting the King's men. Some said that all the colonies would snatch themselves free . . . . The year had spun around; war on the coast; Nancy Webb with a clover leaf in her shoe, meeting Sam in a path.

In this last sentence three aspects of life (grammatically equated in the sentence) impress themselves on Diony as equally significant: the swift passing of time; war; young love (Nancy is significant because she praises Diony's beauty and first makes her aware of it).

The skill with which Miss Roberts lets one scene merge into another (as an indication of fleeting time) is especially well illustrated in a description of life at the fort. Diony has been wishing to see a beautiful river a few miles to the north of the fort, but the trip is too dangerous while the hostile Indians are around.

Her pleasure of a river could wait. She knew herself to be the beginning of a new world. All about her were beginnings. The beginnings of fields took form as the trees were cleared away and the canelands plowed, and the beginnings of roads appeared where a man made a trace by walking to a stream, another following and another, and added to these the footmarks of dogs and horses. She learned to fashion garments of buckskin for a man, working softness into the stiff hide and sewing the seams together with a leather strip of elkskin. Often there was dancing in the stockade. A fiddler would fling out a reel or a jig and the young women would gather in the dusk. Then the fiddler would call for dancers and the men would come, not caring whether they did or not, but dancing nevertheless. Then there were gay ironic curses, compounded of danger and scarcity and the need a man has for revel . . . . There was dancing every night while the fiddler stayed there.

The next week a preacher came, one who had visited the fort at Boonesborough and preached there. He seized upon the rhythm that swayed the fort in dancing and turned it to the uses of religion and he called for repentance, saying that wickedness was rife there. Then there was singing where there had been dancing, and there was a hearty flowing of tears . . . .

Besides the swift passing of time, indicated especially in the movement from dancing to religion, the multifariousness and great importance of this frontier life are caught up in this simple summary passage, the summary, as always in Miss Roberts' writing, being composed, not of general statements, but of sharp, concrete details (even to the exact manner of making a new road). As part of all this life, Diony "knew herself to be the beginning of a new world," and so, the implication is, did all the others there. And how did they go about fulfilling this great destiny? Most American historical novels would have it mainly a matter of grand marches and thrilling Indian fights. And, of course, *The Great Meadow* contains Indian fights because these were a part of the reality—but a negative and destructive part. The positive beginnings of this new world were made, as the next few sentences describe so vividly, in the simple, everyday activities of the fort. And of equal importance with this simple but heroic labor is the recreation of gay music and dancing, the rhythm of which merges, by the preacher's skillful maneuvering, into the emotional outburst of a religious revival. There is, however, none of the easy satire which in much modern fiction has been directed at such revivals; Miss Roberts knew that evangelical religion has been a very important and, on the whole, constructive force in the new world.

The typical passage cited above, then, clearly indicates that the swift passing of time in Miss Roberts' work is not

the tyranny of meaningless time in a Godless world, which
has become a characteristic belief of a great part of Western
civilization (cf. Percy Wyndham Lewis, *Time and Western
Man*). For her and her characters, in spite of the pressure
of time, there is a sense of significant achievement—a structure erected on the foundation of the ever-present past, as
Diony realized on her wedding day when she was leaving
her parents (never to see or hear from them again, as she
knew) to go with Berk over the mountains and into the
distant wilderness:

Suddenly, in the tinkling of the bells [on the horses], she
knew herself as the daughter of many, going back through Polly
Brook through the Shenandoah Valley and the Pennsylvania
clearings and roadways to England, Methodists and Quakers,
small farmers and weavers, going back through Thomas Hall
to tidewater farmers and owners of land. In herself then an
infinity of hopes welled up, vague desires and holy passions for
some better place, infinite regrets and rending farewells
mingled and lost in the blended inner tinkle and clatter. These
remembrances were put into her own flesh as a passion, as if
she remembered all her origins, and remembered every sensa-
tion her forebears had known, and in the front of all this mass
arose her present need for Berk and her wish to move all the
the past outward now in conjunction with him.

The merging of the past, present, and future is skillfully
combined in this passage with the merging of the outer
physical world and the inner world of the spirit (this latter
in the beautiful symbolism of the tinkling bells blended
with the "inner tinkle and clatter.")

The temporal effects in Miss Roberts' style frequently
remind us of Thackeray's method, so ably described by
Percy Lubbock in *The Craft of Fiction*. (The narrative

method of Thackeray, as Lubbock says, is panoramic and pictorial, subordinating instance and occasion to broad effect, giving swift and piercing glimpses but very little continuous display of a constituted scene.) In *The Great Meadow*, for example, Berk's account of his adventures in the wilderness when he returns to Five Oaks to court Diony is rendered impressionistically after the manner of much of Thackeray's narrative:

Back then, Berk told of a succession of single combats, a man against a man or against two. Gowdy grappled with his man once and flung him over an embankment and emptied his rifle into his side while he lay. He himself, intent on Gowdy's danger, had neglected his own, and a redskin was upon him to lay hold of his rifle and wrench it from his hand. The crash of rifles was incessant, the cries of the dying, the shouts of the leaders, the war-cries of the savages, curses and groans and the stab of the knife.

But Miss Roberts is not limited to this swift, panoramic kind of narrative, as Percy Lubbock has shown Thackeray in the main to be; she is equally good at expanding with sharp detail the single scene before the reader as the occasion demands. Consider the scene in which Diony and Elvira are attacked by the two Indians, Elvira being killed and Diony critically wounded. Since this scene is one of the most important in the book (most of the rest of the story—especially Berk's long journey to get revenge— growing out of it), Miss Roberts builds up to it with considerable detail and then describes at length the heroic struggle of the two women to keep the Indians out of the hut. There is none of Thackeray's awkwardness in expanding the individual scene; on the contrary, the dramatic physical action is handled with great skill and then is succeeded (as one would expect of a convinced Berkeleian and an artist) immediately, without a change of paragraph, by a dramatic description of Diony's consciousness just before she fades into unconsciousness from the blow by the Indian's hatchet:

Then Diony saw the hatchet that leaped over her own head, and a great blow fell as a stiffness that tightened through her being and shut pain out . . . . She dreamed of her home in Virginia, of sitting beside Betty in the half-light under the high window, drawing threads of linen off the distaff to the whirr of the great wheel . . . . There was sweetness and security in the dark room, a great rain falling outside and crashing over the dog alley. Then she waked a little out of the pain that throbbed over her and stiffened her head to a tight sheaf that crushed her thought . . . . A light down floated over the dark of her understanding and blew without consequence across a great dark space, and she caught at the first fleck of it which signified that she must close the door. A second lighter thistledown drifted across the dark . . . which informed her that Elvira was dead, that she lay scalped on the floor . . . she tried once again to close her will about the necessity to live, to arise and close the door, but she was enveloped in greater darkness and her pain turned back upon some inner and mightier frame, which had been as yet untouched and untested, and asked it again for some kindlier sign, some final explanation.

Psychologically, this passage renders with great effectiveness the twilight zone (fantasy punctuated with brief glimpses of reality) of a consciousness fading out after a severe wound; but it also goes far deeper than this: the Berkeleian philosophy and religion—as the "inner and mightier frame"—are made to appear the inevitable and solid refuge after the preliminary escape into childhood memories. Technique and theme are completely merged, and, quite unlike his experience with Thackeray, the reader is not aware of the author, but of the immediate and moving drama—the mental quite as cogent as the physical.

And there is another important difference between Thackeray's narrative method and Miss Roberts'. Because of his desire to present a whole complex society, Thackeray subordinates his hero or heroine (if any of his characters can be so called) to the great panorama. In *The Time of Man,* Miss Roberts' method is just the reverse of this: the panorama or pageant (though not a whole society) is there, but it is subordinated to the heroine; in fact, it exists mainly for her sake—that is, in the technique of the novel. In *The Great Meadow,* as we have seen, there is more emphasis on the other characters, more of an attempt to delineate a whole society, but still the consciousness of Diony is the main focus of interest, the technique wedded to the Berkeleian philosophy.

Still another important difference between Thackeray's impressionism and that of Miss Roberts is that she mingles more conversation in her rapid sketches than does Thackeray. In fact, the summary scene in Miss Roberts' work often ends in a series of short sentences that are snatches of conversation, in which the speakers are not identified. The swift impressionistic effect is still there, since in the pressure of time there is no pause to identify the speakers, but the scene is sharply dramatized by the conversation. Such a conversational ending is analogous to the ending of a section of a musical composition with a swift movement of the notes, each small group related to, partly repeating, those coming before, and yet advancing the theme always with variations—somewhat like the movement of waves coming into the shore—overlapping, sometimes seeming to retreat, and yet moving forward gracefully and inevitably to the pause at the end of the movement. This flowing conversational-summary ending to a scene, one of Miss Roberts' favorite devices, is well illustrated by the following, in which the marriage of Berk and Diony by a Methodist minister, when the Virginia law requires a Church of England minister, is sharply criticized by some of the guests just before the bridal couple leave for the wilderness:

"It's only Tories would hold what Stafford holds," a voice whispered.

"If any doubt has come to trouble any man in Albemarle, we'll go away now, this hour," Berk said. "Married we are and married we'll go away from here. We won't have to prove the law of the Tories against we get in the wilderness."

"Hit's a wilderness marriage. Let be." One or two spoke.

"Married for the wilderness."

"Don't trouble their souls with doubt."

"It's a miracle; the old law come back."

"Married fit for the wilderness."

"Without law, but no matter."

"Quiet! A new day. No matter."

"Amen, amen, amen."

Miss Roberts seems to be referring to this impressionistic-conversational technique and indicating the exalted nature of its conception when she writes in an isolated note on *The Great Meadow* of her desire, "To find the Greek inevitables in nature all around us, whatever the station of life presented. Hence the chorus of voices crying from among the 'gossips.' "*

Diony, like Ellen, often seems to see herself as if from an outside point, sometimes by the unaided projection of her imagination, as in the following vision which came to her on the long and trying journey across the mountains to Fort Harrod in Kentucky:

Viewing the heels of the horses as they swam ahead of her against the green of the grassy road, she saw themselves on the way, three men and a woman, as if she saw all from outside point, near but apart.

Again her vision of herself may derive from another's report, as when, a few months after the Indian attack that was fatal to Elvira and almost to her, she "heard report of herself by the mouth of Lawrence," one of the settlers, who had heard it while on a journey among the Indians:

Two white squaws, herself one of them, were named over and over. She was a white squaw among the Long Knives, then. She saw herself from the distance, a long dim vista reaching down from Ohio. She saw a white squaw, a strong young woman with rich life in her, a faint red under her sunburnt cheeks, her linsey dress casting a dull shadow in the dim cabin. She, the white squaw, walked over the earth floor and went into the deeper shadows beside the fireplace.

Diony, like Ellen, though very modest, is aware of her own beauty and vitality, and is momentarily pleased that the Indians should find her attractive—so pleased that she adopts the Indians' point of view in this vision and sees herself as a white squaw. But the tragic memory is quickly resumed as she, the "white squaw," "walked over the earth floor and went into the deeper shadows beside the fireplace," in the hut where the terrible event occurred, and the brief vision is swiftly ended, the next scene shifting forward to the resumption of her work in the fort after the healing of her wound.

In portraying the psychology of Diony, Miss Roberts uses one method which she does not use in presenting Ellen: in her grief for Berk, who has been absent almost two years on his mission to kill Indians, and whom everybody but herself believes to be dead, Diony still clings to a desperate hope and talks to Berk as if he were present and another Berk had left her:

"He forgot me when the year was only half done," she said, addressing Berk, asking for redress. "He went off after revenge, to kill Indians to satisfy the death of his mother." She drew out the thread and wound it on the spindle, her presence turned toward Berk as if she would still recount to him all that concerned herself. "He forgot our child I had here in the wilderness." Berk was bade to witness Berk, to blame and despise. She flung out one long sobbing cry for this and another to follow it when she realized the crookedness of her thought, wailing then without reason, but the tears and the cries of the child stopped her.

In this outburst of grief associated with the delusion of the two Berks, Diony shows a properly human emotion that does not in the least detract from the heroism of her character. Boone himself is said to have wept on occasion, as no doubt on that recorded in real life in his diary, from which Miss Roberts quotes as follows: "My footsteps have often been marked with blood—lost two darling sons and a brother [killed by the Indians] .... Many dark and sleepless nights have I been ... separated from the cheerful society of men ... an instrument ordained to settle the wilderness."* In fact, these characters (both fictional and historic), though presented most convincingly, are so heroic and independent that the primacy of spirit in them becomes almost transcendental self-reliance instead of Christian faith in an all-provident God. Though due allegiance is acknowledged here and there to Berkeley's "great Mover and Author of Nature"—the supreme mind-substance—yet Boone (especially) takes on something of the nature of a demigod, who brings order out of chaos in nature. "Boone the leader," as Miss Roberts says in her notes, "to take us through Chaos," and in her unfinished poem that was to be called "Daniel Boone and the Long Hunters," Boone achieves god-like feats:

> *At last he dug the Mammoth Cave.*
> *He spaded out the rock and the air,*
> *And he said now let it be dark*
> *And it was so in there.*
>
> *And he divided the dark in two*
> *And the bright half he called light—*
> *That's where we get night and day.*
> *The bright half he called light.**

The earth aspect of a tendency toward pantheism has been noted earlier in connection with Miss Roberts' primitivism—her characters at times (as in part of *The Buried Treasure*) being dependent on the ancient Earth-Mother, the Goddess Terra, of whom they become in their closeness to the earth mythical representatives. Especially in *The Great Meadow* (and to some extent in *The Time of Man*) another aspect of pantheism—man's being, as Emerson said, "part or parcel of God"—becomes evident. Diony, though always feeling her inferiority to Boone, longs as a child (like the Berkeleian God) to create rivers by thinking of them, and, as noted in Chapter II, in a sense does so by her heroic and spiritual life amid the rivers and canelands of pioneer Kentucky. From an early age, Diony felt "a sense of grandeur" in the great name given her; she

knew what name she bore, knew that Dione was a great goddess, taking rank with Rhea, and that she was the mother of Venus by Jupiter, in the lore of Homer, an older report than that of the legendary birth through the foam of the sea. She knew that Dione was one of the Titan sisters, the Titans being earth-men, children of Uranus and Terra. She had a scattered account of this as it came from between her father's ragged teeth as he bit at his quid and spat into the ashes . . . . She could scarcely piece the truths together to make them yield a thread of a story, but she held all in a chaotic sense of grandeur, being grateful for a name of such dignity. Her brothers called her Diny, and they were indeed earth-men, delving in the soil to make it yield bread and ridding the fields of stumps, plowing and burning the brush.

Though Diony and Ellen are always humble and modest enough, the emphasis in portraying them seems to be shifted toward exalting their spiritual independence— (in Diony especially) their almost transcendental semidivinity. There is no mention of dependence on Christ in either book: Ellen in a crisis turns to a stronger realization of her self-identity—"I am Ellen"; Diony in her supreme crisis turns deep within herself, to "some inner and mightier frame . . . as yet untouched and untested," which seems more like Emersonian self-reliance (though Berkeley, not Emerson, is the philosophical source) than like true Christian prayer.

In *The Great Meadow,* of course, there are several references to Berkeley's "great Mover and Author of Nature," but this God is more Aristotelian than Christian—which brings up another point about the nature of the religion evident in these books. Thomas Hall, Diony's father, speaks of the pagan gods and the Berkeleian "great Mover" as if both were real. When he has made up his mind not to try to prevent Diony from going into the wilderness with Berk, he talks to the young lovers about "the eternal aptitude of matter."

He talked of Rhea who, he said, signified succession and who was the mother of six gods: Jupiter, Vesta, Neptune, Ceres, Juno, and Pluto; and these took their fitting places in the heavens or in the earth or in the underworld of the ground. The great Mover and Author of Nature, he said, makes himself plain continually to the eyes of mankind through these visible signs . . . .

What, then, is the explanation of this puzzling combination of purely pagan gods and Berkeley's Great Mover, who is part Christian and part Aristotelian, and the pagan tendency toward pantheism—both in a kind of mystical glorification of Mother-Earth and in the semi-transcendental self-reliance of the main characters? Of course, neither Miss Roberts nor her characters deny the Christian God: the church attended by Ellen throughout her life, though it is not much emphasized, is certainly Christian, Berk and Diony are married by a Methodist minister, and the ministers who come periodically to Fort Harrod for religious revivals are of course Christian (in the Protestant evangelical tradition). As Miss Roberts says of *The Great Meadow:*

These people had not the faith in commerce which now colors all our religion . . . . One hears now, "It would not be on the market if it were not safe" . . . . The substitute was heroic solitude, trees, Faith.*

The extra-Christian tendencies in these characters, then, seem to exist, rather contradictorily, along with a simple belief in Christian doctrine as preached in the frontier Protestant churches of that period. Since even professional philosophers are not always consistent in their systems, the appearance of such contradictory beliefs in simple characters like those of Miss Roberts is certainly not unrealistic. These characters, furthermore, were the spiritual descendants of widely varying types of colonial Americans, as she indicates in her unpublished papers by tracing the interconnections among the characters in all her books in one big genealogical table and by the following note:

Tidewater gentry, scholarship, pagan lore, English communicants and Catholics, wealth and ease, family pride, these are met by sturdy races of tradesmen and farmers, Methodists —most despised sect of the century—Puritanic, Quaker, provident, holy, and aggressive, of great bodily vigor and a sturdy beauty. They were on fire with their own flame. These elements gathered into the parents of this woman, Diony.*

When we remember that Dante allows a pagan mythological character, Ulysses, in his *Inferno,* and Milton has pagan gods in his Hell in *Paradise Lost,* it hardly seems unlikely that an amateur scholar like Thomas Hall might believe in both the pagan gods and the Berkeleian Great Mover, and that his tendency toward deism, which was very influential in early Virginia, should be passed on as part of Diony's inheritance. As for Ellen, her lack of formal religious training in the home, both of her parents being very ignorant, and her closeness and sensitivity to nature would help to explain her strong tendency toward a kind of stoical, yet exultantly spiritual, self-assertion. Ellen, too, however, as Miss Roberts' genealogical table makes clear, has no less a rich and complex inheritance than Diony, though of course in Ellen, more ignorant than Diony (who had learned something of Berkeleian philosophy from her father), there is little more than an intuitive grasp of the spiritual reality which is so vitally important to them both.

At any rate, in Miss Roberts' characters, various, and even at times contradictory, types of belief have been welded together at white heat in the intense vitality of their personalities,—a reflection of the intense vitality, and an embodiment of the artistic triumph, of their author. In fact, as this whole chapter has attempted to demonstrate, Miss Roberts' artistic achievement, especially in the two books here considered, is the welding together of poetry and realism, technique and theme—psychology, philosophy, and religion not compartmentalized as is customary in this skeptical age, but completely unified as they are rendered in the intense consciousness of the heroines. Narrative technique alternates between panoramic, impressionistic sketches (to indicate the swift flowing of time) and the detailed dramatic development of crucial scenes—both presented mainly from the point of view of the heroine, now very accurately in her own delightful, archaic rural idiom, again as the poetized essence of her thoughts (with less concentration on Diony than on Ellen, to accommodate the broader scope of *The Great Meadow*). A comparison of Miss Roberts' impressionism with Thackeray's, noting important similarities and differences, leads to the conclusion that Thackeray is superior to Miss Roberts only in the broader scope of his work, certainly not in his technique, which is in several respects inferior to hers.

In concluding this chapter about her two most important books, it seems well to turn once more to her unpublished papers. The following, undated fragment of a letter to some friend (unnamed) indicates a clear understanding of the great tradition in which she worked, and of her lasting success in *The Time of Man* as an artist in her own right within that tradition:

Now my masters are Hardy, Shakespeare, Synge, Beethoven —symphonies—Dickinson, Hopkins. I am still a musician deeply within along with whatever else I am. *The Time of Man* is a symphony brought into words, for I believe that it is, whatever its failings, complete in itself. At its roots, its inception, it might have taken musical form.*

And finally another of her notes on the sources of *The Great Meadow*:

I used to sit near my grandmother to hear her tell of the wonders of her youth and to hear her thrust memory back into the memories of her father and mother, back through the Wilderness by way of the Trace . . . .

Upon this inheritance the odors of old centuries continually blow out of old books to join what is kept treasured thus within, what is identical with the breath of life. These confirmations of things held in family memory give a pleasurable sense of one's own validity, as if, having known by the way of the senses, one knew again by the way of the summaries of human experience that are on written pages. Thus one projects himself into more than one century and knows what it is to be alive in a reach and breadth of existence that transcends three score years and ten.*

In *The Time of Man* and *The Great Meadow* at least, the evidence seems very strong, in spite of the critical neglect of Miss Roberts' work in the last twenty years, that through her art she will in the future project herself into more than one century, that the fragrance of what is finest in the American tradition will blow out of her books to join what in future generations will be "kept treasured thus within, what is identical with the breath of life."

5. *Variations on the Theme*

ᣛᣔ Miss Roberts' major theme is stated in *The Time of Man* and *The Great Meadow*. These novels set forth in a major key her great conviction that through the power of spirit man conquers all. These are positive, unqualified affirmations on a grand, almost heroic, scale. We turn now to a consideration of a group of three novels which set forth variations on that grand theme. These novels—*My Heart and My Flesh, The Buried Treasure,* and *Black Is My Truelove's Hair*—all fundamentally assert Miss Roberts' major theme, but they moderate it to a minor key for reasons which will become evident in our subsequent discussion of them. For the sake of clarity we will discuss them separately and in the order listed above.

1. *My Heart and My Flesh*

My Heart and My Flesh was her second novel (published in 1927), the main portion of it being written at Santa Monica, California. Her health was bad at this time, which may account for the very somber tone of the book. This dark tone is the first impression the book makes on the reader; it is a sort of brooding, lyrical, Hamlet-like melancholy which hangs over all but the conclusion of the book. Too, there is apparent a sort of static quality that seems, at first, to hold the book in retrograde, as if the mind of the creator were continually circling instead of flying off in a straight dramatic line. Counteracting this, however, is the symbolic movement of the novel looming up from the first sentence all along the narrative line.

Of particular significance in this novel are its various levels of meaning and the narrative technique employed to convey forcefully the fundamental story plus its manifold meanings. About these subjects our discussion will center. Consequently, our first need is a fairly complete summary of the plot.

First, then, the actual novel itself. There is a smooth structural symmetry from the first sentence of the novel to the last. The prologue begins with the following sentence: "As a child, Luce was running to the store to get a small can of oil, for it was growing dark and she had the lamp to fill." Thus we are given the point of view of Luce in which we remain for the entire prologue. Thus, also, Luce (etymologically her name derives from the Latin *lux*–light), symbolizing the light, has the lamp to fill to show us the world of the story. Then, quickly and poetically into the prologue come the major motifs of the novel, namely: the rich earthiness of the Negroes; the Bell family and the promiscuity of Horace Bell; the search for the soul; the idea of rebirth; Theodosia and Theodosia's mulatto kin; Anneville, the little Kentucky town: Mome[1], the glorious fan-

[1] Miss Roberts told her friends that the prototype of this city was Cincinnati.

tasy city to the North; Caleb Burns, the true lover and the farmer of fine cattle; and, finally, the historic past of the town, the distant Virginia ancestry, stretching back to the eighteenth century. The prologue, presented as fantasy of Luce's mind, stretches backward and forward in time and gives an impressionistic picture of Anneville, the scene of the subsequent drama.

Chapter One opens on a quiet, peaceful summer afternoon in Anneville. Then, the scene shifts to the farm home of Theodosia's Aunt Doe, where Theodosia and her sister, Annie, go to visit. The visit, in many senses, is idyllic—the great farm is in its prime, and the entire scene is replete with the rich bustle and confusion of farm life. Here, for the first time, Theodosia detects an undertone of sarcasm in her Aunt Doe, an indication that her Aunt bears a certain hostility toward Doe's brother, Anthony Bell, who is Theodosia's grandfather. Negro servants are here, provoking an ambivalent reaction from Theodosia. Here, also, Theodosia displays to us her first doubts of reality. Soon, in quick succession, Theodosia's long train of losses begins: first her little sister, Annie, and then her mother, Charlotte Bell, dies. These deaths are not dramatized so much as lyricized. They are touched on lightly in a minor key. The entire story of Charlotte's death requires only three short sentences, and she disappears completely from the story. Time flies, and Theodosia is now seventeen. Old Anthony wants to send her to the city to study the violin, but his patrimony has been spent, and he is a broken figure. This chapter ends as he mutters futilely to himself—feeling that he must help Theodosia somehow, but not knowing how. The reader feels that he has been observing this scene remotely, from without.

Chapter Two begins as Theodosia visits the farm home

of her aunt, Doe Singleton. The uncle is now dead, and the farm is falling slowly to ruin. This scene is in sharp contrast with the earlier visit, when all was life and activity, and a rich bustle of confusion ran everywhere. Now the jack is old, the hounds are dull, the house is musty, the food stale, and the gutters broken. The scene is symbolic of Theodosia's own life from this point on until her rebirth.

Three young men of the town begin to pay court to Theodosia, but their presence is not quite real to her. She feels them to be a "part of the rich insufficiency which surrounded her." For her, she feels, life itself is insufficient. This feeling of debilitation increases when she discovers that her father is also the father of three mulatto children. Two nights later he attempts to seduce her, and the chapter ends with her complete alienation from him.

This chapter is an important one in setting the "tone" of the novel. The tone of the language is that appropriate to the withdrawal motif. In Chapter Two the master gesture of withdrawal begins to shape itself as the "feel" that goes with Theodosia's character. From this chapter on, she is like one falling away from the world, growing more and more remote from it. The various deaths in her family and among her friends are marks indicating her progressive withdrawal, which continues until she is shut within the sterile womb of Aunt Doe Singleton's house, the nadir of her withdrawal. Miss Roberts has created a kind of "withdrawal prose" that accompanies this motif and effectively maintains the tone.

In Chapter Three heavy blows are struck at Theodosia, stripping more and more possessions from her. Her close friend, Catherine Lovell, moves away. Her sweetheart, Albert Stiles, leaves her for another woman, and she dreams futilely of him, ". . . passing farther away, moving toward the inevitable disaster of doors." Conway, a second sweet-heart, burns to death. Theodosia tries to establish some relationship with Americy, her mulatto half-sister, but fails. She loses her touch for the violin, and as the chapter closes, even her memory of Conway fails when she learns he has fathered a bastard child. Thus, events are spinning her farther and farther from the world.

In Chapter Four her alienation from the world is acceler-ated. Her beloved grandfather, old Anthony Bell, dies leaving her debts but no property. Her father deserts her for good. After losing her mulatto kin by unwittingly pro-voking Lethe to murder and Americy and Stiggins to incest, she falls into a severe illness and loses her health. Thus, in a sense, she is already dead. "She was shut into some remote death although breath came and went in her throat."

In Chapter Five this devolution is pushed to its lowest possible extreme. Theodosia loses all ability to support herself and is forced to seek shelter from her eccentric and mad old aunt, Doe Singleton. Here she virtually starves, managing to get her only nourishment from the rough corn-pone prepared for and slobbered over by the hounds. Her illness grows worse. She passes into a stage of recurring hallucinations, is seduced by Frank Railey, and begins to hear strange voices. Stripped of everything she meditates suicide. At this point, an apocalyptic vision of the soul draws her back to a love of life, and she makes her escape from the farm with the aid of the liniment-man, on one of his periodic visits to the farm.

In Chapter Six we witness the return to life of Theodosia. She settles in a village and teaches school. Under the coun-try regimen, she comes quickly back to physical and mental health. Here she meets Caleb Burns, a good and substantial farmer, who possesses a wholeness and integrity that

Theodosia's life requires. Caleb loves here, and she accepts him. In the midst of a summer night, she lies awake and thinks of her rebirth into life and happiness. A great peace lies on the earth; it is symbolic of the great peace within her. Steps come from the night and pace through the barnyard. "They went across the hollow place and came back again toward the rise where the cows lay. They walked among the sleeping cows, but these did not stir for it was a tread they knew."

One way of comprehending the richness of this novel is to examine the various levels of meaning on which the story moves. It is first of all the story of a girl in conflict with her family and environment; almost defeated by them, she ultimately triumphs. Next, *My Heart and My Flesh* is a story of racial and historical significance, showing the decadence of the Bell family against the perspective of five generations, stretching back to the classic pioneer figures of Kentucky. There is a cyclical movement here as Theodosia, after her regeneration, marries Caleb Burns, the staunch countryman, and presumably starts a new bloodline which will have some of the old pioneer strength and fervor.

There is even a level of meaning which may be thought of as cultural criticism, in the sense that Theodosia represents that familiar figure of the New Criticism—the person of dissociated sensibility, of divided consciousness. There is considerable evidence of this in the story, in addition to Miss Roberts' explicit note which follows:

Do I write about Theodosia less lovingly than I did of Ellen? If so, why is this? Ellen is and was for me life itself. Have I less sympathy for Theodosia? Why? What is she? How does she relate to life? She is a wandering spirit, a lost thing. Why is she

lost more than Ellen is? She is lost through a partial consciousness which leads her to set up standards and anti-standards.
Ellen is not lost because she belongs to the earth itself, to the
swing of the tides of the seasons.*

It is interesting to note from the above quotation that
Miss Roberts felt closer to Ellen Chesser than to Theodosia
Bell, yet psychologically, Miss Roberts was much more akin
to Theodosia, the withdrawn introvert. Ellen was her ideal,
the kind of person she would have liked to be.

The nature of the dissociated sensibility of Theodosia
will become apparent as we discuss the final level of meaning which appears in this novel. It is convenient to discuss
this level under the term *archetype,* meaning that the
action in the novel repeats in its particular way a pattern
of action which has been repeated from the days of the
earliest recorded narratives.

The archetypal pattern in *My Heart and My Flesh* is
primarily that of the withdrawal and return, or rebirth,
motif. This is the major motif, seen in Theodosia's spiritual
death at Aunt Doe's and followed by her spiritual rebirth
into a new life. This basic archetypal pattern appears
frequently in the Old Testament and is, of course, a
great part of the substance of the New. But *My Heart and
My Flesh* is more of an Old Testament novel in its tone and
atmosphere. In the Old Testament, the rebirth motif
appears in such figures as Noah, Jonah, Joseph, and especially Job. Theodosia's situation is analogous to that of Job,
the adversary has his way with her, and she is progressively
stripped of her property, family, good name, friends, and
talent. And like Job, her very flesh is afflicted by a grievous
illness. But unlike Job, her spirit, at first, is not strong
enough to resist disaster and yields temporarily and despairs

completely. But the death passes, the desert is left, the spirit is reborn; and, like Job she is restored to the riches of love and serenity of mind. This is the most moving overtone of meaning in the novel, and in a sense, it possesses overtones within overtones. For the spiritual withdrawal has been prefigured by Theodosia's physical withdrawal from Anneville to the remote farm house of her Aunt Doe.

Another thread of meaning which winds into the rebirth motif is the search for the soul. Luce introduces this idea in the prologue, in her fantasy search for the soul of Charlotte Bell in her fleshly case. Theodosia picks it up as her grandfather, Anthony Bell, lies dying. "Her inner vision heightened, and she began to divide her being, searching for some soul or spirit." This leads her into her grandfather's being, and she probes mentally for evidence of his soul. Later, she pushes the same inquiry into the being of her mulatto half-sister, Americy. This search culminates in her spiritual rebirth, which is her evidence that the soul exists and is found.

So, on this deepest level of meaning, we have an archetypal pattern worked out in terms of a rebirth. Theodosia, a Job-figure, searching for evidence of the soul, divided in her very sensibility, withdraws from life, undergoes an arid death of the spirit, then returns to the world, spiritually reborn, knowing that the spirit recreates itself over and over again from within. This rebirth pattern, symbolically reflecting, in effect, the entire meaning of the novel, successfully extends every major scene into an added dimension.

There are now a few aspects of the narrative technique to be discussed. Miss Roberts was a careful craftsman. *My Heart and My Flesh* underwent a period of cautious planning. Voluminous notes remain, indicating how painstak-

ingly she rewrote and deleted in her attempt to achieve the
precise medium for her story.

The most difficult problem in terms of narrative technique was that of point of view. What point of view could
best sustain all the levels of meaning desired and present
them smoothly and credibly? Her solution was to adopt
the point of view of a central consciousness, suspended in
the world to be known by the reader. Thus, we experience
this world of Anneville, but we experience it in terms of
feelings and insights of the central intelligence, Theodosia
Bell. There is a prologue which gives us our first glimpse
of the world of Anneville through the eyes of Luce, who
has no other function in the novel. Miss Roberts herself
has commented on her purpose in using this device.

The mind here to be entered is the mind of the woman,
Theodosia. The process begins with a Knower, an Observer,
Luce a sensitive onlooker. The narrative moves slowly into
Theodosia's mind, beginning in the mind of Luce, seeing Theodosia first from the outside, moving more closely and intimately into her experience until it becomes identical with her
consciousness. By this process I hope to be able to establish a
spirit the more accurately and to present it with a movement
which will approximate something life-like. So much for the
mechanical process.

The prologue is a phantasy. It begins in the mind of Luce,
but it moves forward and backward in time and presents the
background of what is to follow. We may assume that Luce is
always the knower.*

Originally, Miss Roberts had planned to maintain Luce
throughout as the central consciousness and subordinate
Theodosia to Luce. Thus, Luce's story would have been
the primary one, counterpointed by the lesser one of Theo-

dosia, and it would have given us a novel much larger in scope, although lacking the tight unity attained by the novel in its final form. We can see how this problem concerned Miss Roberts by considering her following note:

In Lucy [Luce] present an aspect of the world so confused that she can make no logic of it nor reduce it to any order or saying. She reads books to try to find some model or criterion of behavior as it appears but finds no real relation between what she sees about her and what she reads, nor any relation between the varying aspects of what she sees. This is youth.

Then in maturity come clarity, statement and logic, sinister, perhaps, but definite even in its indefiniteness.

Then Theodosia's story would be but an incident of the whole. Lucy's story being the measure. Theodosia's story then would come to an end about two thirds of the way to the end.*

Miss Roberts actually prepared a good section of the novel in accordance with the plan indicated above. This manuscript, now in the Roberts Papers, keeps the point of view primarily in the consciousness of Luce, and it introduces other materials which must have seemed extraneous to Miss Roberts since she deleted them from the final version.

Her revisions were in the nature of rigorous cutting to simplify the plan of the story, to make it completely Theodosia's story, and to make it completely unified. There can be little doubt that her revision was wise and improved the novel structurally, although the story of the Negro Uncle Wilse, one of the finest individual studies she ever penned, is among the material deleted. In the final version, we enter the story smoothly through the mind of Luce and gradually enter and possess the consciousness of Theodosia. In this manner: "She [Theodosia] spread a trail of herself down the platform as she went proudly first . . . leaving a comet-train of herself behind to be entered, walked into, known by the knower, the chronicler."

With the major theme, spiritual rebirth, and the point of view established, there remained still the physical setting of the novel to determine and Theodosia's character to flesh out. The physical setting is a familiar one for Miss Roberts —the town of Anneville and its surrounding county, which is merely the real-life town of Springfield, Washington County, Kentucky moved into the realm of art. This setting is realized with the clarity and meticulous care for which Miss Roberts is noted.

The character of Theodosia, the protagonist, presented a more difficult problem. Theodosia bears so striking a resemblance to a very close, youthful friend of Miss Roberts, Sue Ray, that Miss Roberts' fellow townsmen feel that the friend unquestionably served as the prototype for Theodosia. The split sensibility, which is the decisive factor in her personality, we have already discussed. We should add two other stresses which have importance in the total picture of her character: she possesses a certain distrust of physical reality and maintains an ambivalent attitude towards the Negroes.

This distrust of physical reality is akin to the Berkeleian idealism we encounter in all of Miss Roberts' protagonists. In Theodosia it takes the form of a feeling that the realm beyond herself is incomplete or that it is a production, a masque, which is being staged in a vast theater for one sole auditor—herself. For instance, on her first visit to her aunt's farm, Theodosia observes the group gathered in conversation on the portico of the country home; and suddenly it becomes a scene in a play for her. "In the moment all the people present became actors in a pageant and all the words they said seemed deeply significant as if they were proclaiming themselves now in their real and permanent, unillusory aspect, in their true cause and relation."

This questioning of the continuity of physical reality appears over and over again and becomes one of her characteristic traits. As in this scene with Annie, her sister: "She could touch Annie but was she the same, she questioned, that she had touched before and was she herself present?" As Theodosia meditates on her first lover, Albert Stiles, "He was a part of the rich insufficiency which surrounded her."

A second stress in Theodosia's character which is carried throughout the novel is her ambivalent attitude toward the Negroes. The Negroes, who are an important part of the background of the novel, form a sizable portion of the population of Anneville. Although they live a suppressed and segregated life, they have a primitive strain of rich vitality which is in contrast with the dessication of Theodosia's own life. This vigor appears in the prologue—in the scenes of the Negroes in the stores buying and the picture of the Negro laborers strung out in long lines digging ditches for the new water lines of the town. Theodosia admires and likes this rich earthiness of the Negroes and, at the same time, feels a refined disgust towards them. In the first chapter, while Theodosia is visiting her Aunt Doe, she visits the Negro tenant's cabin and observes the small Negro children at play.

She would watch their small dresses, their brown legs, their moving gestures, and she would ask them questions to pretend an interest in their replies, but her pleasure was in her own sense of superiority and loathing, in a delicate nausea experienced when she knelt near the baby's quilt.

* * *

Theodosia knew a sweet loathing of the small dark infant and knew that she herself could not be brought to touch it or to touch Katie. She knew the half-pleasant disgust felt for the young of another kind, a remote species. Their acts sent little stabs of joy over her, sickly stabs of pleasant contempt and pride.

This loathing and contempt increase Theodosia's inner conflict later, when she learns that three mulattoes are related to her, two as half-sisters and the other as half-brother. Yet, feeling pity and a certain tenderness akin to love for Americy, Theodosia fights back her sense of repulsion and makes overtures to her mulatto kin. But as indicated, these overtures are failures, since she unwittingly incites Lethe to murder and Stiggins and Americy to incest.

Of interest here is Miss Roberts' note on miscegenation in her Papers. "Not for a thousand years or ten thousand would the blend be actual and until that consummation it would bring sorrow and be illicit, illegitimate, unyielding."* And so, of course, it does "bring sorrow" to the Bell family and their mulatto kin in *My Heart and My Flesh*.

This particular note, by the way, is strikingly similar to the closing scene of Faulkner's short story, "Delta Autumn," which also treats miscegenation and its tragic aftereffects. Old Ike McCaslin, talking with a beautiful young mulatto in love with a white man, thinks of the possibilities of racial intermarriage in this manner. *"Maybe in a thousand or two thousand years in America,* he thought. *But not now!"* And, then, he finally tells her: "Marry: A man of your own race. That's the only salvation for you—for a while yet. Maybe a long while yet. We will have to wait."

Before leaving the discussion of the narrative technique in this novel, we should sum up the fragmentary comments we have made throughout on the style. The style is a highly mentalized one in the sense that it gives the constant impression of her inner life, and this inner life, in effect, is the story. The mentalization is a smooth and fluent one, however, if compared, for instance, to the jagged and staccato associations of Bloom and Dedalus in Joyce's *Ulysses*. It has the "murmuring" quality previously noted in her other novels, and it is admirably suited to conveying the "world" of Theodosia Bell, clearly and beautifully. More than that, it succeeds in conveying to the reader the rebirth motif, not only as a rational meaning but as a language gesture. If we do not push the analogy too far, we can say that the style is a musicalization of *My Heart and My Flesh*. For instance, Miss Roberts was a great lover of music and constantly sought certain musical analogies in her work. In the present novel, the prologue is equivalent to the prelude of a symphony. All the major motifs, (leitmotifs) of the novel are stated here[2] with their characteristic movements and tones. The novel itself follows in six chapters comparable to the six movements of a symphony. Miss Roberts' papers contain a sort of "program notes" on these movements, as she writes in one place that "the farm prose should be lyric prose."* Within the individual books, the structure, movement, and tone remain analogous to music. There is a fluid movement from the first chapter to the last. The marvelous feel for this musicalization of a scene by the coil and flow of language is ideally represented by the last paragraph of the book. Style here has been brought to virtual perfection. If the book has a fault, it lies in the character of Theodosia as conceived by the author. The language which realizes that character is almost flawless.

In the foregoing discussion, we have attempted to touch on and clarify the most important aspects of *My Heart and My Flesh*. We feel that, in conclusion, we should say why we feel this to be a lesser work than *The Time of Man* and *The Great Meadow*.

The primary reason for the "minor key" quality of this book lies in the very nature of Theodosia as a person. As a "divided sensibility," Theodosia contains an element of negation in her character which is not found in either Ellen Chesser of Diony Hall, who *exist* completely, purely, positively without negation or qualification. Therefore, an abundant vitality flows from them which is lacking in Theodosia. Miss Roberts herself felt less sympathy for Theodosia,[3] and this partial bloc in her imagination is evident in the characterization of Theodosia. Moreover, the remote, dreamlike quality which suffuses so much of the book makes it less massive. Theodosia is a person who feels the "rich insufficiency of her life." She is an *exemplum* of St. Augustine's text—"Our hearts are made for thee, O Lord, and they find no rest till they rest in thee." The "insufficiency" which is the subject matter of so much of the book cannot—all other things being equal—have the grand emotional appeal which emanates from the "rich sufficiency" of Ellen Chesser and Diony Hall.

But having said this, we have made our only major adverse criticism of the book. It still remains the best of her novels after *The Time of Man* and *The Great Meadow*. It still remains a profound poetic and tonal achievement in the American novel; and melancholy as it is in so much of its theme and milieu, it does not end in an agony of naturalistic despair, but in its conclusion, like all her novels, it leads us from death to life.

2 *Vide supra.*
3 *Vide supra.*

Elizabeth Madox Roberts

2. *A Buried Treasure*—Minor Pastoral

In 1928, Miss Roberts, while reading the Springfield *Sun,* ran across a news item about a county farmer who had discovered a buried kettle of old coins on his place. The incident remained in her mind, and later she made this entry in her notes:

"Last year far back on such a farm [she had been discussing the remote lands still in the county], at a place which can scarcely be reached by any wheeled conveyance whatever, a small farmer owner found a pot of silver and gold, a kettle of old Spanish money."*

Her speculations on this incident soon grew into a short story, "A Buried Treasure," which was published in *Harper's Magazine.*[4] The short story, in turn, grew into the novel, *A Buried Treasure,* published in 1931. This novel still strikes the fundamental theme of the primacy of man's spirit, but it is a departure from the somber tone of *My Heart and My Flesh* to a light and pleasant "masquing." For this reason it provides us with the second of her variations on a major theme. Our first impression of the book is one of great simplicity—classic simplicity—of action and atmosphere. Then, gradually, we become aware of overtones arising from the work—connotations and implications appearing. The novel is like a palimpsest. Behind the clear surface writing of the palimpsest, we catch glimpses of older scripts, dimly discernible and giving us vague snatches of older meanings. The palimpsest simile is peculiarly apt, for the rural folk of this novel continually suggest in their talk and actions the pioneer folk of Kentucky and, antedating them, the folk of England in the

4 Published in two parts, December, 1929, and January, 1930.

Middle Ages and on back to even older times, when the folk gathered on Midsummer Day to dance their ancient ring dance and celebrate the old vegetative ceremonies. These older meanings, ancient memories of the race, vague stirrings behind the clear surface of the novel, give it much of its peculiar charm.

This discussion will consider three aspects of *A Buried Treasure*—the different modes or kinds of appeal it exerts on the reader, the nature and importance of its narrative point of view, and the nature and function of the final scene of the book. A discussion of these three subjects will take us into the heart of the novel.

First of its modes of appeal is the plot situation of the story—a middle-aged Kentucky farm couple dig up, by chance, a pot of gold. Buried treasure is thus thrust into their hands by the gods. The problem: Will they be able to keep it? Will they use it wisely? To add interest to this plot, Miss Roberts introduces a number of subplots—the romance of Imogene Cundy and Giles Wilson, plus the presence of two thieving house painters who threaten to steal the treasure, and a juvenile genealogist, Ben Shepherd, who is a sort of *deus ex machina* at key points in the plot. This is the level intended to catch the initial interest of the reader and to provide the basic ingredients with which other more appealing elements will be intermingled.

What are these more appealing elements? One derives from the analogy of the novel to a five-act comic drama; in its five-part division and its manipulation of plot and subplots, it is much like a five-act comedy. The relaxed pictorial character of the novel frequently suggests a masque or a pageant. Speech passages alternate with richly pictorial nature scenes in a somewhat stylized manner, again reminiscent of a masque. This masquing element is most clearly apparent in the sensuous ring dance which climaxes the novel, as will appear when we discuss this scene.

Still another pleasurable element in the novel is its unobtrusive allegory on the theme of treasure. We soon realize that the author is implying that there is treasure other than the one discovered by Andy and Philly Blair. Philly first realizes this at her party. "Philly wished in this instant that she had thought to have a party before a kettle of gold had come into her knowledge. The people seemed to be making sufficient happiness for one another." The real and lasting treasure, she finds, is the human heart in amity with its own kind.

In a sense, the withdrawal and return motif—which appears in several of Miss Roberts' novels—is tied in with the symbolism here. For Andy and Philly Blair, having found the treasure and realized its worth, soon become fearful of thieves. In effect, they withdraw into the safety of their home and hover over their treasure, keeping it from harm and keeping themselves apart from people. But they soon feel this withdrawal is wrong. By giving a certain portion of their treasure to the church, they lose their fear of people and symbolically re-enter communal life as they engage in the ring dance which closes the book. It is this return which brings them contentment.

Still another palimpsest meaning showing unobtrusively through the literal text is the presentness of the past, the conviction that the rural folk in their intercourse with nature are following ageless patterns set for them long before the dawn of history. The great rhythms of nature beat constantly in the background of the novel, although with no tragic force. The climax and conclusion of the novel is set on Midsummer Day. Sir James Frazer in *The Golden Bough* reminds us that, "The Midsummer festival must on the whole have been the most solemn and most widespread of all the yearly festivals celebrated by the primitive Aryans of Europe." So it is not by accident that Miss Roberts has her folk gather on Midsummer's Night for a ring dance which is likened to the great wheel of life. It is a continuation of the great cycle of life running far back into eras before literature of any sort was known. We feel with pleasure this great continuity in the ageless flow of the life of the race.

The land rolled forward toward the harvest, or it rolled backward toward the time of planting, toward the long sequence of harvests and all plantings, moving backward over and over, the soil turning, revolving under the plowings of many springs. ... The men were dispersed to the fields, but at the burying-place they were gathered together, their names written on stone—Wilson, Blair, Rudds, Bonnie, Trigg, Roundtree, Turner, Shepherd, and others, written on the faces of rocks.

The ultimate level of enjoyment in the novel lies in the lyrical beauty of the language at many junctures of the book and in what we have called earlier in this chapter the musicalization of fiction. Miss Roberts wrote of *The Time of Man* that it "is a symphony brought into words .... At its roots, its inception, it might have taken musical form."* *A Buried Treasure* is too slight to be likened to a symphony, but it most certainly suggests a pastorale. Scene after scene glides into our consciousness with the magic suggestiveness of music. The analogy to musical form is just as great in *A Buried Treasure* as it is in *The Time of Man*. In fact, this element seems to be the primary concern of the author, who often employs the plot merely to keep the reader's rational faculties busy while the overtones, which provide the fundamental pleasure of the book, gradually have their way with him. It is difficult to establish this point without using very lengthy quotations. However, the quality of this musicalization will be apparent in the series of quotations at the conclusion of this section.

What we have listed here as separate modes of appeal are not, of course, thus separated in the actual narrative. They are so skillfully blended with the fundamental line of action that they come to our consciousness gradually and unobtrusively as overtones lightly heard behind the primary rhythm.

Almost equal in importance to the multiplicity of appeals is the point of view adopted by Miss Roberts. Of fundamental concern in any novel, point of view is doubly important here because of the intricate effects sought behind the surface simplicity. Miss Roberts' problem was this: what point of view will convey clearly the fundamental conflict, the present situation and contemporary milieu of rural folk, and will convey also and at the same time another perspective on these folk—the perspective of the long past which lies behind them, the generations of Kentuckians reaching back to Fort Harrod, and the presentness of this past in the actions of the rural folk who will be too unsophisticated to grasp it themselves? The problem is a fairly difficult one. Miss Roberts solved it by adopting a third person point of view, but not a completely omniscient one. The author, in effect, employs two intelligences through which the action is viewed—Philly Blair and Ben Shepherd. It is the suspended central-consciousness technique with the author seeing the situation through the eyes of Philly or Ben and unobtrusively ordering it for us.

The burden of the novel is carried by Philly. She is the central consciousness employed in chapters I, III, V. The fundamental conflict of the story is seen through her eyes.

Her consciousness is equipped to show us the *present* with great clarity and simplicity. It is the task of Ben's consciousness to show us the long perspective of time, the presentness of all the past. His is the central consciousness employed in chapters II and IV. Both chapters are retrospective, antiquarian. Whereas Philly is a participant in the main actions, namely the discovery and protection of the treasure and the marrying off of Imogene Cundy against old man Cundy's furious opposition, Ben is a remote and aloof spectator. In practically every scene he is the onlooker, the observer of action. Consequently, as one might expect, Ben suffers as a dramatized character. Philly comes alive as a tough, vital, middle-aged woman. She dominates the book, representing the principle of activism so far as the book has one. Ben was almost universally decried by the reviewers as a pale effeminate shade drifting ineffectually through the book. This was hardly just to Miss Roberts, however, because symbolically he was meant to be a shade. Symbolically, Ben Shepherd represents the spirits of all the Shepherds past, returned to observe what their descendants have become. Indeed, it is obvious that Philly half believes Ben is a ghost, for she becomes frightened on his visit to her, getting up and running out of the room away from him. And the next day, "the apparition [Ben] of the day before still troubled her . . . . It was a terror to her that her farm bell should be waking the dead [Ben] in the old Shepherd burying-place."

Philly gives us the close view, involves us in the action. Ben gives us the long view, remote and aloof from the action. So Ben's Chaper Two goes over much of the same ground as Philly's Chapter One, and both chapters end with the same scene, the beginning of the party. Visually, Ben's scenes are in sharp, hard perspective—seen at a dis-

tance. Philly's scenes are within the action. Ben, suggesting
the past, represents all the dead ancestors of this community. He hovers about the Shepherd graveyard, discovers
and carries off a skeleton footbone of one of his early ancestors; is continually bothered by ants, and sees in his mind's
eye their endless galleries under ground—they symbolize
the endless animal energy of the earth to him, triumphant
over man's limited vitality. Bones, ants, the past—Ben's
view is the long racial view, man against eternity. And he
sees that to these people he has become a wraith, and he so
styles himself in his revery. Thus Ben's two chapters (Two
and Four) are musical withdrawals after the fuller melody
of Philly's chapters, withdrawals in a minor key—"defunc-
tive music under sea." And Ben, who has come from another world, as it were, into this idyllic scene of pastoral
harmony, must withdraw at the end of his magic period.
As he does so, he returns the piece of human bone to the
Shepherd burying ground, seemingly indicating that he
realizes that one can not recapture the past in any antiquarian sense and, moreover, that he has the *living past* in his
experiences with the Shepherds in the *present community*.
So a compulsion takes him back with the bone to undo the
violation he has committed. This time his passage through
the brush is easy (since he comes to right a wrong, the guar-
dian spirits make easy his passage). And his purpose has
been fulfilled.

. . . He had been into the homes of the living Shepherds,
they now wearing other names, and he had seen them at their
working, their living, their play, their lovings. He had walked
through their old orchards . . . . He had fished in their stream
. . . . He had surprised them at forbidden love; he had eaten
their food; and he had prayed with them in their church . . . .

There was no human outcry, none crying "Mine" or "Nine". He dreamed over this remote memory, without malice, letting it become undone and unstated. His passage through the brush was not difficult . . . he found his way and he laid the bone down in the place where it used to lie.

So it is fitting that Ben's next to last appearance in the book (the conclusion of Chapter Four) should recapitulate his function as the observer of the Shepherds, a visiting wraith, as it were, who departs silently without ruffling the tranquillity of the hamlet's life.

The best way to indicate the real quality of this novel would be to quote in its entirety the closing scene, which runs from page 277 to page 296. Since it is not practical to quote so extensively, the next best thing is to point out the artistry of the last scene in unobtrusively catching up and synthesizing all the major narrative modes of this novel and leaving us with a scene of clear and timeless beauty.

This scene is intensely pastoral. Philly and Andy, having secured their treasure from thieves, are walking through an open pasture on Midsummer's Night at twilight. They are searching for a strayed black heifer. There follows a paragraph of description which serves as a transition into the *Midsummer Night's Dream* ending:

The little black heifer came out of the brush into the open pasture and went slowly across the moonlit space. She was no longer an anxiety while she grazed in the open and drifted down toward the feeding pen. The light in the small glade where the calf had been seemed broken into parts that crackled and spun, that drifted and glided in streams, that came to an end each moment and began again in some new drifting of the birch leaves that blended with the white light. A mockingbird began to sing on the top of a high bough and it pushed song up into the wide, lit sky with a passionate throat, mounting and throbbing in the beginning of a song frenzy that turned and quavered, that asked and answered, that trilled and bubbled and ended at length with a slow hush-note. Then Philly knew that something which had seemed to be a part of the quick, sudden, intermittent moonlight that lit the glade, was the noise of speaking voices, as if people were walking together, of people shouting and singing, coming nearer. A drift of floating objects began to form at the end of the pasture, three becoming one and then turning to four, to be one and then three, receding and coming forward. Imogene came first into form and Giles followed soon after, with a circle of girls and boys around, and Rudds and his wife were quickly at hand, and Eliza White and old Mr. Bonnie, with two of the Roundtrees, walking up out of the powdered air.

Thus the folk assemble, walking up serenely, "out of the powdered air," and the climactic scene ensues which clearly catches up, restates, and blends all of the narrative levels (modes) which have been previously stated. This scene is a masterpiece of muted poetic composition, and its pictorial effect (like Keats' "Grecian Urn" scene) is a subtle one; in the poetic realm it seems to catch life at a magic moment —at that magic moment when life is changing easily into legend or myth.

This scene is so skillfully done that it will repay closer examination. The action level is simple and straightforward. The folk gather and form a great circle and begin a game song. Later, Philly sits within the circle and converses with a few of the matrons. Then, the circle breaks apart, and the men practice calling animals—pigs, turkeys, and horses. The great wheel is reformed and goes forward only to be broken later by the sheriff, who arrives to arrest one of the thieving housepainters, much to Andy's relief.

Again the game resumes with Philly conversing quietly with the other matrons. Later, in the moonlit night, they disperse and go slowly homeward.

This brief pictorial passage, however, catches up all that the novel has been preparing; it unites all levels of the narrative. Plot and subplots are resolved; the buried treasure is honorably secured. Giles's marriage to Imogene is proved legal; the threat of the thieving carpenters is removed. The symbolism suggested in the title reaches its fruition in the shared friendship of the folk; indeed, here is treasure in the simple pleasure of fellowship with one's own kind. The withdrawal and return motif is concluded with Philly and Andy now having entered completely and fully into community life. The "presentness of the past" comes to us in the performance of the ancient folk dance and the singing of the old folk song, "Here We Go Round the Mulberry Bush," and the "feel" of ancient games and celebrations of long past Midsummer Days which suffuses the scene.

The point of view has become ostensibly that of Philly, the dramatic present. Ben Shepherd has departed from the story. But Ben's point of view—the long perspective of time—is not completely lost. In fact, it appears and blends with Philly's; it appears in the timeless quality of the folk pursuits in the last chapter. Ben's perspective is retained in the ancientness of the ring dance, the game song, and the agrarian pattern of life of the folk in this climactic scene. The two points of view which have alternated throughout the book are thus brought into a harmonious union in the resolution of the novel.

And over the entire scene hangs a sense of space and light—over all beneficent nature, beautiful and rich, joyous and satisfying. But into this rich, sensuous beauty intrude lightly lyrical hints of frost and death, making a bitter-sweet amalgam and suggesting the sad undertone of life's tragedies flowing always beneath the placid surface of this midsummer idyl.

The lyricism, alluded to earlier in our discussion, is particularly noticeable in this final scene. A few quotations from the scene itself will demonstrate not only this lyrical quality, but the suggestiveness and musicalization of Miss Roberts' fictional world.

The rustics have gathered on Midsummer's Night in a scene of great natural beauty, which transmits its beauty to them.

The light of the moon was almost as bright as the day and Philly could not be sure that the twilight had gone. Bonnie's dress caught the light and flashed a newer yellow, and all the girls were pleased with the new beauty the moon had brought to their clothing; and they made their skirts dart and flutter in and out of the bright glow to feel themselves a part of the flashing color and to know that they were lovely. The throng, set in a circle, made a great wheel that turned about a little thorn bush and sang a game-song:

> *Here we go round the mulberry bush*
> *On a cold frosty morning* . . . .

The great wheel of the game becomes symbolical of the great wheel of life, of the great world itself turning under the powdered moonlight, while an age-old vegetative ritual, but dimly remembered, goes on about a thorn bush.

They joined hands, all in a ring again, and the great wheel began to turn, spread wide to make a moving circle, singing the rhyme of the mulberry bush. The great wheel turned, making ready a world, a world of mankind turning all together, Philly and Andy and Ronnie Rudds and old Bonnie with all the girls and boys of the farms. As the earth itself the wheel turned under the moon, singing . . . .

But into the warm luxury of Midsummer's Night intrude thoughts of the bleak cold of winter, voiced by Philly and two of her friends. Philly speaks.

"They say it's the longest day in the year, Midsummer day . . . . It's long a-plenty. Summer is a warm season and pleasant. I just love summer."

"It's hard to recollect how cold it once was," Ronnie said, "but it was cold enough."

"I'm afeared we might have a cold winter, after the summer so warm."

"Oh, I'm afraid so too."

"And wood so hard to get, and coal so far to haul."

"The dark days. And night settled down soon after four o'clock."

. . .

"But it's a long time off yet till winter."

Finally the night begins to move, the idyl is drawing to a close, and the folk reluctantly prepare to leave the Midsummer Night's magic.

"Day would come in a little while. Come on, we'd best go now," some were calling out. "It must be near morning."

"It's hardly night yet! It's never got dark yet. No. It's not near to morning. . . ."

"Day is right here at us. We must go."

And even as they prepare to leave their pleasure, a faint sound is heard, a katydid, a frost sign here in the midst of

summer, prescient of winter and death. The faint overtone
of death backgrounds the scene.

It sang one faint "did," as short and hard as a pin-prick.
Listening, all of them quiet, some of them heard the faint
"did" again.

. . .

"Midsummer Night, and I wouldn't want to be a-hear'en
a frost token already."

. . .

"It's curious to think about."
"In the midst of the first harvest . . . Midsummer Night and
hot weather all around us, and you hear the first frost-sign
of a frost-sign yet to come."
"Oh, God's sake, think of it."
A sign that a frost-sign is bound to follow."

Then the farmers, maids, and lovers, their game-time
over, disperse through the softness of the powdered moonlight; the comedy is over, and we must return to mundane
reality. All are gone.

Philly and Andy started back homeward, down the pasture,
driving home the little black calf. The bushes and the briars,
the tree trunks and the little saplings, were full of vague,
unbodied lovers, and off a little way in the shadows there were
these, just out of sight, whispering, under the stones, behind
the ditches, under the hummocks. They were all gone from the
moonlight and hilltop.

Thus, in summary, a brief newspaper clipping has been
transmuted into a novel which is a delicate and muted art
triumph. It is a creation in a lesser form of fiction—the
musicalization of themes on a minor scale. Yet it has excel-

lences of its own, and connoisseurs of fiction will always
turn with pleasure to the climactic scene of the ring dance,
where consciousness is caught and suspended forever in that
joyous moment when life is just at the point of changing
into legend.

3. *Black Is My Truelove's Hair*

Black Is My Truelove's Hair was the last novel Miss
Roberts completed before her death. She had been keenly
aware that the critics disapproved of her preceding novel,
He Sent Forth a Raven, on the grounds that its symbolism
was not adequately grounded in the physical narrative.
Consequently, she took particular pains to provide a strong
thread of physical narrative in her last novel. Having done
that, she felt completely at liberty to give her symbolic imagination free rein. It is this multi-layered symbolism which
ultimately expands the story to a commentary on all human
experience and makes it a memorable novel. By the same
token, this symbolism compels two or three careful readings
to catch its full savor.

By taking a broad look at the novel first, we discover
familiar patterns—basic patterns which Miss Roberts
loved. We see the familiar pastoral setting—this time in
Henrytown, a village in the Pigeon River country. Once
again we have a girl protagonist, Dena Janes. Once again
we have the archetypal pattern of death and rebirth. Dena
Janes suffers a kind of spiritual death when her love affair
with Langtry ends calamitously, but she is reborn through
endurance and through the entry of a life-giving love, that
of Cam Elliot, into her own life.

But these are sufficiently mundane patterns. How does
she lift them to the clarity and luminosity of successful art?

The present section will be largely an attempt to demonstrate how she accomplishes this. Here we can make some
general observations as background for our closer examination. First, the point of view is omniscient third person.
However, the omniscient observer hovers so close to Dena
Janes throughout the story—much of the time being within
her mind—that we get the effect of partially identifying
ourselves with Dena. We are much closer to Dena than to
anyone else in the story, and quite naturally she is the most
lifelike character. Of singular importance also is the organization of the novel into five major segments. This five-part
organization suggests both drama and music. Like drama,
the novel introduces a conflict in Part One which goes
through various heightenings and partial resolutions in the
next three parts to reach a major climax and swift denoue-
ment in Part Five. Like a complex musical composition,
the novel introduces a number of diverse motifs in Part
One[5]; these then reappear in various guises throughout the
rest of the novel until they reach a stormy crescendo in the
climactic shooting scene which quickly changes to a diminu-
endo passage as the sound of a single step fades off into
the night. Within each of the five divisions, the tempo of
the novel also suggests a musical analogy. The tempo is
marked by its fluidity, its constant progression; it has an onward, even murmur like a quietly flowing river of sound in
a musical composition. Reading it, one constantly thinks
of a pastorale. Its formal pattern is strong and obvious and
satisfying.

It is necessary first to examine briefly the actual story and
then observe it as it turns gradually from its literal meaning
to various symbolic meanings which together constitute the
totality of the novel. The novel begins with Dena Janes

[5] These will be itemized and discussed later.

pacing along a lonely road at the hour of dawn. She is returning home, fleeing from Will Langtry who lured her away but refused to marry her. So Dena returns as a ruined woman to her village and begins the hard task of taking up her workaday life again. The village gradually and grudgingly accepts her into its life as autumn advances. But a fear that Langtry will come back to murder her haunts Dena. Then, the winter has passed, and it is summer again—with Dena's health restored, and a new vigor about her. Frony, Dena's sister, loses her gold thimble; the old gander sets up a continual screaming, and a strange howling is frequently heard. Dena's fear of Langtry, dormant through the winter, now returns. Strangeness falls from the air. Then, Dena meets Cam Elliot, the miller's son, and begins a courtship with him. Cam returns the gold thimble to Dena and discovers the cause of the strange howl. Cam is clean cut, straightforward. He proposes, and Dena accepts. Late summer approaches; Cam is building their future home. The old fear of Langtry comes back. When Dena hears that he has returned, she flees at night from her home. Langtry catches her and fires twice, but misses and becomes hysterical. He craves the pardon of Dena. Journeyman appears and leads Langtry away—all passion spent. Dena, now completely free from her fear, completely her integral self again, and now ready for Cam and her true marriage, walks peacefully off into the night.

This, in effect, is the basic story with which Miss Roberts begins. But it becomes much more than this, since the symbolism is part of the final form of the book. An attempt to suggest the major threads of that symbolism will be made here.

One of the first things we note about the story is that, as we progress through it, the little village of Henrytown gradually turns into a microcosm of the world itself. All the hierarchical patterns of the great and ancient world appear. Dena Janes is Everyman in this world. Father Grimes represents the church, the religious principle. Mug Banner, the former whore and procuress, representing the principle of ancient evil, tempts Dena to give herself to a prostitute's life. Nat Journeyman is the philosopher, the knowing man, the principle of wisdom. Minnie Judd and her husband, a wealthy farm couple, occupy the status of privilege; they are virtually the aristocrats of the little world. The other families—Bowers, Wheat, McClark, etc.—are the middle and lower classes. Will Langtry is the personification of death, as Cam Elliot is the personification of life. Through Henrytown runs the river which becomes by extension the river of time and the flux of life itself. Over the town hangs that great apple of light, the sun, source of all life and being and source of the ancient nature myths frequently hinted at in the story.

An important figure in this world is Nat Journeyman, who, at the basic level, is a retired school teacher now living his declining years in Henrytown. But as we penetrate the story more deeply, we become aware that he is much more. Journeyman is the knowing man, the mind of man, the rational faculty of man. People in the village come to him with all the questions they cannot answer. Journeyman ponders and answers, "as claiming all knowledge, but humbly or with humor. The orchard was placed in the heart of the glen. From his seat under the largest apple tree he could view the way, north and south. Each one, man, woman, and child, was known to him."

Thus Journeyman sits at the heart of the village and observes with a brooding philosophical calm the spectacle of life as it flows by him. Through his orchard and his fields, he is in touch with the powers of growth and decay—the great rhythms of the earth. "His house alone faced the river; he was the one being in the entire glen who kept the river in his thought . . . apart and knowing, he stood with time, identical with time, as it passed over, as it moved like the river . . . to flow unrecognized and changeless through minor degrees of turbulence and calm." So the river for him is both life and time, and he the knowing mind, the Apollonian element in man, sits and observes, because he is also the observer, and it is through his eyes we often look when the author wishes to affirm some benignant quality of Dena.

Journeyman, then, becomes a kind of control for the novelist, allowing her to promulgate many of her own beliefs without being obstrusive and providing a center of some sophistication in the naïve world of Henrytown. He is also a reserve of strength for Dena when she is in trouble. Moreover, he personifies the masculine element in the novel even more than does Cam Elliot or Will Langtry. Thus, in one sense, he is a balance to the femininity of Dena Janes. This is of value since in a Roberts novel there is always a tendency for the feminine point of view to weaken and emasculate the masculine. Journeyman, however, is solid, substantial, and massive—indeed, he adds authority to the novel.

So much for Henrytown as the microcosm of the great world and Journeyman as its spokesman. By this means the incidents of the novel become not only individual occurrences in the village life, but also waves sweeping across the great surface of racial consciousness. Symbolic significance is thus more easily attained.

The major symbolic meaning of the novel pattern is revealed in the two loves in Dena's life—Will Langtry, the truck driver, and Cam Elliot, the miller's son. Langtry clearly symbolizes death; this is said several times in the narrative. As at the beginning:

"What does he look like?" Grace asked.

Dena made a motion as if she would hide her hands under her frayed skirt. She looked intently at the sandy grass beneath her and answered:

"Oh he looks like . . . death."

"I know the look then."

Then, later, when Dena tells Journeyman of the sexual symbol on Langtry's chest, Journeyman explains to her. "A symbol of life, but tattooed on the breast of a man it is the emblem of death. A man who wears it there is dead already." Again in the final scene of the book, as Langtry stands stupefied after he tries to murder Dena, he speaks to her:

"Ask her, " he said . . . if she will shake my hand and say good-bye to me."

"No," Dena said, speaking slowly, "I will not do so. I will not take his hand. Maybe a long while from now, if he comes, I will shake his hand and speak to him so."

Dena is clearly thinking of death as she makes this last remark. Thus Langtry comes to be the emblem of the not-life. In the core of himself, there was no heart to be invoked, because the roaring hate-lust had grown inwardly to eat out the vitals. By depriving himself of the essence of life, he becomes death. Dena sees this nothingness for herself when Langtry compels her to look into his eyes.

"Down a long hollow space that reached almost to the end of the world. Black like night . . . but hollow. I screamed at what I saw. In the bottom of the black hollow passage that was made out of his words I saw his soul. I saw the end. I saw the bottom. It was blank and empty and dark . . . . It was nothing. It was a black nothing stretched across the way."

And, later, Dena thinks of Fronia confronting the enraged Langtry: "Perhaps she would see the murder in Langtry's face, and see death there." Langtry's death symbolism is not only the nothingness of physical death, but also the nothingness of the hollow men who live a death-in-life. It is this death-in-life that Dena is fighting against in the opening part of the story. Her struggle to be reborn into the world of the spiritually alive is one of the major themes of the novel.

This theme is articulated partly through Cam Elliot. In contrast with the mystery of Langtry is Cam, whose mystery is the mystery of life. His father remarks of him, ". . . Cam he's drunk with life. And hardly knows what to do with it." And later on, still speaking to Dena, he adds:

"He's shy now. That's because he's got so much life inside him and is afraid he won't use it right, and afraid he'll use too much of it and offer too much all at one time."

It seems clear therefore that Dena's change of lovers— from Langtry to Elliot—is part of the allegorical structure of the book. Gradually drawing herself away from the memory and the fear of Langtry, she begins her period of spiritual gestation which results in her spiritual rebirth when she and Cam are joined in their new love. Allegorically, she moves from death-in-life to life. The general allegory will become more apparent if we look at Dena's affair a little more closely.

As the novel opens, Dena walks over a country road in the quiet light of the dawn, fleeing from the death that is Will Langtry. Even as she walks, her mind phrases the basic conflict of the novel, rejecting death and turning toward life.

"I'm alive," she said. "I got a right to live then."

. . .

"I got a right to live." She began to weep softly again.

. . .

"A right to a life that makes good sense . . . ."

The novel, then, becomes the story of the manner in which she gradually wins "a life that makes good sense." But it is only with difficulty that Dena is able to throw off the ties that bind her to Langtry. Out of her abundance, she has loved too much; and though she feels that her love for Langtry is gone, a certain ambivalence[6] pervades her emotion toward him. She hates him, and yet she loves the first picture of him that still lingers in her mind. This ambivalent emotion is her first great barrier in her journey toward real life. She broods over it, and finally takes the problem to Nat Journeyman.

"I can't cure myself," she whispered.

. . .

"I've got the two [Langtry as the person she loved and Langtry as the one she grew to hate] divided. I can hate one and want the other with my whole body and I can't cure myself, but I know they are all one and all Langtry, and I know cruel, and would kill me, and will maybe, but what can I do?"

. . .

"I still think, somehow, of the first one [Langtry as loved],

[6] This ambivalence will be underscored in importance by a strange howl Dena hears. *Vide infra.*

and I want for something I can't name or call, with all my whole life . . . ."

"Can you cure me?"

"It is a great sickness," he said.

Thus Dena is caught in the orbit of Langtry's fascination. She must be pulled out of it in order to establish the integrality of her life again. So Journeyman prescribes for her. First, prayer; then, rich foods and work and joy in the rhythms of the year. In an earthy monologue reminiscent of Chaucer, he sweeps the rich pageant of the revolving year of the farm before her eyes. This is his way of telling her that time will cure. Dena accepts his advice, and by the following June, she is hearty and vigorous again. Her love for Langtry recedes into the background, but her fear remains. A new and powerful counterforce is needed to overcome this fear.

This counterforce comes in the person of Cam Elliot. Cam's courtship is swift, and Dena soon falls in love with him. He proposes to her, and a new world appears for her.

The broad light of a sunny day spread over them . . . . It was the new world, the new day . . . . It was the human world beating over the inanimate world.

. . .

She would be sitting within his warm embrace . . . .

The true warmth and power of life would be sitting beside her. There was no terror in the passion of it. If it leaned over her, strong and terrible, she went with the strength of it, as strong and as kind.

Thus Cam draws her by the force of his love away from the negation and death of Langtry. Yet there is another stage that must be passed through. As August of the second

year draws near, Dena feels that she must relive imagin-
atively her love affair and flight of the previous summer.
Like a shell-shock victim reliving his traumatic experience,
Dena goes painfully back through all the details of the
affair, seeking vaguely some catharsis for the pain she has
known and seeking some answer for the disastrous ending
of the Langtry episode.

She wanted to understand what had happened the year
before and to bring it to some end, not threat or death. Sudden
violence and unreason had drowned it.

Then, in her mind, she recapitulates the entire experience as she goes about the farm chores. But the catharsis
does not come. Fear comes instead, and then there is the
message that Will Langtry is in town. She attempts to flee,
is fired upon by Langtry, and finally confronts him. As soon
as she does this, the fear spell is broken; Langtry loses any
hold over her, and she walks away into the night, peaceful
and content and able to give herself completely to Cam.
Life wins over death, and Dena is spiritually reborn.

Miss Roberts had an extremely acute sense of form, and
it did not permit her to leave the symbolism without
further development. In order to give the richness of overtone to the story, she added three devices which are like
shadows cast across the main action of the story. In effect,
the devices are a sort of lighter and minor accompaniment
to the major theme. The three devices used are the thimble
episode, the screaming gander, and the strange owl-like
howl of a hound which sounds through certain key scenes
of the story.

The incident of the thimble runs about like this. Dena's
sister, Frony, has one precious possession, a little gold

thimble. It has belonged to Judd's wife; Frony, who has had an affair with Judd, received it from him as a love token. Dena, through carelessness, loses it. The loss occurs at the beginning of the second section of the novel. Frony's continual concern and troubled search for the thimble run throughout much of the novel until the thimble is returned by Dena's lover, Cam Elliot, at the time he proposes to her. This incident, in itself, would seem unimportant enough. But as the story moves forward, the thimble bulks larger and larger until the reader begins to attend closely to the meaning of the incident.

In the context of the total story, the thimble becomes the symbol of the love lost and love at last found;[7] that which Dena lost in her disastrous affair with Langtry and regained in her final union with Cam Elliot. More than this, the thimble is felt to be overtly a sex symbol. It is flaunted by Frony openly before Mrs. Judd as the token of Frony's adulterous affair with Judd. As Dena speculates on the thimble, it grows to a giant size in her mind and is thought of as a silo, a tower or a mountain with a thicket at the base; or when it is reversed she sees it as a cup or some kind of hollow container. Miss Roberts' own notes on the thimble episode are helpful and specific. She writes thus:

> The thimble is a symbol. Compared more than once to a silo tank, a great round tower that stands beside a barn, it here assumes great size and importance. The search for it dominates the three middle chapters of the book. It was small and shapely and gold and precious. Once Fronia had it, but she lost it . . . . Rather she tossed it away. Then Dena had it, but she lost it.
> When it was found at length it was in the hands of Elliot who proved to be Dena's lover, who brought it back to her. Then Dena gave it back to Fronia and she, possessing it again,

[7] As Miss Roberts points out in her notes on this novel. Roberts Papers.

was free to turn her mind toward loving Rodney Baker, her permitted and admitted lover.

Fronia had taken it away from Mrs. Judd. Winning it thus, she was careless of the thing for which it stood, but loved the symbol and liked to wear it before the Judd woman as a testimony of power, and before Judd himself, as if she might any moment renew the relation for which it so carnally stood.

Dena had it for a brief space. But she lost it. In Cam Elliot's hands it was kept, a locked and a secret thing, much wanted and awaited, but retained by him until he was sure of the relation between himself and Dena. It was returned to Dena in a love-basket, such as Ormstead could give to a maid, but the basket here enriched by the gold prize that lay in the heart of the fine cabbage.*

Thus the thimble episode becomes a dramatization of the power of sex which can be good or bad, depending on the manner in which it is used.

Another shadow theme used is the screaming gander. Early in the novel, our attention is called to the turbulent howling of the gander, "Old Charlie," who walks amid his flock of geese and terrifies all with his terrific blast of sound hurled defiantly toward the heavens. Somewhat later the howl becomes so persistent and repeated that Dena investigates and finds that "Old Charlie" has moved to the neighboring flock, and the ousted gander there has been forced in turn to service Frony's flock. As a consequence of being supplanted and being in strange surroundings, the new gander howls in continual protest, setting the nerves of all the neighbors on edge. Since the reader's point of view is hovering close to Dena throughout the novel, her constant concern with the gander impresses the reader to the point of feeling that this incident (which stretches through some seventy pages of the novel) has far more than a surface significance in the story.

It is at this point that the reader may well cavil at Miss Roberts' symbolism. There is no doubt that a careful reading gives us the feel that symbolism is intended here, but it does seem obscure, and needlessly obscure. We know from her notes a good bit that she intended by this symbolism. Here, for instance, are some of her comments:

The Screaming Gander . . . a part of the great body of man's woe.

The screaming gander is the principle of unrest and protest. Man protesting his fate. Man bursting the bonds. Man unwilling to stay fixed in his ordered place . . . . Hence Judd has burst from bonds of his marriage and courted Fronia.

Once alone in his orchard, hidden in the midst of trees . . . he [Journeyman] flings up his head and screams a protest toward the sky . . . .*

Such were her intentions, but it is doubtful if the transfer of meaning from the image to the symbol is clearly enough made to see the gander as a symbol of man protesting his fate. It is easier to see him as another exemplar of the masculine principle in the novel, another strong assertion of "maleness" to be placed alongside Langtry, Cam Elliot, and Journeyman.

The third and last of the shadow story-motifs is that of the strange owl-like howl heard by Dena for the first time on the night that she lost Fronia's thimble. It appears here as a concomitant of the fear and loneliness felt by Dena in this night scene. It occurs first in May and then recurs again and again throughout the novel right up to the climactic scene.[8] On its third occurrence, Fronia hears it also, and it gives her "cold shivers of fear." Dena is made fearful too, and says, ". . . it seems fearful and strange. I wonder what

[8] There are eight key scenes in which the howl appears, beginning on page 117 and running over to page 238.

☆ 193 ☆

it is, and where it's hid. Is it far, or near? I can't tell. Like something a body knows but can't quite remember."

Dena's last sentence is a significant one since it states plainly what the howl is intended to be in the novel: the howl functions as the objective equivalent for the psychic trauma created by her unfortunate experience with Will Langtry. The fear and strangeness are not particularly in the sound, but in the mind of Dena, where the fear is transferred to the sound. The cry has a strange, ambiguous quality, neither clearly a howl nor the hooting of an owl but somewhere in between. This ambiguity presumably represents her attitude toward Langtry, which is ambivalent, containing both love and hate. It intrudes into her consciousness even as Cam makes love to her. She mentions it, saying: "I heard it as far back ago as May, and . . . I wish I knew just what kind it is for sure."

Then the howl occurs later, and in her overwrought imagination, the sound articulates, by a kind of synesthesia, the visual image of Will Langtry's pistol. "Terror grew into each syllable of the cry, scarcely to be endured . . . ."

Cam proposes to her and at the same time discloses that the strange sound is caused by a young hound, whose howl is caught by Judd's barn and echoed to Dena's farm. This dispels some of the fear, but not all.

The echo followed her and left its meaningless force even among the meanings which she and her lover had given it. A dark face [Langtry's] which sometimes had its first beauty often floated in her pleasure that she had found out the mystery of the baying owl and pleasure re-echoed from half-remembered distresses of a long while past.

From this point on, her fear of the strange cry gradually disappears until, in the climactic scene of the book, she repudiates completely her fear of Langtry and thus ends forever the fearful significance of the howl.

Taken together, these three shadow themes seem successful enough—with the single exception previously made. They do increase the unity of the novel, and they do add a richness of connotation which increases the pleasure of the reader. Moreover, they are reinforced by the strong, pagan nature symbolism running through the novel, which is best represented by Dena's love of the sun. Dena, through the summer, lies naked in the sun, "for the great flood of being that poured into her from above." The sun is like a sentient being, a great lover: "She turned her right side to the rays and stretched out her thighs." The fullness of life streams into her from the sun. "She had been born again into the sun." At one time, Miss Roberts evidently intended to make much more of this sun relationship since she set down *Naked in the Sun* as one of the tentative titles of this novel.

There are certain minor defects in the novel which should be mentioned before a final evaluation is attempted. There is Dena's Catholicism which doesn't ring quite true to a Catholic, although a Protestant would see nothing artificial in it. Dena's remarks about confession to Frony are not true to the idiom and manner of the Catholics of central Kentucky, and her reference to the "sacrarium" on page 127 is out of character. Occasionally, also, Miss Roberts' controlled style lapses into overwriting as in, ". . . the busy corner where an oil station dispensed fluids of three kinds out of tall blue and red fountains."

A more serious defect is the thinness of both Will Langtry and Cam Elliot. Neither of these lovers of Dena is strongly presented as a physical personage. They remain, in the final analysis, unconvincing as men. This difficulty with her male characters is a frequent one in Miss Roberts' work, and it may account for a certain weakness in the conclusion of the novel. After twenty-five or thirty pages of objective suspense, the three characters are suddenly overwhelmed with their symbolic import and become too allegorical. Journeyman's actions and his explanations might suffice in a poetic drama, but they seem too abrupt a break from the physical reality of the story—they induce a narrative discontinuity here. As a consequence, the shooting scene, while it fulfills its symbolic purpose, is not completely convincing on the physical level.

In conclusion, then, we may say that in her last novel Miss Roberts strikes once again her grand theme—the endless resurgence of life out of death. Yet in this novel it never reaches the sublimity of pitch attained in *The Time of Man* and *The Great Meadow*. Very likely this novel must rank behind *My Heart and My Flesh* also. It is definitely a variation in a lesser key than the above works. Yet *Black Is My Truelove's Hair* has excellences of its own, and it is superior in the hierarchy of her work to *A Buried Treasure, He Sent Forth a Raven,* and *Jingling in the Wind.* If we feel some twinges of disappointment that this work does not rise to the brilliance of *The Time of Man,* we must always remember that the woman who wrote this was in the advanced stages of a fatal disease. Her intellect was shadowed by disease and care.

Yet, in spite of this disease, Miss Roberts achieved scenes here which are rich and carefree and joyous—scenes earthy and fragrant with meadow and flower and Chaucerian to their very core. The novel opens with the beat of footsteps and closes with a single tread dying off into the night—signifying the beat and swell of the great flux of life. It is her valedictory. Facing death, she overcomes it and renews the earth and man in her giving and telling. In this sense, it is a noble and stoic valedictory.

6. *The Allegorical Novels*

ॄ᠊ Earlier chapters have demonstrated Miss Roberts'
mastery of poetic realism; this chapter will explore her ex-
cursion in two novels into allegory, the characters of which,
existing in a realm that lies somewhere between fantasy
and reality, are used to convey some penetrating satire
against our complex industrial civilization. The main characters in these works have a twofold purpose: (1) their
words and thoughts point out the ills of our age, and (2)
their own lives finally exhibit the antidote; that is, they
may themselves at first embody some of the evils which
they see, but their clarity of vision and basic goodness finally
enable them to react against those evils and return to the
simplicity and happiness of a life close to nature. Miss
Roberts seems to have felt that a realistic story with well-
rounded, realistic characters would detract from her main
object, satire; and yet her second purpose, to exhibit the
antidote in the lives of these characters, would have been
accomplished better, it would seem, if they had been developed with more convincing realism. At any rate, her

poetic fantasy, while definitely inferior to her poetic realism, has a charm of its own with its mingled tone of satire
and idyl.

1. *Jingling in the Wind*

In *Jingling in the Wind*, Jeremy, the rain maker, goes to
a rain makers' convention in the capital, mainly because he
wishes to meet the beautiful Tulip-Tree McAfee, also a
rain maker, whose charms have been described by his
friend Josephus. On the way to the capital the bus breaks
down and the travelers pass the time away by telling in
Chaucerian fashion (with Jeremy as moderator) stories
which illustrate the ills of our age. From the story told by
Tulip, who joins the waiting group out of a cloud, Jeremy
learns that she has become hard and cynical like the age.
At the convention, with the city and even the sky above
it full of advertising, Jeremy against his will is elected principal rain maker and finds that he owes all his unwelcome
honors to Tulip. After he succeeds in making rain, he is
almost forced to head a great parade organized in his honor.
Jeremy finally slips away without being noticed by the noisy
crowd and goes to a beautiful park near by. Here, with the
advice of the symbolic spider, he summons and courts
Tulip. These two, reborn into the simple life close to
nature, will give up their scientific profession (in which
they have impiously interfered with nature), marry in true
love (hitherto frustrated by their profession), and perform
the most important of nature's tasks, raising a family.

In this story that seems so simple on the surface, Miss
Roberts has directed against many aspects of our complex
industrialized civilization a very penetrating satire. The
whole story basically is a primitivistic allegory in which
Jeremy and Tulip-Tree represent the basically good and

innocent portion of the human race that has been corrupted by the complex and artificial life of modern civilization, the corruption here represented by their adopting the blasphemous profession of rain making. Of these two, Tulip-Tree has become more corrupted since she was closer to nature to begin with—indeed (perhaps originally a wood nymph inhabiting the beautiful tree for which she is named), she is a kind of nature goddess, "the very flower of the dawn," from whom "no beauty that ever gathered to her ever departed" and in whom dwell "gentleness and a fine faith in the earth, in the air, in the sun . . . . So attractive is she even in Josephus' description that Jeremy is in love with her before he meets her, even to the extent of saying, " '. . . when she comes into his presence all the birds of the man's heart will begin to sing and the whole sunrise of his soul will begin to dawn in the east.' " Then, when Jeremy meets her and discovers that she has become, in spite of her loveliness, hard and cynical, he devotes himself from then on, neglecting and finally rejecting completely his profession, to " ' bringing fountains and the ways of fountains back into her heart.' " The archetypal pattern here would be something like the Biblical fall of man and his spiritual rebirth, both Jeremy and Tulip-Tree finally giving up their complex scientific life in something of the spirit of Christ's "Except ye become as a little child, ye can in no wise enter the Kingdom of Heaven."

The organization of this book is perfectly adapted to its beautiful poetic theme. The flowing temporal quality noted in Miss Roberts' other books is even more pronounced in this one—a swift and graceful (impressionistic) movement from one scene to the next, often enhanced by the lyrical quality of the individual scene. The leitmotif in this graceful progress is the frequent inclusion of snatches

from beautiful folk songs about love (some of them
traditional and some composed in the spirit of tradition
by Miss Roberts); the final love scene contains several of
these complete, sung by the lovers to each other.

Only once is this swift movement retarded to any appre-
ciable extent—in the series of stories told in Chaucerian
fashion by the travelers to the capital while they are waiting
for their bus to be repaired, and even this retardation is
not very noticeable because of the dramatic liveliness in the
telling of all the rival tales, even the broken narrative of
the dyspeptic optimist and the ungrammatical story of the
bashful farmer, Bolingbroke. Besides the obvious resemblance of the machinery of narration in this series of stories
to that of the *Canterbury Tales,* there is a further parallel
in the resemblance of the tone of Miss Roberts' satire to
that of Chaucer: a very witty and good-natured but penetrating disclosure of the ills of the age presented dramatically in the stories, the characters and narrators of which,
as well as those commenting in the audience, unwittingly
reveal their own follies. The conversations after the completion of each story are always lively and witty—indeed
throughout the book this ever present wit keeps the idyllic
portions from becoming sentimental at the same time that,
without being vicious, it forcefully discloses the evils of our
modern age.

The point of view is most frequently that of Jeremy
(with occasional modified omniscient-author assistance),
but we are also taken into the minds of other characters—
once in the beginning (most charmingly) into the minds
of the insects in the wet grass on a beautiful spring morning
after a rain. Some of them are disturbed as,

a sound, swaying movement of tone mingled with felt percus-

sion began to drag and strike on the wet. It came nearer, in
the midst of the running whisper a great throb or beat that
was a regular and blithe drum-tap widely muted . . . . The
crickets were unaware of the approach and the caterpillar
made no stir of recognition, but the quail under a brush heap
crept more inwardly toward the shadows of the twigs and
snags, and a toad leaped softly away.

This sound is made by the boots of Jeremy, who enters
singing a delightful old folk song, "Oh, could you be . . .
oh, have you seen . . . oh, would you be my true-love . . . .' "

It is now necessary to trace in some detail the broad ram-
ifications of the satire that accompanies the simple story
outlined above and to determine whether its conclusion in
any way strains the fundamental unity which we have at-
tributed to this work. The first important passage of satire
occurs in Josephus' account of the capital:

Committees investigated charms, spells, hoodoos, the influence of stum-water or warts, on moles, on styes, the influence
of natural forces on prognosticators. Other committees investigated love charms and tokens, or weighed the potency of
passion or measured it with a measuring apparatus and issued
cards of permission. The psychologists were there . . . .

Having destroyed the exhausted classical myth, they were
investigating the dreams of the happily married: Did they
dream? How often? What? . . . . There were assembled all the
forces of science, religion, art, politics, and business, and their
anti-forces, together with their wives, amours, offices, heirs,
affiliations, and charges. Learned theologians sat in tense
postures in a hall answering one another with weighty dis-
courses, their questions calling to mind the great ages of the
past when doctrines were made solid as cannons. Metaphysi-
cians weighed delicate hairs of thought and substracted faint
essences of meanings, pushing gently and more inwardly upon

words, trying to find the whereabouts of a substance which Josephus with his stammering breath could designate only as the what-is-it. There was a group whose concern was to relieve thought of language, but over against these labored a group whose struggle it was to relieve language of thought.

This passage has been quoted at length because it summarizes many of the most vulnerable aspects of our contemporary civilization—the excesses of congressional investigations and psychoanalysis, the futility of theological argument in an age of unbelief, and the oversubtlety of various types of linguists. In this last category may be included now most of the New Critics—for example, William Empson with his faint essences of meaning so extended that by a "rich ambiguity" a word used once in one passage may have several different meanings. Such for Empson is "the structure of the complex word" that it is "rich" in proportion to the number, variety, and even contradictoriness of the meanings it may be shown to possess and the feelings it may be said to arouse. The description of the group who try to relieve language of thought is especially applicable now to a prominent school of philosophers who contend that "mental entities" (thought or thoughts) do not exist; there is, they say, only language, which is not a description of, but determines, what we call the structure of the world. It is to be noticed that Miss Roberts satirizes both this group and those who, at the opposite extreme, would "relieve thought of language"—this latter group presumably those who rely heavily on "ineffable" intuition or pseudo-mystical inspiration.

This attack on both extremes indicates a pattern in her satire—a concern for the Greek ideal of measure and decorum. In her attack on very different aspects of modern civilization, including both science and religion, she might seem to be following the method of Butler's *The Way of All Flesh,* but the tone of her satire is much gentler than his, and she is not, like him, a skeptic, her attack on religion, for example, being directed only at the futile or insincere or fanatical followers of it. Among the futile would be the "learned theologians" in "tense postures" mentioned in the above passage. The insincere would include "many churches" (as reported by Josephus in the capital) which "had entered the business world and served food or sold shares in mines which were jointly owned by Divine Providence and a board of deacons." Among the fanatical, who receive Miss Roberts' strongest thrusts, are the Reverend James Ahab Crouch, a shouting evangelist (perhaps Billy Sunday), whose tirades are directed with equal zeal against "the men of the rain science" and "the divine Zelda," the most famous dancer in the capital. Crouch "beat the air each night in his great tent, a hurled curse for the swift-toed Zelda," because, it was said, he "had some secret knowledge of her which he could not reveal without exposing himself." Another report had it that Crouch was jealous because Zelda, although really very old, kept youthful by having new glands, while he was physiologically unable to have his glands successfully renewed. As the stranger, Breed, said, "If all the rest of mankind was of a sort with Zelda, Crouch would be, as they say now, out of a job. He's jaundiced with the new disease," which, he explains later, works on "the within-sides of a man that can't take the glands . . . ."

But this John B. Breed has moral defects of his own: he is the perfectly respectable pillar of society who would do anything for money. He has a sales bill offering for sale at bargain prices a farm, including abundant livestock and

"One wife, a woman in sound health, thirty-two years old, excellent housekeeper and gardener . . . . Average 85 in Johnson Intelligence Test. Teeth in excellent condition. Fair skin, brown eyes . . . a faithful wife, a capable mother, an excellent cook, a good nurse . . . ." Breed would have bought the property himself if he had not already owned enough like it to engage all his attention.

Breed's story of the "divine Zelda" and her associates indicates that Miss Roberts is attacking the exorbitant claims of science quite as much as she attacks the ranting evangelists who denounce science as interference with the Divine Plan. Eugenics has perpetuated the youth of some, including the popular dancer, Zelda, whose charms are flamboyantly advertised by being written across the skies on the stars. Jeremy finds himself discouraged by this scientific paradise. "Oh, what a world," says Jeremy.

"Already there's a new disease by reason of what it does to the within-sides of a man that can't take the glands, that knows he will never be able to exchange his old ones for new . . . . That's what took Jimmie Crouch. Jaundiced so bad, he is, he can't see Zelda without he goes into a rage . . . .

"It's a disgrace to grow old. Old age is a disease and it begins to take a man as soon as he is born. The young are likely to be doomed and only the old are young and happy. The world will be fixed, and no new combinations will appear, and we will continue forever without hope. Let Spring go to rot in a cellar! Give me back a world of the old sort where a man lived out his three score and ten and then went to his heaven. Oh, what a pass things have come to!"

Zelda and her group of rustics with their artificial barnyard and cow (located in an extension of their apartment on an upper floor of the Keepsake Hotel) have about the same relation to true nature-as-norm simplicity as the commercialized radio hillbillies have to the genuine folk singer and the genuine farmer. And the advertising of the Reverend James Ahab Crouch, which also appears spread in super-neon fashion across the skies on the stars, has the same relation to the simplicity and sincerity of the rural churches near the home of Tulip as ranting preachers like Billy Sunday (and even Billy Graham?) have to the truly self-effacing and genuine pastors who do not attempt to become known outside their parishes.

Of course, even the simple churches—the Bethelerian and the Carmelist—near Tulip's home are by no means perfect: they have their doctrinal quarrels, as did Tulip's father and mother, the mother being "in all things fundamental" in religion and her father, as Tulip says, being "unfundamental." "And," as she says to the group waiting for the bus to be repaired,

"to add to the complication of things it so happened that those children allotted to Father inherited from Mother and those allotted to Mother changed their dispositions and vacillated between the one temperament and the other, while the two environments became crossed likewise so that the two heredities and the two environments, interlaced and drawing as it were contrary-wise, were complicated by conflicts between conditions and attitudes, the whole producing a snarl which no geometrician would unravel."

Even the simplest, most sincere person, like Tulip, Miss Roberts seems to be saying, has great difficulty making a satisfactory adjustment in this very complex, modern age. In fact, Tulip, to Jeremy's great distress, has become rather hard, almost cynical: " 'I have always observed,' " she says, "that parents derive far more pleasure from the begetting, conceiving, bearing, and rearing of offspring than the offspring derive from being begotten, conceived, born, and reared. And in view of the fact that my own begetting, conceiving, bearing, and upbringing yielded me so little of anything which might be described as pleasure, I have often thought that I would be quite justified or forgiven for deriving any pleasure I could from the begetting, conceiving, the bearing and upbringing of some people on my own part, in spite of the fact that this might cause the people themselves some inconvenience . . . ."

In fact, she admits that, at the agricultural college which she attended, she had fallen in love with a young man who turned out to be a " 'non-existent personality. I had been willing to mate for life, even eager to so copulate, with the Amalgamated Irrigation Corporation of North America and Europe.' " Tulip had finally rid her mind of " 'this phantasmagoria, this ex nihilo nihil fit' " and had become relatively content in her profession of rain maker, had become, as one of the travelers called her, " 'a "hard-boiled" virgin.' " All this greatly disturbs Jeremy, who says again and again: " 'But, oh, if only Tulip could take her place again beside the fountain, if only romance and sweet waters and a belief in an actuality . . . .' " Here, then, Miss Roberts implies in presenting Tulip's difficulty, is one of the greatest problems for even the best people in this age: to "believe in an actuality." And that ultimate actuality can be neither art nor science. With all her devotion to art, Miss Roberts never forgets that art is not actuality, that it can be no more than a representation of reality.

And neither art nor science, she seems to be saying, can be a satisfactory substitute for religion. As Mr. Breed said at the end of his story about the wonders of eugenics, which had depressed Jeremy and some of the other listeners:

"I think we have fallen into a too melancholy cast of thought. Some managed to keep going all this while by conjurations and enchantments—until science should perfect her own witchcraft."

Then Breed suggests that the clergyman " 'give us a bright fable or a yarn,' " the implication being that this is about all a clergyman can do in a world ruled by science. Miss Roberts here, it seems, is attacking the prevailing As-Ifism in the modern world, the idea that truth is either nonexistent or at least unattainable and therefore the purpose of thinking—whether devoted to art, philosophy, religion, or (for that matter) even science itself—is not to find truth, but simply to make the machines (ourselves) function more smoothly and harmoniously—after the fashion of most branches of pragmatism, Cabell's "romance," Santayana's "realm of essence," I. A. Richards' "emotive" use for poetry, the surrealist dependence on the "magical" powers of the unconscious, and various other evasive or escapist treatments of reality in modern times.

The clergyman obliges with an ironic "fable" about Adam in the year 4004 B. C. Adam wanders around telling everyone that he is the first man. An old philosopher says to Adam: " 'I expect to see the day myself when mankind will get into control of his environment. Complete control.' " The philosopher tells of the wonderful progress made since, about ten generations back, washing was begun by the human race. The witch doctor and the medicine men said that the first man who learned to wash himself was neurasthenic. But soon washing developed to such an extent that it lost its hygienic function in one tribe and became a rigid ritual. Adam meets numerous people, including cavemen drawing animals on the walls of their caves, and tries to convince them all that he is the first man. Discouraged and confused, he returns to Eden, and " 'presently there was nothing to show where he had been . . . . Thus ended Adam of the year 4004 B. C. ' " This story seems to satirize both the excesses of scientific optimism—the belief in the ultimate "complete control" of the environment—and, in the opponents to washing hands, the excesses of primitivism. In Adam's inability to understand that he is not the first man, she seems to be recognizing, perhaps with reluctance, the futility of the Fundamentalist contention that mankind began in 4004 B. C. Science, for better or worse, has destroyed this story.

Miss Roberts satirizes the excesses not only of scientific optimism, but of optimism in general, the latter in the melancholy, dyspeptic man who gorges himself on the contents of his large stuffed lunch bag, and, while groaning from pain, constantly affirms: " 'Only good is. Evil is not. Nothing which is not can have being. The pork is good . . . . The pickle is good . . . . There is no pain.' " His parents planned to have a " 'refined and delicate woman, a sylph.' " They arranged for the exact measurements of the forthcoming child; they were correct on breadth and thickness, but missed out on length and sex and got the long, thin, dyspeptic male instead. " 'Two [dimensions] they got, eighteen in the waist and twenty-two in the hips, but oh, but oh . . . . All is for the good. Good is. Six foot nine in length. Two dimensions they could control but the other two . . . . All is, on every hand, good.' "

"A paroxysm of such intensity overtook the melancholy optimist at this moment that his conserve and biscuit rattled from his hand and fell to the grass." Jeremy's comment, in which the others concurred, was this: " 'We can do nothing, nothing, in the face of absolute affirmation.' "

The rain makers' convention at the capital is held in an old barn containing livery stables. "Here space, air, light, water, pleasure, old story, tradition, all mingled to give comfort." Among "the ghosts of sound" that hovered about the place were:

The faint bray of an ass . . . gabble of foot-rot, hamstring, crupper, fetlock, haimes, drenches, and glanders . . . . Curry combs clinked in the morning and hay fell in dull whispers into dark mangers that were no more visible. Barn rats, their ghosts, ran before the barn rat-dog that was, too, a barn goblin that hid under the frame of an old quern where corn was ground, all now removed, all gone, all bright clean gray stone.

The use of the barn indicates another phase of Miss Roberts' attack on industralized civilization. Since its exponents do not wish to be accused of destroying tradition, they make this deferential gesture by having their convention in an old barn full of "old story, tradition." But the emptiness of their gesture is apparent, first, in their selecting a barn, and, still more, in their inability to discriminate between the best and the worst parts of even this tradition. They recall the famous race horses stabled here, but "the ghosts of sound" that impress them even more are "the faint bray of an ass . . . the gabble of foot-rot," and barn rats.

The city and the sky above it are full of advertising. Business is so completely dominant that even the stars and the signs of the zodiac are now used as super-neon signs for advertising, with messages like the following blazing in different constellations:

Ursa Major: Zelda, dancer. Lady of three worlds.

Cancer: And one of them the underworld. Beware Sodom.

Serpens: Beware the new disease. Dr. Jett warns you. Ladies and gentlemen, take the Castor Kiss.

The Seven Plowing Bulls: Zelda. Lady of nine veils.

Cancer: Ought to be dead. By every law of right and decency. It is a terrible thing to subtract . . . .

Plowing Oxen: We carry the woman of light. The eternal woman. Zelda, dancer.

Cancer (screaming across the heavens): Get an injunction! Out with the siren. Down with the jade. Daughter of Babylon. Hear Ahab Crouch. (Donated by Pike the Pickle Man.) . . . .

Virgo: For maiden sanitation use Shamrock, the wise shampoo. Tulip McAfee uses.

Ursa Major: See Zelda, dancer.
See Tulip McAfee,
Blue Wing, Fleet Mare.
Time is a fleet mare
And the mare is on the wing.

The Crouch type of evangelical religion, it will be noticed, is advertised quite as flamboyantly as a laxative, a vaginal shampoo, and Zelda's dancing.

The first business of the rain conference is to advertise for a poet to celebrate the great event with an ode, but scarcely a poet is left since the philanthropists have offered so many scholarships and prizes to poets on condition that they leave this country to pursue their work.

But finally one was discovered, one who had been masquerading as something else, pretending that he had a living from some more genteel calling when actually he had no living whatever. Discovered in a small town far in the South, he was granted security, dragged out of hiding, and promised the fee. He agreed then to furnish odes of designated length conveying useful sentiments.

But the author is so overcome to know that he is to have pay for what he does that he suffers complete amnesia and has to be nursed back to health by psychiatry.

In the meantime, Jeremy's main concern is to win the love of Tulip and restore her to the simple, wholesome life of nature, since she, corrupted by the influences of the age, is an associate of the great capitalist, Breed, and has arisen "to vast proportions" as "directress of events, creatress of powers" in the forthcoming rain carnival. Jeremy is selected to be the principal rain maker and finds that he owes all his unwelcome honors to Tulip. He succeeds after a brilliantly described struggle, in making rain (in which phrase there seems to be a cleverly vulgar pun, perhaps suggested by Gulliver's method of extinguishing the Lilliputian fire) and is hailed by the throngs as "The Rain Bat!" which he considers a humiliating title. A great parade is organized in his honor; it goes through the streets of the city with him at the head.

In the great procession among many other repulsive creatures are two monsters: Forbidding, representing our legal experiment with prohibition, and Ginbreath, representing alcoholism. Miss Roberts' attitude toward this problem is clearly indicated in the following comment:

"It was said that they engendered each other, for they were
of such a substance or kind that where they touched together they were continually renewed." A still bigger
monster, Bruitabout, followed close to these two. "Men had
nicknamed him Advertising. He was the chief cyclops of
the world." Then followed in close rank "more familiar
monsters from the lowly walks of the world."

Finally came the Chicago adjectives, bringing the parade to
a magnificent finale, the Chicago epithets—enormous, brutal,
unscrupulous, pathetic, amateur, gigantic, huge, heavy, animal, turgid, pulsing, and Titan.

This, of course, indicates that in the poem "Chicago" and
elsewhere, following an important trend in Whitman,
Sandburg prostitutes his art by confusing quantity with
quality quite as sordidly as any other advertiser.

While he is riding at the head of the parade, Jeremy is
haunted by the thought that Tulip "will sit invisible in
some elegant salon, Breed at her right hand, he affable,
obsolete, archaic, diabolical for all I know, his right hand
invisibly clutching the right hand of Mephistopheles himself, rich, a capitalist, suave. May he go off in a consumption
and may his blind gut rot." Jeremy at last is able to slip
away unnoticed because the throng is so intent on shouting
and merrymaking. He goes to a beautiful park near by and
finds a spider spinning her web near the pool. This symbolic spider is spinning "the whole of culture." " 'I draw
it all out of myself,' " says the spider,

"with my long supple fingers, I pattern it on the air. I make
it as I go, but it is made already within me, spinning . . . .
This segment here is a science, and this a renaissance, or I go
thus, spinning, and here is a psychology of love. Or a univer-

sity. We come now to a dark age, a knot here, my long pliant fingers turning. I draw it out with my hands. A dark age is followed by an age of enlightenment, and here is a new religion. Votes for women, moral prescriptions, Egypt, India, Babylon, I make a knot, a rise and a decline. Morning, noon, mathematics, a one-god, Isis, I make a knot, St. George, Diana, St. Brigid, war, a romantic era, an enlightenment, a new art, a new disease, jewelry, a new vegetable, sin, savagery again, I make a knot, and I am back again, a new philosophy, a Pyramid . . . ."

All this seems at first to be almost a Spenglerian theory of history as cycles of rise and fall, or even like Henry Adams's discovery of chaos in history. Such an impression seems reinforced when we consider that Miss Roberts' symbolic spider is a female who tells Jeremy that she will not be weaving tomorrow because she is going to eat her husband.

"Why, where is your husband?" Jeremy asked.
"I have not seen him yet," said the spider, "but he will turn up tomorrow. I will eat him down to the last mouthful. Then I will begin a new race of spiders, each one as complex as myself. It is all very intricate."

Furthermore, Jeremy at last noticed that the spider

had become repetitious, having finished all possible figures and patterns, or she twiddled inconsequently at last strands, dribblings and leavings of infinities that had gone on without one care for the which or the whether of webs.

But the key to Miss Roberts' meaning comes in another remark of the spider that, " 'There is nothing so humorous as history,' " because " 'History always neglects the most salient points.' "

What these salient points are becomes clear in the succeeding and final scenes of the book. Jeremy decides to " 'found a Masculine Renaissance' " by winning and marrying Tulip and establishing himself as the undisputed head of the family. The spider approves, but advises him not to write the demanding letter that he has planned, since " 'The first step toward a Masculine Renaissance will be the restoration of flattery and chivalry. They go before in the design.' " Jeremy takes this advice and writes a chivalrous letter pleading for Tulip to come to him. She does so, and we have a very delightful scene of courtship with the two lovers singing beautiful love songs (similar to the old folk ballads but created by Miss Roberts) and the farmer, as the appreciative chorus, singing a charming version of the old ballad "Lord Thomas and Fair Annie." Jeremy and Tulip "sang together, the loud song and the soft song, and what they sang made a round that spread about the china tree and built a fugue to the evening." The spider, too, "sitting quietly beside the subjunctive mode, one long finger touching Babylon," sings a beautiful "vesper song." "Then that most exquisite spider," the same symbolic spider,

that crouches at the hub of the web that is the mind stirred, feeling a tremor pass over the web as if some coil of it were shaken by a visitation from without. Life is from within, and thus the noise outside is a wind blowing in a mirror. But love is a royal visitor which that proud ghost, the human spirit, settles in elegant chambers and serves with the best.

There is no contradiction between the spider's spinning "the web of culture" and her "crouching at the hub of the web that is the mind," since from the Berkeleian point of view the former would be identified with the latter: "Life is from within, and thus the noise outside is a wind blowing in a mirror." In other words, the "noise outside" is simply a reflection of, and dependent on, the human mind or spirit. But the greatest activity of the human spirit, "the royal visitor," is love, and when this great event is being introduced the spider "left her spinning and stood poised on the top of a fine thread," recognizing, as does Miss Roberts, that love is more important than all the events that had been spun on the web, that marriage and family life based on love are indeed the climax of history. Simple love, rather than all the pomp and ceremony of monarchs, is the truly "royal visitor which that proud ghost, the human spirit, settles in elegant chambers and serves with the best."

In the above explanation, the proliferation of the satire directed against so many aspects of our civilization might on the face of it appear to be only loosely connected with the simple love story of Jeremy and Tulip. But actually all the way through there is a very close relationship because it is complexity that interferes with simplicity—each of these many distractions must be overcome before Jeremy can win Tulip; some of them, like the feeling of power in his profession, are temptations for Jeremy, and far more for Tulip, whose corruption was greater because she was closer to nature to begin with, the feminine principle (of motherhood and reproduction) being, as it were, at the very heart of nature. In the end, love, which will result in marriage and the raising of a family, triumphs, not for all but for the few who, like Jeremy and Tulip, can see its value; that this remnant may eventually be sufficiently enlarged to save the rest is an implied hope which can be realized, if at all, only in the fullness of time.

2.   *He Sent Forth a Raven*

He Sent Forth a Raven is a more complicated book than *Jingling in the Wind,* and is the least realistic of all Miss Roberts' works, although there is considerable incidental realism in the lively conversation and in the general background, especially the descriptions of nature. The somewhat dreamlike atmosphere is reinforced by the impressionistic transitions and the irregular chronological arrangement of the scenes. As in *Jingling in the Wind,* the allegory is based on a simple love story in which true love must overcome the numerous and difficult obstacles that characterize our complex modern world.

The story, briefly, is this: Stoner Drake, a diligent and upright farmer, having lost his dearly beloved first wife, Helen, in death, has made a vow during the fatal illness of his equally beloved second wife, Joan, that if she too should be taken, he "would never set foot on God's earth again." He carries out this defiant vow, continuing to direct the activities of his farm from within his house. He is very stern with the other members of his household—particularly with his granddaughter, Jocelle, who has come to live with him after being deserted by her sensual mother, and with his daughter, Martha, who becomes an invalid after he drives away her sweetheart by unjustly accusing the two of sinning together. Jocelle receives her greatest injury, however, from her cousin, Walter, who brutally rapes her before he goes away to war. Like Dena in *Black Is My Truelove's Hair,* she finally recovers from the shock by living a wholesome life outdoors and by thinking of her true sweetheart, John Logan Treer, the idealistic and impractical young county farm agent, who is now also away because of the war.

Frequent visitors at Stoner's home and opponents in numerous heated arguments are the blasphemous but intelligent carpenter, Dickon, and the ignorant but sincere rural preacher, Briggs. Drake can accept the world view of neither of these men and is rudely impatient with them both. Always unhappy himself, he tries to interfere with the marriage of Jocelle and Logan after Logan returns from the war, but finally after their marriage and after the birth of Jocelle's child, Stoner, now an old man with a failing memory, agrees to let Logan manage the farm.

The broad outline of the allegorical pattern is very similar to that of *Jingling in the Wind*. One of the lovers must save the other from the distractions of modern civilization before true love, resulting in marriage and a family, can triumph. This time it is the girl, representing average wholesome living with a simple religious faith and without too much theorizing in cosmic terms, who must win over the boy, representing the inadequacy of excessive theorizing, however idealistically motivated. The main obstacles otherwise to be overcome are Jocelle's mother, representing feminine sensuality; Walter, representing an overweening impulsiveness brutalized by the stress of war; Dickon, representing rationalistic skepticism; Stoner, representing blasphemous defiance in the face of adversity. The position of Briggs, representing the Hebraic relation of man to his God, is much closer to that of Jocelle, and he finally unites Jocelle and Logan in wedlock. But his position needs to be supplemented, as at Martha's insistence he finally does supplement it before he blesses this union, by emphasis on the Redeemer. The archetypal pattern for the whole book is that of withdrawal (into the complex evils of our war-torn civilization) and return (to the simple, close-to-nature, and religious pattern of love, marriage, and family); or the archetype, as in *Jingling,* may be said to be the fall of man and his spiritual rebirth: towards the end of the book, after the birth of her child, in all Jocelle's thoughts, not very clearly understood but strongly felt through faith, "somehow or somewhere came the Redeemer."

Point of view, as in *Jingling,* is usually that of the main character (with modified omniscient-author assistance); and even when other characters briefly occupy the center of the stage, Jocelle is present and her reactions are recorded. This does not mean that even Jocelle is presented with great clarity; she, like the rest, is seen through the dreamlike atmosphere of poetic fantasy, not poetic realism. Such an approach, again as in *Jingling,* gives a kind of objectivity through aesthetic distance that makes concentration on the theoretical subject matter easier, but it is highly questionable whether this fully compensates for the loss here of the dramatic human interest that characterizes her best work.

The fantasy in *He Sent Forth a Raven,* unlike that in *Jingling,* is extended even into the jumbled chronology of the first two sections of the narrative. Different scenes in the first section give a very unchronological series of glimpses into Stoner's home life (including a brief flashback picture of his happy life with Joan before her illness) and the lives of his various children and grandchildren. One scene is devoted to Martha, whose later tragic life is foreshadowed in the statement that "she had an incandescence that seemed to come from the flowing filaments of her haunted mind." But most of the scenes are devoted to Jocelle. There are brief glimpses of her life at Wolflick, Stoner's home, both before and after her mother deserts her, and then a section beginning with her life at Anneville before her mother elopes with the crude salesman. The unsettled chronology of the narrative seems in a way to reflect the troubled uncertainty of Jocelle's childhood. At least after the first two sections, which take Jocelle up to the age of thirteen, the regular chronological order of the narrative is never disturbed. The satire is conveyed less effectively here than in *Jingling,* because here much of it is given in lengthy conversations in which the characters simply express their disapproval of certain characteristics of the age: dramatic force is attained, however, when these conversations erupt into heated arguments—especially those between Dickon and Briggs, with Stoner shouting down first one and then the other.

In the main part of the book, to repeat, the satire is conveyed, in rather obvious fashion, by conversations within two groups of characters who, in this secluded place with almost no social life, spend their leisure time discussing matters of paramount importance for the nature and destiny of man—discussions especially appropriate against the background of the terrible war, World War I, then in progress in Europe. It is necessary to examine in some detail the content of these conversations because they exhibit, as forcefully as is possible through such a medium, the struggle between the allegorical protagonist, innocent simplicity, and the antagonist, evil complexity.

After her return from a session at a girls' school—a brief idyllic interlude in which she is for the first time really happy, feeling that strong sense of her own identity, the (Berkeleian) power of spirit, which is so important for all of Miss Roberts' main characters—Jocelle joins in the frequent midday sessions at the barn with the first of these two groups, composed, besides herself, of Martha, Walter, J. T. (another cousin), and John Logan Treer. Logan, from the standpoint of an idealistic socialist and primitivist, de-

plores the machine age and the perversion of religion in
the interests of big business. " 'Under cover of the popular
religion,' " he says, " 'the Barons of the Big Fortunes grew.
Learned how to sell things to the government . . . . Fifty
years of Lincolnmania. The worship of the cabonman.
The cult of Jesus grew parallel with the growth of empire.
Merged then . . . .'" Logan thinks that when Europe gets
through fighting there will be a " 'new man . . . . The
co-operative man.' "

"He's a smoke dream, your new man," J. T. said. "I don't
see the fellow. Try to get one and you'll get an engine. He'll
always go down. The mob-man wins. Goes where he's told in
the end. Wants a full paunch . . . . Goes down, your man does,
in the vapor of his own thought."

But Logan, the idealist, does not accept this as opposed
to his view; he will accept the idea of man as vapor, if it is
good vapor: " 'What we want is good vapor. Acts according
to the rules of all vapor. All right. We are such stuff as
dreams are made on. The good dream.' " But immediately
Logan is afraid that he has hurt Martha, "since she is the
one present whose little life seemed more nearly rounded
to its sleep." Martha, surprising Logan, seems to agree that
the vapor may be good, but, influenced no doubt by her
own suffering, emphasizes its dissolution—in a poetic interpretation of Shakespeare somewhat like that of Edwin
Arlington Robinson in "Ben Jonson Entertains a Man
From Stratford":

"The hand that wrote that dandled baby Hamlet, I reckon,
and kissed hands with Ben Jonson . . . said furtive rosaries,
perhaps, and at last knuckled down to death's handshake, the
vapor wanting to thaw and dissolve itself into dew. What's

dew? Put under ground at Stratford and crying out a dare by the way of some rude country cousin poet, and cursed be he that moves those bones . . . ."

After some further talk of this kind, the subject of the war intrudes itself. The impetuous Walter, though he believes that big business has caused the war, wants to rush into it to get it over with quickly.

When America enters the war, Walter immediately enlists. Just before he leaves to go abroad with the Marines, Walter returns home—"a frantic, careless, frightened, fouled, war-shocked man, in fervor of impatience and imaginings"—and rapes Jocelle. In her agony Jocelle, "With the passing of the days entered a delirium in which she thought that she would give birth to some further monstrosity of war, as if war would tear a Gargantuan, incestuous birth through her breasts." Like Dena James in *Black Is My Truelove's Hair,* Jocelle finally recovers from the shock by living a wholesome life outdoors (raising chickens) and by thinking of her true love, now also absent in the war—Logan, who will become truly devoted to her if she can win him away from his eternal theorizing. "She wished for Logan to be near her that he might see here the unified flock, the collective, that he might feel with her the rush of their short flights and their brief resting on her arms and her shoulders." She realizes that he will never see a human flock unified like this, that his dreams of "the farm-unit, the land-collective, the labor-general" are futile, but, "flushed by her constant inner wish," she says to him when he is home on furlough, " 'Oh, I wish you could have it so, whatever 'tis.' " When he is gone for two years and does not write to her, she thinks she will forget him and destroy all the voluminous papers

on collectivism that he has entrusted to her. But she remembers his goodness and rejects another, much more
ardent, lover to wait for his return.

The other group which discusses questions of great
moment includes Drake, Dickon the carpenter, and Briggs
the itinerant rural minister. Around the fireside at night
their talk thunders back and forth, while the children
listen around the circle and Martha rests in her bedroom
upstairs. Dickon is the intelligent but confused and cynical carpenter who knows a great deal of pagan mythology,
and in his book, *Cosmograph,* traces the development of
the universe from Chaos. " 'Chaos,' " he says,

"produced Earth, Love, Erebus, Night, and the Universe.
Void space, that is. Earth comes first, though. The broad-
breasted Earth they called 'er, like she was a wench. Mankind
comes a long way down . . . .
"Thus we see that Man, the upstart, the prig of the Universe, holds no place. Not even a cog among the wheels. The
whole mechanism turns, grinding out forms to pitch them
over as the engine goes humming along at a merry pace, and
nothing in the whole panoply of phantasmagoria cares if he
falls out or in, but you might hear a thundering guffaw on
Mount Olympus when he tumbles headlong back into Chaos."

Drake wants to know the origins of everything, and,
although he has rudely rejected Jocelle's vision (as a child)
of a beautiful City of God, yet he does not like Dickon's
complete paganism. Briggs, the itinerant preacher, says
that God still protects the faithful in a world of violence
as He did Noah and a few with him at the time of the
Flood. Drake is often rudely impatient with Briggs and
seems to accept his simple faith little more than he does
the pagan skepticism of Dickon; at times Drake appeals

to Jocelle to help him decide which, if either, of the two is right.

On the night when Logan is coming to marry Jocelle, the argument runs stronger than usual among the three older men: "Thus, thus, natural laws [Dickon], defiance [Stoner], or Hebraic relation of man to his God [Briggs]. Each argument was heightened by the coming lover, each man striving to state himself anew." None of the three seems to be interested in encouraging Jocelle in her plans for a happy marriage. In fact, Dickon has previously lent her his *Cosmograph* and tries to convert her to a pessimistic skepticism like his; and Drake, so unhappy himself, does not wish Jocelle to be happy, although in his rough way he is fond of her. He scorns Logan, who is the county farm agent, as " 'The bean beetle. The registered shorthorn. The stomach worm in the stomach of the Supreme Sheep. The big tapeworm . . . . The Phosphate Philoctetes. Caesar among the cabbages . . . . The Species Man. The Collective Almighty. The grand Bull Durham.' " He tells her that Logan can stay only one hour, hoping thus to discourage the lovers and prevent their marriage. Dickon tries to convince her that Chaos will reign in this projected marriage, as in the history of mankind heretofore. Even before Logan arrives, however, Jocelle has an ally in the the invalid Martha, who calls down to her from her bedroom upstairs:

"If he can't come where you are, you blow hell straight through Chaos. God! Jocelle, don't let anybody tell you . . . ."

"Who is she, up there?" Dickon asked, listening.

"It's Francesca," the voice from above hissed in whispering, sobbing. "Don't let anybody talk . . . ."

Martha's comparison of herself to Francesca seems at

first to be a defect in Miss Roberts' allegorical structure—
a kind of self-conscious, too obvious, allegorizing, inap-
propriate also because Martha's lover unlike Francesca's,
had deserted her in a critical time. But we must remember
that Martha, an invalid since Stoner drove her lover away,
has brooded so much over her condition that she is subject
to distracted flights of fantasy; at this critical moment she
pathetically imagines her situation to be like that of Francesca, as indeed in some respects it is. Her days are passed,
as it were, in an Inferno of regret, and she is almost frantic
in trying to keep Jocelle from a similar tragedy.

When Logan finally arrives, he brings the marriage
license and seems to be very much in love with Jocelle, but
he cannot even now refrain from his eternal theorizing—
this time on the injustices of the present war:

"They talk about the unknown soldier, and the *unknowing*
soldier he was, rather, out to kill and get killed to make fifty
men richer. Oh, God pity us. I always held no man could
make more than a million dollars in a lifetime and make it
honestly, but here, of late, men, a few men, made a million
in one year and made it off this blinding, tear-gassed, shell-
shocked wretchedness that ruined us . . . ."

A sudden cry from above aroused them from these contem-
plations, a warning. Martha was calling from above in a half-
spent whisper: "Jocelle, Jocelle, twenty minutes is all left."

Logan then produces the marriage license, and Briggs is
asked to marry them. He does so while Drake sits, "as if he
were in some partial coma or trance." Thus, Jocelle is
happily saved from Martha's fate and Logan, though
never completely, from his theorizing. Miss Roberts certainly does not imply that the evils which trouble Logan
are not real; she implies only that his proposed theoretical

remedy is fantastic, that he will not only be far happier but help much more to lessen the ills of the world by marrying a girl like Jocelle and making a home of his own than by dreaming about the "collective man."

In the next chapter, Briggs and Dickon continue to argue about the origin of the world, Dickon emphasizing the indifference of the cosmic forces to man and Briggs telling the story of how God cared for Noah and the other few faithful during the terrible Flood and how after the Flood, Noah " 'opened the window of the ark which he had made: and he sent forth a raven, which went forth to and fro, until the waters were dried up from off the earth . . . .' " Briggs and Dickon argue so violently that they come to blows, and Stoner helps Briggs eject Dickon from the house, defiance (in terms of the allegory) temporarily yielding and joining forces with religion against cynical skepticism. Briggs then preaches to Stoner, begging him to give up his blasphemous oath never to set foot on God's green earth again. Stoner is strangely moved, but finally refuses to revoke his oath.

In the final scene, Jocelle has her child, and Stoner, now very old and forgetful and mellowed, agrees that Logan, expert in agriculture, will be the manager of their farm.

The implications of the allegory may now, by way of summary, be repeated. Dickon represents rationalistic skepticism; Stoner, blasphemous defiance in the face of adversity; Briggs, the Hebraic relation of man to his God, with more emphasis on the Redeemer (at Martha's insistence) in his final plea to make Stoner revoke his oath and before he joins Jocelle and Logan in wedlock. Jocelle represents average, wholesome living, which does not attempt to choose among all these sytsems, finding all of them unsatisfactory compared to simple family life close to nature, with a simple religious faith and without too much effort to theorize in cosmic terms. The inadequacy of theory, however idealistically motivated, is illustrated in Logan, who finds himself fully only when he turns at last to Jocelle. On the eve of Logan's return from war,

Jocelle's thought was sweetened by a will to leave armies and treaties and international blunderings and predictions of after-war disasters, and to make, here, an order, a peace, through her own person set to rights, and to make comfort and pleasure for the other one.

Such a course will bring peace and order like that resulting from Noah's "sending forth a raven, which went forth to and fro, until the waters were dried up from off the earth." In an age of violence, Miss Roberts seems to be saying, the approach to anything like peace and order must be on some such simple basis as this. Individual men and women can best achieve happiness for themselves, and eventually contribute most to international good will, by marrying (if they really love each other) and raising a family, the most important part of any lasting civilization. This is the solution for Logan and Jocelle in *He Sent Forth a Raven,* as for Jeremy and Tulip in *Jingling in the Wind* and the main characters in almost all Miss Roberts' stories—the age-old theme that needs emphasis now perhaps more than ever if our civilization, with all its evils (so well indicated by the satire in these two allegorical novels), is to survive.

The power of love as a manifestation of spirit is evident in Jocelle, who "had drawn life out of Woldlick where a lonely tomb had closed over Drake years ago," and who now, married to Logan, "was hearty, living from hour to

hour between these two, the one man shut into the house
and the other shut out of it"—until at last Drake agrees to
let Logan become the manager of the farm. On the day
following the birth of her child, Jocelle, even through the
pain, is full of happy thoughts:

Sleeping, and waking, she saw within the act of seeing, as if
the brain itself were a prism, a crystal-clear design, a mathematical form, and as such common to all men. Common-to-
all-men drowsed over her and brought Logan from the garden
where he now rested from the long night of sharing with her
the coming of the child, where he sat within the reach of her
calling, but she lay still, letting him rest. And thus, a clear
design, the mind, common to all men, it pointed an index to
a communal sharing which was religious, the sharing of the
common mental pattern where individual traits merged . . . .
    Under this again . . . the will to believe, to live, to hate evil,
to gather power out of emotion, to divide hate from love
where the two are interlocked in one emotion, the will to love
God the Creator.

And in the middle of these thoughts, not very clearly
understood but strongly felt through faith, "somewhere
or somehow came the Redeemer."

Thus there is resolution and happiness at the end, as in
all of Miss Roberts' work, because spirit has triumphed
over all the evils, even the horrors of a world war, in our
modern civilization. It is as if "somewhere or somehow,"
to follow Jocelle's thoughts, the words of the Redeemer are
again heard through the pages of this book, saying, "Be
of good cheer; I have overcome the world."

We have spoken of the defects in realism that keep
these two allegorical novels from being major works of
Miss Roberts, but it should be kept in mind that this is

a weakness only in physical realism; the powerful emotional impact of spiritual realism may be felt surging through these pages. In fact, it may well have been the strength of her idealistic (Berkeleian) reliance on spirit that made her, in these books, neglect the solid physical foundation and buttresses that support the spiritual structure of almost all of her other work. This was the same kind of reliance on the power of spirit that enabled her to continue to produce beautiful works of art while she was suffering almost constantly from an incurable disease during the last years of her life. If these two allegorical novels, then, appear somewhat fragile physically, they are nevertheless strong and moving in the realm of spirit.

7. Technique in the Short Story:

The Haunted Mirror

and Not by Strange Gods

&⤳ The material in Miss Roberts' two volumes of short stories (*The Haunted Mirror* and *Not by Strange Gods*) is, as might be expected, more concentrated than that in her novels. Instead of the elaboration of a pageant (the type of narrative movement most characteristic of her novels), we are given in most of the short stories a sharply dramatized psychological crisis in the life of the main character rendered with swift strokes. Miss Roberts is still, fundamentally, a poet in prose, but the poetry of her short stories compared to that of her novels is like a folk ballad compared to an ode. The poetic beauty is rendered implicitly in the situation with a minimum of choral (lyrical) embroidery. Even the stories that are predominantly idyllic rather than dramatic (like "Holy Morning" and "Love by the Highway") accentuate the swift flowing of time that we have noted in her novels. Eleven of the thirteen stories in these two volumes are excellent, and even the two relative failures—"Record at Oak Hill" and "Love by the Highway"—reveal careful craftsmanship marred by effects that seem, in spite of their simplicity, too much contrived.

It seems even more evident in her short stories than in her novels that, in spite of the fundamental optimism which she derives from her emphasis on primacy of the spirit, Miss Roberts never refuses to face the somber and is quite as skillful in presenting abnormal as she is in presenting normal psychology. Her short stories, for example, contain more Freudian imagery than her novels. In "The Scarecrow," Joan, a timid girl morbidly averse to marrying and yet attractive to boys, spends most of her time guarding her father's corn from the crows with the aid of a scarecrow. As she goes to sleep in the field, she dreams with mingled attraction and loathing of Tony Wright, who is in love with her, and of an image of herself that she planned to build to free herself from the task of watching:

The image was built of a bony frame over which was drawn a quivering curtain of skin and blood. Three smiles [representing Tony] walked under the tent of shrinking skin and began to fondle the blood. The image screamed lightly when it was touched, but the touch made its horror drunk, so that horror flattened to a plane and then drew downward and inward to a line or thread that lay as an unwilling serpent crushed beneath a weight of willing blood . . . . Tender and unprotected, she was wrapped in hands. He smoked his tobacco and blew his smoke over her. He rubbed gently downward on her face and her throat and stroked her body. He laughed with her, and he took her shoes from her feet, and he bent her this way and that, glad of his power over her.

She waked when a flock of geese went noisily along the creek, going home for the night. She brushed whatever bound her aside and sat upright, and she took her shoes to her feet. She stood up in the glade, and when Tony came near to her again she flung him aside, her strength gathering. Anger and renewed horror made her strong, and she warded herself from his fingers.

The symbolic scarecrow erected by her embattled virginity, however, is apparently no more successful than the actual one she erected in the cornfield, concerning which her sister Betsy has said: " 'I believe Joan draws the crows . . . . No other farmer has such a blight of crows in his field.' " While she has been asleep in the cornfield, Tony, it seems, has been sufficiently intimate with her so that he can persuade her parents that she ought to marry him to protect her honor. As Joan, having run away and climbed up to the roof, listens to these negotiations, "The voices came to her as loud, flattened speech, such as the crows use, a dull continuation of opinions and a sudden outcry of demands and admonitions." Almost forced into marriage by her parents, she provides herself with a scarecrow that is at last effective: while Tony is out feeding the stock during the first evening at their home, she secretes a knife in the bosom of her dress; Tony, observing this through the window, goes away and leaves her alone. She returns home the next morning after an all-night vigil, and her father agrees to consider her as unmarried.

A far more somber theme is dramatically presented in "Death at Bearwallow," with a most effective use of counterpoint to unify the two divisions of the story. The theme is reinforced at the level of diction by the frequent use of words like *night* and *dark*. In the first part of the story, the little boy, Dave Nally, finds himself alone as night comes on in a secluded rural area and is prevented from getting home by a swollen stream. Night becomes for the frightened child a symbol of all terror. "A sudden increase

of fear arose suffusing the entire night that threatened to
split asunder to let terror out, a threat like the threatened
crack of doom. Crack-of-doom stood in his path and waited
upon a thunder crash." Then, ironically, when he flees for
refuge into a lighted house, he comes upon another kind
of darkness just as terrifying as the physical night from
which he has just escaped—two evil men watching by the
bedside of a dying old man, Terry Polin. Except for a brief
troubled sleep, he sits crouched in terror in the corner and
finally, before daylight, flees outside, preferring to wait
"among the cold shadows" at the dark ford. This experience, including the vulgar langauge of the two watchers,
is so firmly imprinted on his memory that years later, as
a grown young man, sitting by the corpse of a girl, Valeria,
whom he has loved though she was engaged to another,
the early experience becomes mingled (contrapuntally)
with his present reverie. In the fantasy caused by his inner
disorder, the most horrible parts of his childhood experience with death are relived ("His entire self from first to
the present moment lay back in his being, and he was one,
breathing and living, the same he had always been"), but
since he is now a man with a mature love for Valeria, he
imagines that he is old Terry Polin dying, and his own
desire for Valeria then becomes, in his fantasy, Terry's
desire for his wife Kate. In this rather grotesque but vivid
struggle for psychic supremacy between the juvenile and
the adult, a juvenile erotic experience is briefly recalled
in his reverie:

He was with a pack of boys, hunting across the fields and
into woods. A pack of boys, himself one, and a little girl hiding. She was running down a thicket, her skimp little dress,
drab, showing now and then in the brush. Hoarse cries, un-

known to themselves, were coming out of their throats. Four
boys, himself one. She was gone, swallowed up by the ground
or slipped away through some fence, Sallie Bent, lost to them,
safe. Down into a deep hollow where the path ran cool, and
she was lost to them, two of the boys off after a rabbit and one,
Wes Hyte, lagging behind in the cool brush, lying on the moss,
loving the moss.

The youthful eroticism of this subsidiary dream is the
result of Dave's repressed desire for Valeria combined
with his vivid recollection in the main dream of the sexual
reminiscences of the two rough men watching by the dying
Terry. " 'Her dress gapped open and I see her naked meat
a-showen.' " Adult eroticism finally reasserts itself in his
fantasy, and Dave once more becomes the dying Terry
longing for his wife Kate:

There was something he, Terry Polin, had always been wanting, needing, and he could not now gather the name of it or
the meaning . . . . It was something that ran in his limbs, in
his legs and arms and sides. It was Kate; he had found the
name for it . . . .
Slowly this sense grew definite and firm, and gathering a
person about it, Kate, a warm moving body, a blood-contain-
ing flesh, hands lifted and rising before the puffed breasts as
she sewed . . . . A great cry formed in his body and rushed up
into his throat, into his loose throat, and there it hung on
folds of flesh entangled with breath and struggled forth in a
dry hissing sound. "K-k-k-k-ka-Kate!"

In this whole scene, the mingling of elements both erotic
and horrible, both juvenile and adult, both past and present, that struggle up from Dave's subconscious under the
impact of the death of the girl he loves, is handled by Miss

Roberts with great dramatic force and precision. The story ends with the reading of the prayer for the departing soul —a reading brought forward from the earlier experience but omitted in the account of it at the time it happened, one of the two vulgar men (as Dave recalls the scene) taking up the reading immediately after their quarreling and fighting with one another. Once more, significantly, as in the earlier experience, Dave goes out into the darkness, which "was complete, no part of it distinguished from any other part."

The intimate connection of the past and the present noted in "Death at Bearwallow" is, of course, nothing new for Miss Roberts; we have noted her skillful use of this technique again and again in her novels—its success apparently enhanced by the fact that the presentness of the past was for her not only a device to render antecedent exposition and unify fiction, but in her own life was one of her deepest spiritual convictions. (If spirit, which is eternal, is the ultimate reality, then in her opinion nothing can be more natural than the persistence of the past into the present with an intensity which cannot be explained merely as memory.) We have considered this device in detail in this story because she has never before within the same scene shifted between past and present, between the juvenile and the adult, between the erotic and the spiritual in such a complicated, and yet completely convincing, fashion. In one sense, there is a struggle between the past, the juvenile, and the erotic, combined against the present, the adult, and the spiritual, and yet this is complicated by the fact that the adult itself alternates between the erotic and the spiritual, and the juvenile aspect of the fantasy is complicated by a dream within a dream. Finally, the dramatic immediacy conveyed in this whole scene with perfectly normal sentence structure and punctuation makes one wonder whether much of the obscure structural fragmentation often used in stream-of-consciousness realism is actually justifiable.

It is an emotional relief to turn from the above somber story to "Holy Morning," a story in which night is associated not wth death, but with youthful love and with the birth of Christ. The beautiful legend of the cattle kneeling at midnight on Christmas Eve is made the background for a love story whose poetic richness and idyllic simplicity make it worthy of comparison with the folklore drama of the early Yeats or with Hardy's *Under the Greenwood Tree*. The preternatural clarity of the scene in which Sabina meets her lover at midnight on this very cold Christmas Eve is carefully prepared for by the sensuous precision of earlier descriptions at the natural level:

Sabina lifted the lantern high and looked about over the huddled animals. The hens and the cock were perched on the rim of the manger, sitting close together. The horse had lain down in his stall. Overhead on the rafters a few pigeons stirred softly and cooed a low gentle complaint at the frozen fields and the north wind that would search into their feathers and find their soft shrinking skin. Sabina left them when she had given the old ram one more bite of hay. All together the beasts made a gentle warmth inside the barn, with their breathing and the odorous breath of their bodies.

So far in this investigation of the short stories, Miss Roberts' skillful use of symbolism has not been as fully considered as it now needs to be in the two stories—"The Sacrifice of the Maidens" and "The Haunted Palace"—that make most extensive use of it. In "The Sacrifice of the Maidens," the outward scene at the beginning does not seem to promise much dramatic power, but as Felix Barbour, an adolescent boy, watches in a small chapel of a rural convent the religious service in which his sister and several other attractive young girls became nuns, the whole scene becomes symbolically a dramatic conflict between life and death and between paganism and Christianity. From the standpoint of a pagan, sensuous love and beauty and devotion to nature, this dedication ceremony is indeed a "sacrifice of the maidens," almost as futile as the old Aztec custom of human sacrifice to which there seems to be an oblique reference in the title. Felix remembers with nostalgia a March day three years earlier when "the wind was hurling laughter about among the trees" and "there was sweetness in the high blades of the corn and abundance in the full shocks as he tore each ear from the ripe stem," and when "he knew suddenly that there was a loveliness in girls and knew that he had only of late become aware of their prettiness, of their round soft flesh and the shy, veiled laughter that hid under their boldness . . . ." But into this sensuous reverie the voice of the priest broke with the intoning of the "Hail Mary":

> Hail Mary, full of grace,
> Blessed art thou among women
> Blessed is the fruit . . . .

To which the people responded:

> Holy Mary, Mother of God,
> Pray for us now and at the hour of our death . . . .

The silence of the people after they have finished their response each time seems to symbolize death—" ' hour of our death . . . our death . . .' the last dusty patter, the last expiring utterance." But each time the priest's renewal of the "Hail Mary" seems to be "the onward rush of a new creation . . . ." "The great intoned word" seems to be indeed the very "Word" of life itself, so that the antiphonal chanting becomes over and over again symbolic of "regeneration and death continued, running around the entire cycle of the Rosary, the Our Father of the large bead partaking of the same pattern, borrowing from the general chant." (Cf. the Alleluia sequence in the Easter Mass: "Life and death in a strange duel fought . . . .") Of course, the obvious inference for Felix would be that the death of his sister Anne's worldly life would be swiftly followed by her regeneration in the life of the spirit. And so, though we are not told, it no doubt is for Anne, but apparently not for Felix: the story, presented mainly from his point of view, ends on the death note without the regeneration. As the priest prepares to communicate to Anne her new name (which will be hers as a nun from now on), "The world [in terms of the symbolism]"

broke and disaster followed. The ashes of a burnt-out creation rattled and pattered down endless cliffs of shales and Felix was aware of the rasping breath in his throat, was aware of Anne, of the last of the kneeling postulants, the smallest figure.

Of course, this could mean that the idea of regeneration would soon come to Felix, but if so, there is no indication of it beyond the fact that it has followed each time in the cycles of the "Hail Mary" earlier in the story. Its conspicuous absence here may well indicate that Miss Roberts, herself a Protestant, considered the cloistered life as something of a tragedy (though by no means so much of one as Henry James made it appear in *The American*). Her own secluded life, we know, was the result, not of choice, but of ill-health and other unfortunate circumstances.

The other story in which symbolism plays an especially important part is "The Haunted Palace," whose title is borrowed from that of Poe's poem and used symbolically in a somewhat similar manner. Hubert, a tenant farmer, and his wife, Jess, move into a wing of an old, deserted Southern mansion, about whose inhabitants Jess has been informed earlier through numerous conversations with Fannie Burt:

The Wickley farm was called Wickwood, she [Fannie] said. Miss Anne's father had gone there in old Wickley's lifetime. . . . Fannie had something that Miss Anne had in mind. It was told imperfectly, thrown out in a hint and retained in a gesture, put back upon Miss Anne, who could tell with fluent words and meaning gestures . . . . Miss Anne speaking through Fannie's speaking, reports fluttering about, intermingled, right and wrong, the present and the past.

Then bits of the life in the old mansion are told with such vividness that Jess seems to know those whose words and deeds are reported. She is especially impressed by, and envious of, the beauty and gracefulness of Mollie Wickley, but attempts to conceal her envy and her ignorance by professing angry scorn of this great life of the past. So vivid indeed are Jess's impressions of this reported past that when she first enters the big rooms at the front of the old mansion, "suddenly without plan, scarcely knowing that her own lips spoke, she flung out an angry cry, half screaming, 'Mollie Wickley! Mollie! Where's she at?'" And on a windy night, while helping Hubert bed down their sheep in one of the big rooms, she sees by the light of her lantern what she takes to be the ghost of Mollie.

Cursing and screaming, she rushes forward and hits furiously at the figure with her club,

while it beat at her with identical blows. Herself and the creature then were one. Anger continued, shared, and hurled against a crash of falling glass and plaster. She and the creature had beaten at the mirror from opposite sides.

The mirror scene here becomes an almost perfect objective correlative for the struggle within Jess's mind. Jess is utilitarian in her point of view and thus blind to the aesthetic. Symbolically, she has taken the superstitious, rather than the truly spiritual, view of the presentness of the past. What she sees in the mirror, then, is distorted into something hideous and menacing in her warped vision; she is afraid of and wishes to destroy that which she cannot understand. As Miss Roberts says in her unpublished notes on this story:

The House is the point of view, or has the point of view. The action then moves into the mind of the ignorant and insensitive woman, Jess, who represents Destructive Ignorance . . . . This is the 'haunt' that haunts the House. But Jess is herself a haunted palace.*

This story from one standpoint might seem to indicate that Miss Roberts is turning against the simple country folk whom she represents in most of her stories as living a very stable and wholesome life close to the rhythms of nature. But it must be remembered that she has never recommended "envious ignorance" as a component of simplicity. The characters who receive her approval may lack formal education, but they have a certain kind of native intelligence and devotion to tradition that are notably lacking in Jess. Of course, not even Jess is hopeless; after all, ignorant and envious as she is and however haunted by fear of that which she cannot understand, her mind is called a "palace," and she is represented as a faithful wife who diligently labors in the strenuous task of maintaining the family livelihood. From one point of view, Jess's looking into the mirror and breaking it may be said to be a kind of reverse narcissism; what she sees in the mirror (her mind) is in a way her own evil nature,[1] which, when she has seen it in all its ugliness, she wishes to destroy. This may help to explain why the story does not end with the breaking of the mirror. Her husband, Hubert, busied elsewhere, has not noticed the crashing glass, and the two continue bedding down the sheep on this cold winter night in the deserted Southern mansion, the "palace" at the physical level. "It was near midnight. Jess felt accustomed to the place now and more at ease there, she and Hubert being in possession of it." Of course, this could mean purely utilitarian possession, and it is true that their joy is mainly in the number of lambs that are born. Nevertheless, there is a kind of idyllic simplicity in the ending—"The sheep were becoming quiet. Each lamb had nursed milk before they left it"—that seems to indicate that, to some extent at least, Jess has made peace with all that she formerly hated and feared.

Another type of story uses the past, in the Shakespearean manner, as source material for a story which Miss Roberts makes fully her own without doing violence to the old theme. "Children of the Earth" is based on "The Second Shepherd's Play"—even to the concealing of the sheep and

[1] Cf. a brief note by Miss Roberts in the Roberts Papers under the title *The Haunted Mirror*, which is the title of one of these two volumes of short stories: "The Haunted mirror is the human mind, in the illusions of which is seen a reflection of reality."

the attempt to explain its bleating as the cries of a human baby. But Miss Roberts' story is a delightful idyl about Kentucky country folk. Indeed, in humor, psychological penetration, imagery, and conversational impressionism, and in the magic atmosphere of idyllic beauty in the closing scene, this story is one of her best. In spite of their human frailty, these "children of the earth" never lose their simple dignity even though their little drama is set against a cosmic background that is majestic and awe inspiring. To consider the story briefly: Dovie Green, whose lazy farmer-husband, Eli, does not provide for her, has driven into the shed back of their house a wandering sheep belonging to a neighbor. She is about to force her reluctant husband to slaughter it when neighbors drop in unexpectedly for a dance. In the meantime, with Eli's lazy imagination stimulated after his own cold and insufficient supper, we get the magnificent passage in which he plans to feast on roast lamb:

Eli thought of a cup of hot coffee rich with cream, and the cold food of his supper stuck in his throat. He saw a large roast of tender lamb frying in the oven, hot in its own grease, and he would take a fine plateful. The rest of the business would be high up in Bancroft's thicket, torn up by the dogs, and nothing would be left but a few scattered and mutilated fragments of wooly skin tangled in the brush, never to be discovered. He would make no plan, but he would let his hand do whatever came to it in an easy way, no fuss, no knowledge, no loss of sleep. Nobody would know. He would not know . . . . He would have the feast early in the day, before people were stirring about. He would take all easily, careless, no worry. He would sleep all night in his bed, his head thick with sleep, and all the while his hands would do what they had in mind, his feet walk up to the high thicket with the now unmentionable and unrecognized residue, the that, the not-no-nothing whatever of his thought.

This passage skillfully indicates the lazy futility of Eli's character. Because he is too lazy to act decisively, he lets himself believe that even while he is asleep the secretive slaughter of the sheep and the preparation of it for his feast the next morning, "before people were stirring about," can be accomplished simply by "letting his hand do whatever came to it in an easy way . . . ." This kind of approach, so his reverie implies, is wise for two reasons: (1) it will avoid detection, and (2) it will leave him guilt-less, since the "mutilated fragments of wooly skin" in the thicket, to be left there by "his hands," personified as independent agents doing what "they had in mind," would be "the not-no-nothing whatever of his thought."

But Eli's reverie is interrupted when the guests hear the bleating of the lamb and are not convinced that it is the little Green child crying. Dovie slips out and releases the lamb, and it strolls into the house, "crying out once in excited pleasure," among the dancers, who "were noisy and happy over the lamb's presence, disputing of its good sense":

"Flossie came to Eli Green's surprise party . . . . I doubt if Flossie knows so much as she makes out . . . . I got my doubts about Flossie . . . . She's only mutton . . . . I doubt iffen Flossie's knows her name . . . . She does now . . . . Look at Flossie, God's sake!"

The dancers, who thus jovially pretend to doubt Flossie's ability—since she is only "mutton"—to recognize her name, probably fail to see the full implication of their humor: if she were, as they say, only pretending to be able to recognize her name, such pretense would indicate far more intelligence than the ability she would be pretending to have.

When the dancers, now that the stars are out, decide that they must leave and when they go together out at the door into the beautiful night, "The sheep kept among them, as if it would know among them the security of flocks." Inspired by this "myriad of small sparks over the great roof of the sky," the group, walking along as couples, arm in arm, sings religious songs—"Beulah Land," "Shall We Gather at the River," "When the Roll Is Called Up Yonder"—to the accompaniment of Amos's fiddle. Then follows another of those very moving and beautiful conclusions into which most of Miss Roberts' stories glide with easy grace and simple dignity: she makes the very simplest of characters, ignorant country folk, full participants along with the fragrant, moist, and cool rural landscape and the stars in a scene of cosmic serenity and exultation:

The night was moist now and the heat of the day was gone from the hilltop. The voices, now well blended, now broken apart and struggling to be one again, clung about the song, letting comment pass, rolling slowly through the long lines of the song which Amos sometimes sang alone until the words were heard once and learned. Johns, the peddler, was farther gone, the wheels of his wagon creaking and rattling slowly down the highroad far to the left, heard when the song was momentarily stilled by a rest in the measure. The lamb had lain down in the cool grass at the roadside. The song was well liked by the singers, and when it had been sung through they wanted to sing it again, their voices beating forward with it now without halt or delay, singing of eternity and jasper walls.

Amos sang well, and the others borrowed of his talent, looking from one to another with pleasure . . . filled with wonder and delight, feeling themselves to be a part of the great body of the stars and the world without end. Voices crying out in the interval:

"That bright star up yon way, I heard a man say it mought be called Mars, or maybe he said Jubiter, I disremember which."

"They say the stars are worlds or suns. People there like the people on the earth."

"A better kind, maybe."

"God help 'em, I hope so. Better."

"Sing again. Sing one more. Sing what we sang awhile ago."

"Sing one more and we'll go."

"Sing 'Beulah Land.' "

"Sing 'Shall We Gather at the River.' "

"Sing what we sang first."

Analogies to music have been indicated again and again in Miss Roberts' work, her love for both literature and music apparently making her feel that there is an intimate connection between the two arts. But we must remember that she connects the two in a way quite different from Poe, whose belief was that poetry is greatest when it approximates music because poetry should give an indefinite pleasure, and, for Poe, the art that best exemplifies indefinite pleasure is music. For Miss Roberts, literature, both prose and poetry, must be clear—the pleasure to be derived from it must be a very definite one, inseparable from the union of truth, beauty, and goodness. The emotion, in other words, must be very clear and definite, its clarity and definiteness a result of its being evoked by a specific dramatic situation or, to use Eliot's term, objective correlative. And this emotion, for Miss Roberts, will be a spiritual experience because the definite objective correlative is most often, in her concept of the close relation between the two qualities, both phyiscal and spiritual. The serious function of music, then, is to make an identity of this close relation. When Theodosia in *My Heart and My Flesh* utters the following words, she is expressing Miss Roberts' view: " 'I'll say, "Where are you?" I'll climb all the musical stairs there are.' " So far as the nature of the medium will allow, indeed Miss Roberts throughout her work has climbed these stairs, the steps of which it may be well to recall here: rhythmical sentences; euphony in word, phrase, sentence, paragraph, and even, by extension, in the graceful transitions between paragraphs; beautiful imagery, often containing specifically musical terms; conversation progressing slowly and emphatically by partial repetition of significant phrases; and, finally, analogies to musical compositions in the structure of her stories.

The short story that best illustrates Miss Roberts' extensive use of musical devices is "The Shepherd's Interval." At one level this story deals simply and realistically with the life in prison of a farmer convicted of bootlegging and with his final release and return home just in time for the sheepshearing and for his daughter's wedding. The analogies to music, however, soon become apparent, the general form perhaps being most nearly like an operetta presented in a kind of twilight atmosphere between comedy and possible tragedy, with the comic triumphant at the last in what promises to be an idyllic wedding scene. The narrative moves slowly with portions of speeches and thought often repeated as in a musical composition. The characters are Flynn Thompson, in jail for bootlegging, and his fellow prisoners, Leck Wolsey and Jinnie. Since

Leck and Jinnie (Jinnie, "soft and white like a woman," formerly called Jimmie) may be said to be the chorus, their comments, mainly on Flynn, tend to flow together contrapuntally as a kind of composite speech rather than realistic dialogue, their language notable almost as much for its rhythm and euphony as for its content, though the idiom of ignorant small townsmen is always accurate and the subject matter is always carefully related to the center of interest, which is the consciousness of Flynn. Leck and Jinnie at the beginning of the story are discussing the "villainy out in the world":

"Outside is a muck of villainy . . . ."
"Outside is a squash-shise of dirt and slime . . . ."
"Men and women . . . ."
"Both kinds . . . ."
"At it day and night."
"Villainy."
"A squash-shise of blood and slimy juices."
"Wherever blood runs is villainy . . . ."
"Heave-ho, all together, and they all heave-ho."
"They ho-heave, prittle-prattle, dumb, dam, dim."
"Pass the gravy."
"Pretty pill, pass the gravy."

For Flynn, whose meditations have become very gloomy during the long summer days in jail, these voices of his fellow prisoners

continued to knock at the air. They were flattened to the thinness of paper and were set against the air as fixed patterns . . . . The voices that knocked from wall to wall, flat and hollow among the heavy stones, were a continual repetition of common sayings that passed between the speakers.

Then at the end of an interval of this composite speech, when Flynn comes out of his reverie, "The speakers came clear again" for him.

Gradually, in the thoughts of Flynn and in the oral speculations of Leck and Jinnie about Flynn's affairs, we get the antecedent exposition necessary for the story. The speakers are commenting on the difficulties besetting Flynn's beautiful daughter, Mirandy, with Flynn away at sheepshearing time:

"Mirandy, she'll have her hands full against eighteen she-sheep get two lambs apiece and maybe some three. I heard it prophesied this would be a three-times year for ewes," question and reply, neither belonging to the stones, shed and rejected by the firmness of the rock . . . .

Although he replies to them only intermittently, the questions that his fellow prisoners ask him about Mirandy lead Flynn into an extended reverie recalling her past. He recalls her beauty and her popularity with the young folk in the neighborhood, his recollections of her and the remembered voices of her friends mingling in a delightful passage, the rhythm of which parallels the youthful festivities recalled:

Randy, Mirandy, Randy, with six, eight, seven, ten friends coming and going. "Where's Miss Randy? Where's she at? Whoop, Randy! Out of it! Come on downstairs and light up the lamp for a party we're here for. Twang on the banjo and tinkle-tinkle on the juiceharp . . . . Get up outen the bed, Miss Randy, and come on downstairs or we'll send Pat Doran up after you. Come on down and light up the lamp.

Then the remembrance of their merry dances (in Flynn's reflections) becomes symbolic of the dance of life and then, even beyond that, the cosmic dance of a revolving star cluster:

They were all turning around and around in a group, but now and then two turned faster than the rest, turned together, and floated off, married. They would float off together then, settled and out of the whirlwind. Mirandy and all that pertained to her, all that turned about her, floated away, seen apart, going, as a pictured whorl that made a far heavenly body, a little star cluster dancing around in a picture in a book.

But Flynn's cosmic reflections with Mirandy at the center suddenly take an extremely pessimistic turn as he feels himself excluded:

The world, the earth, continued, himself being outside of it. Suddenly it was swept far outward in space, drawn by some powerful star. It hurled plunging, turning first one way and another, and it was wrenched completely out of its track . . . . A great cold settled on the planet where the world had been . . . . The people were all dead . . . . Time was gone. The world—the earth—moved slowly back toward some sun.

So gloomy do Flynn's thoughts become that he contemplates suicide, even to the extent of imagining what his body would look like as "it would break into many kinds, and each kind would find its own, some of it as matter and some as force." Flynn's near deification of Mirandy and then his thoughts of suicide as he feels himself excluded from the world of which he makes her the center seem to indicate that there is, subconsciously, something of the incestuous in his attachment to her. The "powerful star" that in his fantasy draws the world disastrously out of its orbit is probably Pat Doran, Mirandy's fiancé.

But this fantasy is happily ended as the jailer announces, what Flynn had completely forgotten, that tomorrow is the day for his release. The gloomy thoughts now completely cast aside, the coda of this operetta establishes a happy equilibrium as Flynn arrives home in time for both the sheepshearing and Mirandy's marriage to Pat Doran:

"We waited for you to come. We allowed you'd be here by the tenth of the month, and the law said the tenth for you, as we remembered. And so we said we'd wait, Randy said. We brought the sheep into the calf pen by the barn to be ready to shear tomorrow soon in the morning."
Randy was taking Pat Doran's arm and she was walking up before the preacher. She was ruddy as the sunset had been, and she was smiling while the preacher called her name.

Mirandy's charm and beauty, "ruddy as the sunset," are still of great importance to Flynn, but now his attitude is the normal one of the father happy in her happiness and in the re-established conviction, so vital for Miss Roberts, as it should be for all of us, that, in spite of suffering, life itself is fundamentally good, even blessed.

These examples, selected as typical of her work in the short story, demonstrate that Miss Roberts is almost as fine a craftsman in this field as in the novel. Her buildings erected in these two fields of art are both beautiful and sturdy, their beauty greatly enhanced by poetic qualities all too rare among modern prose writers; and the next chapter will demonstrate that in still another field, poetry as such, she is equally competent. Such a combination of solidity, depth, and creative versatility should, the final chapter will contend, give Miss Roberts a far higher rank in modern literature than has so far been assigned to her.

8. *Elizabeth Madox Roberts as Poet*

ᠵᠥ As a child of eight, Miss Roberts saw a picture of
Elizabeth Barrett Browning under which was printed the
single word, "Poet." She was so impressed by this that she
pointed to the word and said, "That's what I want to be,
a poet." And that she became. The very essence of her art
is her poetry. The real key to the subtle appeal of her
novels is poetry. As a result, much of her finest poetry has
already been discussed in the chapters dealing with the
individual novels; we will, therefore, confine our discussion in this chapter to her two published volumes of poetry
—*Under the Tree* and *Song in the Meadow*[1]—and attempt to describe here the nature and value of these
volumes.

We need to discuss briefly Miss Roberts' beliefs about
the nature of poetry. These beliefs necessarily overlap her
general philosophical concepts and necessarily derive from

[1] "In the Great Steep's Garden," a pamphlet consisting of seven brief
poems accompanying a series of photographs, was privately printed by Miss
Roberts in 1915. We will not discuss it, since it is a fugitive piece of little
consequence.

her basic pattern of life. This means that many things relevant to her theory of poetry have already appeared in the chapters devoted primarily to biographical and philosophical aspects of her life and training. We will attempt a succinct statement of her poetic theory here and refer the reader to the above chapters for fuller treatment.[2]

Since Miss Roberts made an explicit statement about her poetic theory, we will quote from it at some length as an introduction to our discussion of her poetry:

I find that I have tried for a poignant speech, as direct as cause and effect is direct . . . .

Poetry must appeal to the emotions each time it appears, with the freshness and vigor and the charm of a clear first impression. It flashes into media where the intellect goes crawling and groping . . . .

. . . Poetry is forever trying to make clear obscure relations in the worlds and systems of things and ideas . . . .

. . . I believe that it is the high function of poetry to search into the relation between mind and matter, into the oneness of flesh and thin air . . . spirit.

. . . I have discarded all poetic fancies and pathetic fallacies and have kept close to my own experience and the truth of American life as we live it here in Kentucky . . . .

I have avoided all literary words and all literary phrases. I have worked for a poignant statement . . . .

I have tried for organic rhythms . . . . I have used contemporary speech and contemporary thought.

I have used child speech and child psychology for my images . . . .

If I can, in art, bring the physical world before the mind with a greater closeness, richer immediacy than before, so that mind rushes out to the very edges of sense—then mind turns about and sees itself mirrored within itself.*

2 Cf. Chapters I and II.

The preceding statement is an excellent analysis of exactly what Miss Roberts achieved in her best poetry. Perhaps the chief distinction of her poetry lies in its double impact. It is at one and the same time children's verse of the highest quality[3] and adult poetry with a distinctly metaphysical character and appeal. That these two qualities coexist in a true imaginative unity in her best verse is an achievement of no mean consequence. True, in her later poetry, there is a break down in some of the poems where social propaganda is implied without a true integration of image and concept. A look at her two volumes of poetry will, we believe, show the justness of her self-analysis.

The first volume, *Under the Tree,* is very likely the better of the two. Done mostly in her Chicago period, it presents with great clarity her "remembrance of things past." Here, however, the things are not really past; they are present, eternally present, in the first clarity of a small child's world. The point of view throughout is that of a small child, say five to eight years old. Most of the poems are in the present tense, a few are in the simple past.

If we ask what the specific subject matter of this child's world is, we find it to be first the physical objects she discovers in her home and in the small Kentucky town at the turn of the century. She sees the cornfield, the cow at milking time, the red-hooded woodpecker, the crescent moon, a child asleep, and an August night. She has a vivid imagination, so she composes fantasies about the "little people" who live in the pulpit at church, about a night fear in the form of a panther who crawls under her bed

[3] From the date of its publication in 1922 up to today, the poems of *Under the Tree* have exerted a great appeal on children. They have appeared in magazines, readers, children's texts, and such well-known child encyclopedias as *Child Craft*.

at sleep time, and about a strange tree that looks at her as she walks by it. She has a grandmother who tells her fascinating stories of how it was in the old days, of her ancestors who lived in Maryland and came through the "Gap" long ago into Kentucky. All these strands are worked into the rich cloth of the child's world.

This world is a pristine world, a clear, transparent world where the viewing senses are washed clean of all impurities. It is T. S. Eliot's first world, "Through the first gate, into our first world, shall we follow the deception of the thrush," and it has some of the white innocence of Blake's world. It is even analogous to that blessed state of childhood frequently referred to in the New Testament in such passages as, "Suffer the little children to come unto me for of such is the kingdom of Heaven." This primal childhood innocence appears with effortless sincerity in such a poem as "Christmas Morning," particularly in the last three stanzas quoted below:

I'd watch his breath go in and out.
His little clothes would all be white.
I'd slip my finger in his hand
To feel how he could hold it tight.

And she would smile and say, "Take care,"
The mother, Mary, would, "Take care";
And I would kiss his little hand
And touch his hair.

While Mary put the blankets back
The gentle talk would soon begin.
And when I'd tiptoe softly out
I'd meet the wise men going in.

There is yet another dimension to this child's world, which, in a sense, is man's world too, since man is but a child in the vast scope of the universe. Thus, as the little girl probes aspects of her village world, she is man probing the pitiless universe. We see this dual import in "August Night."

August Night

We had to wait for the heat to pass,
And I was lying on the grass,

While Mother sat outside the door,
And I saw how many stars there were.

Beyond the tree, beyond the air,
And more and more were always there.

So many that I think they must
Be sprinkled on the sky like dust.

A dust is coming through the sky!
And I felt myself begin to cry.

So many of them and so small,
Suppose I cannot know them all.

Here the child becoming poignantly aware of one of the grand mysteries of the universe is recapitulating an archetypal racial experience; thus, she is man, suddenly and frighteningly aware that the fixity of the world crumbles, that mind as a knowing instrument is inadequate and recoils appalled before the horrors of what we know as space.

This dual appeal in a single poem, appealing truly and directly to the child mind and by overtones to the adult mind, must be assessed as one of her fine accomplishments in poetry. Anyone who has attempted poetry knows the almost insuperable difficulty of such double allegiance. Surely Miss Roberts displays in *Under the Tree* clear evidence that she possessed a unique poetic knowledge of the subject matter discussed above. Jacques Maritain, in *Creative Intuition in Art and Poetry,* says that poetic knowledge is a particular kind of knowledge through inclination or connaturality (connaturality, i.e., you know a virtue, fortitude, because you possess and practice that virtue and *are* that virtue yourself). Thus Miss Roberts knew this unique mind expressed in *Under the Tree* through connaturality; the book is, in effect, an anatomy of her own mind. Such poetic knowledge can be fully expressed only in the work. *Under the Tree* expresses a dual subject matter, reflecting the dual character of her mind.

Of equal interest with her subject matter is the form she employs to express that subject matter. First, there is the strong physical element of her poetry. Some of her poetry is purely a poetry of things. She employs great skill to give the exact look and "feel" of the object or scene. It is her desire to present the physical world with absolute immediacy, to see small things clearly, exactly. She would have mind rush out to the very edge of sense. To this end, she employs a terse, monosyllabic, Anglo-Saxon diction, pared to the quick. The physical effect is extreme and immediate, as in "Little Rain."

Little Rain

When I was making myself a game
Up in the garden, a little rain came.

It fell down quick in a sort of rush,
And I crawled back under the snowball bush.

I could hear the big drops hit the ground
And see little puddles of dust fly round.

A chicken came till the rain was gone;
He had just a very few feathers on.

He shivered a little under his skin,
And then he shut his eyeballs in.

Even after the rain had begun to hush
It kept on raining up in the bush.

One big flat drop came sliding down,
And a ladybug that was red and brown

Was up on a little stem waiting there,
And I got some rain in my hair.

This physical exactness is one of the major factors in guarding these poems from the sentimentality, coyness, and posturing which so frequently mar children's verse. Certainly Miss Roberts has succeeded in avoiding this pitfall. There are other reasons for her success besides the physicality of the poetry. One is the unaltered use of the child's point of view. She establishes it at the beginning and never allows adult condescension suddenly to appear within the poem. Another factor is what we might call "control." The sense of "control" is very fine and exact in "Little Rain." Her usual technique is (1) to describe at the beginning of the poem a physical object or scene, then (2) place herself in the poem in a particular relationship

Elizabeth Madox Roberts

to that object or scene, and then (3) conclude the poem by a meditation which suddenly lifts the poem to the level of a haunting emotionalism (frequently close to mysticism) which implies far more than it says on the surface. This conclusion adds great power to the poem, having the effect of music which goes on in the imagination long after it ceases to sound to the physical ear—*"Heard melodies are sweet but those unheard are sweeter."* Her sense of control and proportion in unifying these three elements of the poem and preventing any one from being exaggerated at the expense of the others definitely contributes to the "guarding" effect of her form. Her short poem, "The Pilaster," is a fair enough example of this controlled style and the techniques of controlling it.

The Pilaster

The church has pieces jutting out
Where corners of the walls begin.
I have one for my little house,
And I can feel myself go in.

I feel myself go in the bricks,
And I can see myself in there.
I'm always waiting all alone,
I'm sitting on a little chair.

And I am sitting very still,
And I am waiting on and on
For something that is never there,
For something that is gone.

In terms of rhyme and meter, Miss Roberts has been content to remain within conventional forms—this in spite of the fact that literary Chicago led the revolt against poetic conventions during her stay there. *Under the Tree*

☆ 258 ☆

stays well within the bounds of traditional English poetry: the most frequent stanzaic form is a quatrain rhyming either *a b a b* or *a b c b,* and the prevailing meter is iambic tetrameter, employing frequent substitutions. Next to the quatrain in frequency come rhyming couplets, varying from a four- to seven-beat meter. A few iambic tetrameter triplet stanzas appear, but these are exceptional. There is no use of free verse. Rhymes are usually perfect rhymes. Miss Roberts has realized that conventions need not be dead weight, but that, properly used, they are a means of gaining new strength and freedom. These traditional forms blend well with the strong song element of the poems. Probably their strongly incantative character is their outstanding formal mark. Song lay at the very base of Miss Roberts' imagination. Poetry, in the broad sense of imaginative literature in general, may be thought of as moving in the three fields of song, novel, and drama. Miss Roberts' forte was poetry as song, and *Under the Tree* is a prime exhibit of this fact. A great many of these poems have been set to music and sung successfully.[4] There is a strong sound element in the majority of these poems, but it is not used to override and obliterate the meaning and sense of the poems. The sound and the sense reinforce each other, and we savor them together. Both are simple and straightforward on the surface. Almost all the poems in *Under the Tree* seem to be on the verge of song. The sense of musical form, so strong in all of Miss Roberts' imaginative experience, is especially apparent in these poems. We cite the poem "On the Hill," emblematic of the mind trying to see itself in relation to physical objects, as an example of this blend of song and meaning.

4 Very likely, the beautifully lyrical "Christmas Morning," already cited in this chapter, is the best known.

Elizabeth Madox Roberts

On the Hill

Mother said that we could go
Upon the hill where the strawberries grow.

And while I was there I looked all down,
Over the trees and over the town.

I saw the field where the big boys play,
And the roads that come from every way,

The courthouse place where the wagons stop,
And the bridge and the scales and the blacksmith shop.

The church steeple looked very tall and thin,
And I found the house that we live in.

I saw it under the poplar tree,
And I bent my head and tried to see

Our house when the rain is over it,
And how it looks when the lamps are lit.

I saw the swing from upon the hill,
The ropes were hanging very still.

And over and over I tried to see
Some of us walking under the tree,

And the children playing everywhere,
And how it looks when I am there.

But Dickie said, "Come on, let's race";
And Will had found the strawberry place.

To sum up our observations, we can say that *Under the Tree* is a book of strong, simple poems appealing to both children and adults. Its delicate psychological probings and metaphysical overtones suggest very closely the quality of the inner reverie and pure sensory imagery of the inner world of Ellen Chesser in *The Time of Man*. The poems usually proceed in a simple, straightforward diction with a strong lilting quality. The object or scene is stated and then begins to glow (her magic is in making it glow). This incandescence is an attribute of the entire poem; it grows from the total effect. The poems are little flames which flare up in our imagination and then glow for a long time in our memories. We will not soon forget them.

In 1940, eighteen years after the publication of *Under the Tree,* Miss Roberts brought out *Song in the Meadow,* her second and last volume of poems. As we would expect, it bears definite similarities to *Under the Tree,* but shows new and different influences at work. It is more experimental than *Under the Tree;* there is a wider range of ideas and verse forms, and a new note of social propaganda appears. More is attempted here than in the earlier volume; yet there are occasional failures, which is certainly not true of *Under the Tree.* Her technical experimentation seems motivated primarily by Gerard Manley Hopkins, whom she discovered in the 1930's. Obvious also is the influence of Whitman and, to some extent, Carl Sandburg; this latter influence is less fortunate. The folk song continued to interest and influence her, as is evident in the latter part of this volume.

Much that we have said about the formal characteristics of her earlier poems would apply equally well to these later ones. To avoid repetition we will touch primarily on some of the new influences which appear here. For example, the dedicatory poem is a sonnet, "Sonnet of Jack,"[5]

5 Cf. this poem in Chapter II.

and it is particularly reminiscent of Hopkins. It is Petrarchan in its octave and sestet and in its rhyme scheme—as were most of Hopkins' sonnets. The meter is like Hopkins' "sprung rhythm," having usually five or six beats to the line and an irregular number of unaccented syllables (running up to eleven for one line). Her great use of alliteration, consonance, and assonance, her coinage of compound words and extreme use of Saxon diction, along with familiar Hopkins figures of speech (e.g., "bony house")—all these display the influence of the British poet. Her very title, "Sonnet of Jack," suggests an affinity with Hopkins' poems of the common man, "Tom's Garland" and "Harry Ploughman"—particularly with the conclusion to his "That Nature is a Heraclitean Fire and of the Comfort of the Resurrection," which reads:

> *In a flash, at a trumpet crash,*
> *I am all at once what Christ is, since he was what*
> *I am, and*
> *This Jack, joke, poor potsherd, patch,*
> *matchwood, immortal diamond,*
> *Is immortal diamond.*

If we compare the above conclusion with the final couplet of "Sonnet of Jack," . . . see the probable source of Miss Roberts' title in "This Jack,"[6] and a further analogy in the startling peripeteia which closes both poems:

[6] In each poem, "Jack" is Everyman. It is of interest to consult one of Miss Roberts' notes on this poem to see how she followed the universality of "Jackness" in our langauge.

Jack, a portable machine for lifting...	J—a–diamonds,
	J–a–clubs,
Jack	J–a–hearts
The house that Jack built	J.—John is so long at the fair
J. Spratt	J. in the pulpit . . . Union Jack

Spread free of the bony house toward
heaven, their joy, his or theirs, say
What you will,—dead Friday and
born again already on Thursday.

The poem "Summer Is Ended" is another excellent example of the Hopkins influence on Miss Roberts, as the first stanza quoted below will indicate.

Summer Is Ended

Summer is ended.
Leaves a-tatter and stippled with rust,
Great leaves and little, brown brittle
and green,
Red, yellow and bitten, frost-eaten,
Summered and weathered, full-seasoned,
clattered and cluttered,
A dust in the winds, sweet mass,
Leafmas.

Somewhat noticeable, though quite secondary to that of Hopkins, is the influence of Whitman. It is most easily seen in her "Conversations beside a Stream." The form of the poem is reminiscent of Whitman's "Song of Myself," employing a loose, free-verse line, frequent catalogings, Indian names for their romantic effect, and some rather vague generalizing about "the people." The same

Jack-Straw, J–a–napes
Jacks (The Great Common Man—
the pawn, the worker, the lover,
the richman, poorman, beggarman, thief)
Jackdaw
Jackal, Jackass————Jackboat
Man's common Jackness

Jack-a-lantern . . . Jackknife . . . Jack
Rabbit
Jack Scren— (Jacobin)
Jackie be nimble and turn me a
sault
Jackie be nimble and think me a
thought.*

poem echoes portions of Carl Sandburg and Vachel Lindsay and seems less like her best vein and certainly is not among her best poems.

Her interest in the tradition of folk song shows itself in a number of the poems in this volume. She frequently employs the ballad stanza, ballad techniques, and diction reminiscent of the Middle English lyric. "The Fox Hunt" uses the question and answer monologue of the folk song with fine effect, while in "Tapestry Weaving, A Ballad Song of Mary," the diction and phrasing are strongly Saxon with an admixture of archaic words like "sweven" and "stear." Both these poems are good. In general, the folk song influence has been more fruitful for her poetry than has the influence of the moderns.

The experimentalism of *Song in the Meadow* displays itself primarily in the use of slant rhymes, long poetic lines, free verse, sprung rhythm, mixtures of different stanzaic forms in the same poem, and a diction which is frequently more stylized and abstract than that of *Under the Tree*. Also, there is a tendency to write on broad social or political questions, to engage in a type of poetry which is overtly a propaganda poetry. Examples of this would be such poems as "Corbin the Cobbler," "Man Intolerant," and "Conversations beside a Stream." These are not among her most successful poems. Her best poetry in this volume is an extension of the mode she inaugurated in *Under the Tree*. This observation is supported by a look at the three categories into which she divided this volume.

The categories indicate their content by their titles. The first category, "Maidens and Loves," is the largest of the three, and its tone is nearest to that of *Under the Tree*. The early poems in this section represent the little girl of *Under the Tree* grown slightly older and indulging further her idealistic probing of the universe in such poems as "Self-Haunted Girl" and "The Fox-Hunt." Then comes the idyllic poem of harvest time, "Love in the Harvest," marked by its exuberant love of life and its strong singing quality.

Love in the Harvest

Harvest now, and all are in the hay.
All the men at work now and all
    the teams a-jingle.
The cutting knives are quick and the
    bright traces dangle
And tinkle with the swingle-tree, to
    put the grass away.

Windrows now, and the heat is from
    the South.
All the boys are gay now and sing
    along the raking.
They shout it from the bottom
    land and make a play of stacking.
A song in the meadow and a song
    in the mouth.

The poems of love—a clear, simple, untroubled love—come now with many echoes of the refrains and singing syllables of Middle English and Elizabethan song. Then the more somber note of "The Lovers" appears, in which the speaker thinks of slipping into the ease of death to escape the pain of life, but is saved by her instinctive vitality:

But I loved life
And life loved me.

Then back to a praise of the sweet mass of the summer for which we "Praise Now the Lord!" in the poem "Summer is Ended." The "Maidens and Loves" section concludes with a series of five, softly lilting cradle songs, including the very beautiful "Blessed Spirit, Guard" with its fine last stanza—

> *At thy cradle side adoring,*
> *Life renewed and here restoring*
> *Blessed spirit guard thy sleeping.*[7]

Altogether, this first section, "Maidens and Loves," creates a tone of positive love, a tone of the joy of life, and at the same time a feeling of the perpetual mystery of life which is present in all our knowledge. The scene is pastoral—always and deeply so. The love is love of man and love of life; it is a happy love, and from this clear mood arise the "Song in the Meadow" and the "Song in the Mouth." Although the poems do vary in aesthetic importance, many being relatively minor, they all are completely realized; that is, they accomplish what the poet set out to do.

The second category of poems, "The World and the Earth," is more disturbing artistically than the first—disturbing for the note of social protest. We, of course, do not object to social protest in poetry; we object here because the poetry seems forced and strained. It lacks the air of complete inevitability, of total integration, achieved in her successful poetry. This sense of incompleteness appears in such poems as "Corbin the Cobbler," "Man Intolerant," "A Man," and "Conversations beside a Stream." In reading these, we have the uneasy feeling that Miss

[7] This last line appears on Miss Roberts' tombstone as her epitaph.

Roberts is writing not what she really intends, but what she thinks she should intend under these circumstances.

Yet another note intrudes here—darker emotionally but finer poetically. This note is that of an old time, a time running back to a prehistoric past, long before the human race had appeared. This note expresses itself in images of the ancient sea and rock, of cold and nonhuman seasons, of fossil shells bearing witness to an ancient and lost flow of life—a note that lies below the floor of preracial memory but never breaks through. Sad and resigned but not bitter, it is what man thinks of after the glad exuberance of the "Song in the Meadow" passes into the mood of reflection and meditation. This vein is well exemplified in such a poem as "The Ancient Gulf."

The Ancient Gulf

The shells are packed into the rock
Life has eaten into the stone, edged
Its way through the hard lime,
Seen now where the fields are ledged.

A lean time under the grass.
A cold season for the rock.
A perilous wait in the still cliff
Where the hard beams of stone lock

To hold the leavings of some leaping tide,
The wash of gulf fog, and the swift
Tang of salt spume on a shore,
Now sealed in fossil and drift.

This emotion leads naturally to the pantheistic mysticism of "Child in the Universe," where the speaker feels herself to be merging with the physical universe. It passes on to the organistic idea of the universe expressed in

"A Man." The theory here, in brief, is that everything is
implicit in anything, so it doesn't matter where you start
because you will always be led inevitably to the answer.
This idea was attractive to Miss Roberts as an artistic
theory as well as a way of life. Its general import is expressed
in the first stanza of "A Man."

A Man

> *Start anywhere.*
> *Build on the eyes or the feet or the hair,*
> *Build on the want of a pen or a ring.*
> *His name, Ben, Bob, Jack, or Jim.*
> *Start with the gallows beam . . .*
> *Start anywhere.*
> *Start with his hat.*
> *Start with his face.*
> *This way or that.*
> *Start any place.*
> *Start with his end or his plan.*
> *Start anyplace to construct a man.*

This poem leads naturally to the extended effort of
"Conversations beside a Stream," in which two voices
speaking antiphonally attempt to sum up America in an
impressionistic mélange of bits of folk song, historical allu-
sions, and democratic mottos. The poem, while it has fine
phrases, suffers from too many passages like this:

> *Of George Washington and his Gentlemen.*
> *The signers who wrote their names, large*
> *and small, to the mighty document of*
> *Jefferson's brain. George Washington*
> *and his ragged regimentals, they of the*
> *bare feet and blood-stained tracks on the*
> *frozen ground.*

Or, like this:

> *Start with democracy*
> *In county, in township, in hundred,*
> *   and shire.*
> *His first aspire.*
> *He, strong speaking and singing*
> *   his will.*[8]

Fortunately, this section closes with an excellent poem, a little prayer, "Evening Hymn," which is complete and satisfying.

Evening Hymn

> *The day is done;*
> *The lamps are lit;*
> *Woods-ward the birds are flown.*
> *Shadows draw close—*
> *Peace be unto this house.*
>
> *The cloth is fair;*
> *The food is set.*
> *God's night draw near.*
> *Quiet and love and peace*
> *Be to this, our rest, our place.*

Part three of *Song in the Meadow* is a brief section bear-the title, "Legends"; it is the slightest of the three sections both in length and aesthetically. The first poem, "The Meeting," presents a situation familiar to those who read Miss Roberts closely. The poem is a brief dramatic lyric describing a meeting between the speaker and an un-named entity within the house. The poem is plainly sym-

---

[8] These excerpts are too much like Edna St. Vincent Millay's "Lidice" to comfort the admirer of Miss Roberts.

bolic, and Miss Roberts herself suggests that it represents the consciousness meeting the soul.* It is a twinning of the ego, a dramatizing of the two personalities within each of us. It is suggestive of the scene at the climax of her short story, "The Haunted Palace," when, Jess, in attacking her own image in the glass, is attacking the brute fear that lurks in her own mind. The poem builds up through six stanzas to a symbolic meeting which comes thus in the last two stanzas:

> *My hand goes up*
> *To reach for the latch,*
> *And a hand inside*
> *With identical touch.*
>
> *Blue eyes look in*
> *At the cloudy glass;*
> *Blue eyes inside*
> *Look out of the house.*

After this dramatic psychology, the poems turn to racial legends such as Cinderella and Adam and then to the family legend dealing with Miss Roberts' great-grandfather seven generations removed. The story of this ancestor's stowaway voyage to America is told impressionistically in "Sailing to America." The Orpheus legend is domesticated in Kentucky in a series of three poems, followed by three others on Daniel Boone. The Boone poems are simple, lilting poems dealing with Boone as a woodsman; they have no suggestion of Boone as the symbolic omnicompetent figure to lead us from the chaos of modern thought —the theme which her notes indicate she hoped to develop in an epic composition on Boone.

The last poem in this section and in the book is "Jack

the Giant Killer," a ten-page poem and a fairly long one for Miss Roberts. It tells a folk-idiom version of the story, with symbolic overtones, suggesting that Jack, in a certain sense, is Everyman; and the Giant is the great forces of nature which are subjugated by Jack Everyman in the nature-myth ending of the last two stanzas.

> *The earth made a cave of the giant's mouth,*
> *And a mountain out of his stomach.*
> *His legs became two mountain chains,*
> *And his head became a hummock.*
>
> *Then Jack brought up his trusty plow*
> *And he plowed himself a field.*
> *He grew his corn on the giant's breast,*
> *And he reaped a mighty good yield.*

It is on these two volumes, then, that her reputation as a poet must rest at present. There are other poems, as yet unpublished, which are not represented in this discussion. Those unpublished poems in the Roberts Papers would in no way alter the judgments made in this chapter. There are yet other poems which are in the possession of the family and remain an unknown quantity. Presumably, they will one day be published, and they may enhance even further their author's name as poet.

The first volume seems the better, all in all. It is a clear, direct poetry, less troubled by the overt intellectualizing that sometimes obtrudes into *Song in the Meadow*. The experimentalism of the second volume is interesting and frequently effective (as in the organic rhythms of "The Meeting" and Jack the Giant Killer," where the beat and rhyme clearly suggest the appropriate physical movement of the poem's story) though occasionally forced. Both volumes, however, have the magic feel and incandescence of good poetry, and they are pre-eminently a singing poetry. And as we listen to the unique cadence of this poetry, our hearts lift up, and we too sing, "A Song in the Meadow and a Song in the Mouth."

9. Conclusion: Integrity in Life and Art

ဦ&ာ Again and again we have indicated and briefly discussed the close and harmonious relationship between Miss Roberts' life and her art; it seems now appropriate to discuss in more detail this happy unity so often lacking in many of our great writers, whose lives too frequently exemplify the evils against which their art expresses eloquent protest. The ensuing final summation, then, will be specifically directed toward a fuller explanation of this unity.

It seems desirable, in the first place, to consider both in her life and in its expression in her notes, stories, and poems the great theme of the close relationship between earth and the spirit. Such a relationship, as she treats it, raises some philosophical problems resolved, as one would expect of an artist who is not a professional philosopher, not in the realm of logic but only in the paradoxical tensions of her art. For example, in her notes she speaks of the "High function of poetry to search into the relation between mind and matter, into the one-ness of flesh and thin air . . . . Spirit. Into the wedding of grass, intellect, instinct, imagination."*

This statement has a strong element of pantheism, as do all those primitivistic aspects of her life and work in view of which the phrase "Children of Earth," the title of one of her short stories, could be applied to most of her characters and indeed to Miss Roberts herself. In *A Buried Treasure* the characters are at one level cosmic figures, children of "Terra, the most ancient oracle, the most profound deity." Characters like Dena Janes (in *Black Is My Truelove's Hair*) and Theodosia Bell (in *My Heart and My Flesh*) who suffer disaster are often restored to spiritual and physical health by living in the open air and healing sunlight, close to the rhythms of earth.

It should be emphasized, however, that in her own life Miss Roberts used discretion, if not strictly consistent logic, in her devotion to this principle of co-operation between spirit and matter, and when she found the two mortal enemies, as in the fatal illness from which she suffered almost constantly in the last decade of her life, she depended on spirit as the gallant warrior that to the very last enabled her to endure with serenity the bodily ills which could not be overcome. Nor do her characters by any means depend altogether on a primitive attachment to Mother Earth for their spiritual triumph. They often assert their strong awareness of self-identity—"I am Ellen!" "I am Diony!"—and in times of crisis turn for solace to something deep within themselves, "some inner and mightier frame," which seems more like transcendental self-reliance than dependence on either the Christian God or a pagan Mother Earth. The heroism of Miss Roberts' characters, both fictional and historical, in one way seems to exalt them into a kind of semidivinity, though they are at the same time made to seem realistic and by no means free of human frailties.

Diony as a child longed to create rivers and forests, like the Berkeleian God, by thinking them into existence, and, as a heroic and faithful wife and mother on the frontier later, in a way realizes her early dream. "Boone the leader to take us out of chaos," as Miss Roberts says in her notes for an unfinished and unpublished long poem, in part of which she has Boone achieving godlike feats like digging Mammoth Cave and dividing the realms of day and night. In her own life, Miss Roberts says that she has known tragedy and has again and again been recreated, "forever recreated," by the power of spirit she means. It is interesting to note that Miss Roberts, like her characters, attributes her recreation to the power of spirit, but not specifically, in Christian fashion, to the grace of God, and it is perhaps significant that she never affiliated with any church. This is not to say that either Miss Roberts or her characters repudiated Christianity. She taught a Sunday-school class for a time and, especially as she grew older, seemed to make religious use of some of the resources of the Roman Catholic Church, especially the Missal. It is usually implied, and sometimes stated, that the characters in her books attend church services, mainly Protestant evangelical, and the later books give more emphasis to the specifically Judeo-Christian tradition: the rural preacher in *He Sent Forth a Raven,* for example, plays an important part in the allegory. But the fact remains that the predominantly pagan approach to the realm of spirit appears in her work about as important as, sometimes more important than, the Christian.

The fact that spirit often depends for strength on a primitivistic attachment to the rhythms of earth might seem to exalt matter above spirit in this co-operative relationship —a conclusion which might seem further indicated by the rich, sensuous immediacy of her work, the result, as her notes make clear, of deliberate planning on her part. This note, for example, on her intention in *The Time of Man*:

The most that I care to do is to present the sweet soil, the dirt of the ground, black earth, bitter and foul of odor, full of worms, full of decay which is change, not evil—black earth, ground, soil . . . and the other one, white sun, light . . . these two forever mingled and mystically braided together in life form, all life, which is Ellen . . . . Life a slender thread running like a ripple through the brown crust of the earth.*

Ellen is indeed one of the children of earth, and is not the parent more important than the child? The analogy is not quite the one intended, however, for it is more as if the elements of matter "mystically braided" (by a divine Creator, one would suppose) evolve upward into life, which in its physical fragility is like "a slender thread running like a ripple through the brown crust of the earth," but which spiritually, as we have seen, soars upward into the regions of semidivinity. The philosophical reason for the emphasis on sensuous immediacy in her work she explains in another note:

If I can, in art, bring the physical world before the mind with a greater closeness, richer immediacy than before, so that mind rushes out to the very edge of sense—then mind turns about and sees itself mirrored within itself.*

Mind or spirit, then, receives aid in becoming strongly aware of itself from sense. Why? The answer for Miss Roberts would be in this respect like Emerson's: a natural fact symbolizes a spiritual fact, from which it would follow that the more vivid the symbol the stronger the realization of the reality symbolized.

Other aspects of her technique can likewise be directly related to this spirit-matter alliance. For example, her poetic realism, her consciousness of which is indicated in the following note, already quoted above:

Two ways seem always open to me as one having such environmental influences as mine, and such mental and physical equipment. One way the way of satire, the other the way of symbolism working through poetic realism.*

Again the symbol would be the natural fact, the sensuous immediacy, the realism which is transformed, elevated, into the realm of spirit, the higher reality symbolized. This transformation she calls a "poetic" process, in making which she calls to her aid a number of the devices of formal poetry: subtle rhythms, consonance, assonance, onomato-poeia, inverted syntax, euphonious names, and archaic expressions. But it cannot be too strongly emphasized that for Miss Roberts the aesthetic process is only an aid to, never a substitute for, the spiritual truth which is her constant goal. The same is true of her use in the structure of her work of analogies to formal music: in her notes, for example, as we have seen, she refers to *The Time of Man* as a "symphony brought into words," in which she has an "overture," "return," etc.

But this transformation of earthy realism into the higher realism of the spirit is preceded by another form of the poetic process which at first seems to be the opposite of what we have been describing. This initial operation with language in her art is what appears to be a perfectly natural and sincere mythopoeism, almost as if she literally believed in the primitive identification of word with thing, and a very earthy thing at that. But then her affinity for the philosophy of Berkeley led her to believe that language and physical objects are far less real than the ultimate reality, which is purely spiritual and of which the lower reality of the realm of matter is symbolic. For Miss Roberts indeed there is no contrast between knowledge of the earthy and that of the spiritual; epistemologically, the two were the same for her, as they were for Berkeley, but the emphasis of the artist and her philosophical master, as might be expected, is different: whereas Berkeley as a philosopher is engaged in transforming what is called the physical into that on which it is dependent for its existence, the spiritual, Miss Roberts as an artist seems at one level to be transforming the spiritual into the physical, the sensuous. But, as we have seen, this is not a linguistic reductive exercise after the fashion of the logical positivists, but the artistic counterpart of the religious word made flesh—a way of expressing (even communicating) the inexpressible, akin to Dante's use of the simple figure of the Rose to communicate in his *Paradiso* the ineffable bliss of heaven. The sensuous in her work, then, as an incarnation of the spiritual is given a far richer significance than in the work of a simple realist or naturalist. Miss Roberts has summed it up thus in her notes: "We go into the unseen by way of the visible, into the unknown by way of the known, into nous by way of the flesh and the dust."*

The success of Miss Roberts as a symbolist in fiction and poetry, then, was no doubt due to a great extent to her wholesome understanding of the nature of a symbol, concerning which she was wiser than the French Symbolists and their modern imitators in two respects: (1) she knew that a symbol cannot be a successful substitute for that which it is supposed to symbolize, that art, however valuable aesthetically, can be only art and not a vital religion.

She resisted the temptation to play the pure aesthete, even though the cult was very much in vogue in her own day. There was a great deal of talk about the "priesthood of Art"—about the superiority of the artist to the crude bourgeois citizens of Chicago, Louisville, and that "Sahara of the beaux-arts," the deep South. Life, said the aesthetes, exists only to provide material for Art, but Miss Roberts never succumbed to this decadent doctrine. (2) Miss Roberts knew that a symbol, to be really effective, must be clear (not esoterically "private"), and firmly grounded in the basic and eternal human emotions—of the type that in her notes she called "large symbols":

> Only large symbols are lasting.
> Hence the indestructible nature of the ancient Bible.
> Noah's Ark. The Earth itself.
> God made a covenant with all living flesh.
> The Tower of Babel. Vain sciences and isms.
> They think they can climb out of the way of God's flood of
>   life and death.
> How poor, how vain to tie the spiritual truth to sciences.
> The Tower of Babel.

Although Miss Roberts, as we have seen, found two ways open to her as an artist—satire and poetic realism—she made use of the first of these in only two books—*Jingling in the Wind* and *He Sent Forth a Raven*—recognizing no doubt that they are her least important works. Even so, these works deserve high rank as effective attacks on many of the evils of our complex industrialized civilization. Both the strength and the weakness of these books lie in their tone, which is predominantly poetic fantasy. The fantasy on the positive side gives free rein to the delightful flight of her good-natured but far-ranging and penetrating wit, the tone of which, as well as the serial arrangement of the travelers' stories in *Jingling in the Wind,* reminds us of Chaucer. The main characters in these works have a two-fold purpose: (1) their words and thoughts point out the ills of our age, and (2) although their own lives at first embody some of the evils which they see in others, their clarity of vision and basic goodness enable them to react against those evils and return to the simplicity and happiness of a life close to nature. At the end of each of these books, as at the end of all her other novels and most of her short stories, we see the triumph of that kind of love which, combining the best of the earthy and spiritual, results in marriage and family life. This happiness comes only to those who, like Jeremy and Tulip in *Jingling in the Wind* and Jocelle and Logan in *He Sent Forth a Raven,* can see its value; that this saving remnant may in the fullness of time be greatly increased is an implied hope on the fulfillment of which the fate of our civilization depends.

Miss Roberts seems to have felt that a realistic story with well-rounded, realistic characters would detract from her main object, satire; and yet her second purpose, to exhibit the antidote to modern evils in the lives of these characters, would have been accomplished better, it would seem, if they had been developed with more convincing realism. *He Sent Forth a Raven* has the additional weakness of a somewhat weak plot structure, the satire being conveyed often in conversations that are insufficiently motivated; the allegory, as a result, seems rather rigid and contrived. The delightful mingling of satire and idyl, however, has a charm of its own and more than compensates for these weaknesses: even these two books, her weakest, are well worth the attention of an intelligent and serious reader.

Just as Miss Roberts considered the whole universe, physical and spiritual, as one great and basically happy unity, so she looked upon the whole body of her work as an architectonic structure, the plans for which may be found in considerable detail scattered here and there in her notes. On one huge genealogical sheet she has all her main feminine characters traced back to one marriage so that they are all, however distantly, related by consanguinity. The key name for the heroine, who was, according to her notes, apparently intended to be used in a series of novels, was Luce. Jocelle in *He Sent Forth a Raven* was originally to be called Luce Jarvis, and there are the following additional notes:

Luce Cycle . . .
I. *My Heart and My Flesh*
II. *The Great Meadow*
Luce
Agricultural vs.
Machine Age

Luce: Her Symbols
My Heart and My Flesh
The Great Meadow
Noah's Raven

Build back the forebears of Luce . . . . Bring it forth several times as a litany.

Build it back to the Litany of the Saints which rises backward to God.

In one genealogical table, Luce Jarvis's ancestry is traced back to Imelda Montford, and in another, that of Theodosia Bell is traced to the same Imelda. Other notes indicate that Ellen Chesser was originally intended to be called

Luce. The name Luce actually appeared only as that of the observer in the fantasy that forms a prelude to *My Heart and My Flesh*, but, as has been indicated, Luce was the original fictional prototype from whom all Miss Roberts' heroines evolved. Though the heroines are thus connected in the familial relationships indicated in the genealogical tables and though they all have in common the qualities of heroism, devotion to duty (especially that of mother), and reliance on spirit, no one appears as a repetition of another. There is artistic variety enough to satisfy the most rigorous comparison between any two of her works, and yet among them all, there are interweaving filiations of both content and form that make her total art structure—composed of novels, short stories, and poems—one of rare symmetry and proportion.

It seems appropriate, finally, to attempt an estimate of Miss Roberts' place in the history of our literature. It is of course impossible to rank novelists in any exact numerical order of ascending or descending merit, but it seems safe to say that Miss Roberts is an important figure in American literature whose quiet but genuine talent has been temporarily obscured by the popularity of more sensational writers in our confused and restless age. She dramatizes the deep central passions of the human race and man's relation to nature and God in universal symbols that are conveyed to the reader in clear, beautiful, and unmannered language. The result is a poetic regionalism that should in her best works have a universal appeal, especially in *The Time of Man,* one of the truly great novels in our literature. In all of her life and work there is nothing shoddy, nothing second-rate. In the long perspective of time, when the works of many whose reputations now overshadow hers will have been forgotten, it seems reasonable to predict that Miss Roberts' best works will endure, because in them discerning readers will always find in very truth, both artistically and spiritually, "a glory from the earth."

University of Oklahoma Press

Norman